Praise for *Lessons from the Mountain*

"Somewhere inside that frightened, shy, freckle-faced little girl, who *just* wanted to please everyone, to *just be* "*good enough*," seethed the heart of a brave activist, willing to take on all comers in her fight to save women's lives. Mary starts out writing a heartfelt "love letter" to her *Waltons* co-stars and fans (no whining here, there's not an ungrateful bone in her body!). But no sooner has she finished happily regaling us with her 'behind the scenes' *Waltons* tales, and the moral lessons she took to heart along the way, she reveals the terrifying challenges that forced her to become more 'Erin Brockovich' than 'Erin Walton'! For someone who started out as a sweet little girl afraid to speak up, it certainly is a pleasure to hear her *shout* from the top of the mountain now!

—Alison Arngrim, *New York Times* bestselling author of
Confessions of a Prairie Bitch

"I can't wait to read my Walton sister Mary McDonough's memoir! Her intelligence, wit and insight guarantee that she will tell her story and ours in a moving and delightful way. Also, her status as a successful child performer qualifies her on the fascinating subject of children in show business."

—Richard Thomas

"Mary has had the courage to face her fears and pain, and consequently is living a richer, fuller life. That's Mary, full of life!"

—Michael Learned

"Waltons fans will treasure an opportunity to see the woman behind the pretty face of one of their favorite family members, and even non-Waltons watchers will cheer her perseverance."

—Judy Norton

"Mary went on a personal odyssey and self-discovery that took her through very turbulent times. I have kept in contact with my 'little sister' over the years and she always seems to impress me. On a personal side, I like the 'child stars gone good' story that so many of us are, and Mary is one of my oldest and dearest friends."

—Eric Scott

Books by Mary McDonough

LESSONS FROM THE MOUNTAIN:
What I Learned From Erin Walton

ONE YEAR

Published by Kensington Publishing Corporation

LESSONS FROM THE MOUNTAIN

What I Learned From Erin Walton

MARY McDONOUGH

KENSINGTON BOOKS
http://www.kensingtonbooks.com

Kensington Books are published by

Kensington Publishing Corp.
119 West 40th Street
New York, NY 10018

Library of Congress Card Catalogue Number: 2011921029
ISBN-13: 978-0-7582-6367-4
ISBN-10: 0-7582-6367-8

First Hardcover Printing: April 2011
First Trade Paperback Printing: June 2012

10 9 8 7 6 5

Printed in the United States of America

*For anyone who has felt like
they were not enough.*

Contents

Acknowledgments

There are so many people to thank for this book. First and foremost, my parents, for providing a strong foundation and teaching me to climb. To my brothers, who have stood by me through great difficulties and our biggest laughs. I love you and appreciate the men you have become. Mom, Dad . . . don't worry, we made it.

To Beverly Nault, without whom this book might never have happened. She does all things writing that I don't do, or don't like to do. Her dedication and commitment to me and this process was what allowed me to write my story. Bev, I thank you for being a confidante, sounding board, great researcher, and friend through all the ups and downs. We did it!

To John Scognamiglio, for championing this book and being so patient, professional, and kind every step of the way. I feel lucky to have you as our editor. Your guidance brought it forth.

To Dr. Karen Seratti, who provided direction at the perfect time. To those who read it in all its stages, encouraging me to go on: Maria Calleia, Rozanne DeCampos, Carol Douglas, Chris Epting, Alexandra Paul, Tiné Hayden, June Dowad, Sybil Goodrich, Claire Peterson, Claylene Jones, Angie Umbarger, Glen Woodmansee, and Sylvaine Capron. Your input and support were invaluable.

To Maureen Pratt, Caroline Paul, Rod Mitchell, Alison Arngrim, Laura Hillenbrand, Dr. Ron Zodkevitch, Stephen Shearer, Scott Vestal, and Eve Golden, whose ideas, insights, and advice were integral to the book.

To Rick Ellis and Stephen Anderson, for having our backs on all things legal. To Paulette Cohn, for being the connector. Dr. Daniel Wallace, for everything lupus-related and so much more; to Tom Sheridan, for lessons in integrity and never letting the bus hit me. Earl Hamner, for his generosity of spirit. Kari Lizer, for her friendship, inspiration, and Mrs. W. To Mark Tinker, Johh Putch, and Bob Yannetti, for supporting me personally and believing in me professionally. To my Walton family, for loving me; and the Walton fans, for all their encouragement from the moment they heard I was going to write this book. More thanks than I can say to my dear friends, who lift me up on a daily basis. I feel so blessed to have you in my life.

To Syd, my light and purpose on this planet, for the lessons you continue to teach me. To Kylie and Robyn, who have added love and learning to my life as the "step*monster.*" To Runtie, who taught me how to love again. Without you, I would likely be lost and alone.

To my Don—my mate, partner, best friend, and love. I feel more appreciation that I am capable of expressing. I love you more than you know, and without your complete support and unwavering love, there would be no book.

Now . . . read it!

In 1971, CBS aired The Homecoming, *a Christmas movie written by Earl Hamner Jr., about a depression-era mountain family based on Hamner's own childhood in Schuyler, Virginia. The movie was a ratings success and inspired the dramatic series* The Waltons, *which aired for nine seasons. Even after it was retired from official production, the show inspired several reunion specials, and is still one of television's most celebrated and beloved series. To this day,* The Waltons *airs in syndication around the world, is sold on DVD, has its own museum, and is adored by members of its national and international fan clubs. In this first book written by a former cast member, Mary McDonough, who played Erin, takes us on a behind-the-scenes, poignant, funny, and sometimes heartbreaking journey up Walton's Mountain and beyond.*

Cast of *The Homecoming: A Christmas Story*

John Walton	Andrew Duggan
Olivia Walton	Patricia Neal
Grandpa Walton	Edgar Bergen
Grandma Walton	Ellen Corby
John-Boy Walton	Richard Thomas
Jason Walton	Jon Walmsley
Mary Ellen Walton	Judy Norton
Erin Walton	Mary Beth McDonough
Ben Walton	Eric Scott
Jim Bob Walton	David Harper
Elizabeth Walton	Kami Cotler

Cast of *The Waltons*

John Walton	Ralph Waite
Olivia Walton	Michael Learned
Zebulon Walton	Will Geer
Esther Walton	Ellen Corby
John-Boy Walton	Richard Thomas (1972–77)
John-Boy Walton	Robert Wightman (1979–1981)
Jason Walton	Jon Walmsley
Mary Ellen Walton	Judy Norton
Erin Walton	Mary Beth McDonough
Ben Walton	Eric Scott
Jim Bob Walton	David Harper
Elizabeth Walton	Kami Cotler

Foreword

By

Earl Hamner, Jr.

In the summer of 1971, an event came about that would change my life, as well as the lives of many others. I had written a script based on my book *The Homecoming*. CBS liked it and ordered it be made into a two-hour movie to be aired as a Christmas special. Fielder Cook, who had accomplished such distinguished work in "the Golden Age of Television," signed on as director. This was a special stroke of luck, because in addition to his taste and talent, Fielder was also a Virginian. He knew the country I was writing about, and he knew the people.

We were again elated when Patricia Neal accepted the offer to appear as the mother, and equally happy when we were able to persuade Richard Thomas, a promising young film and stage actor, to accept the starring role of John-Boy Walton.

Several other adult roles were cast, notably Ellen Corby as the grandmother and Edgar Bergen as the grandfather. Then came an equally challenging task—finding competent young actors to play the roles of children ages six to thirteen. Pam Polifroni, our casting director, brought in teams of young actors. One exceptionally appealing group she had selected primarily because they appeared to be brothers and sisters. We hired that group, and one of those children was Mary Beth McDonough, the author of this book.

Mary Beth was a pretty little girl of ten when she was first cast. She had taken dance lessons, but she had never acted professionally. Little did she (or any of the rest of us) know that in time, she would be seen by as many as 50 million viewers on a single night.

Mary Beth was to play Erin, a character based on my sister Audrey. I was especially pleased by the casting because, like Audrey, Mary Beth was very beautiful, and had a winning smile. I saw some of Audrey in Mary Beth—also a middle child—with an outgoing, accepting, happy disposition.

During the weeks when we first started working together, I came to know Mary's family—her strong, caring father; her pretty, patient mother, with her warm smile; her big, protective brothers, Michael and John; and her little sister, Elaine. You could sense the strength that Mary brought with her from such a family, whom she describes more fully in this book.

There is a cliché in the television industry. Even though there may have been fistfights on the sets, and even if they hardly are on speaking terms, every actor, director, writer, producer, or crew member who worked on a feature film or television series will claim, "We were just like family."

That they were, and are, a family is honestly true of *The Waltons*, because the actors were actually playing members of a real family. They are still bound together because of their experiences growing up as actors playing brothers and sisters. Compounding this equation is the fact that Michael Learned and Ralph Waite saw their responsibility as adult actors and gave the young actors caring and knowing support. Richard Thomas, too, realized the vulnerability of the child actors and assumed a supportive role that he filled during the filming and even to this day—that of the older brother.

Over the many years they worked together, they developed relationships very similar to those of the characters they portrayed. Even today, after the long run of the series is over, the actors still have familial feelings for each other.

When I first read Mary's manuscript, I was struck by the honesty with which she describes her early experiences. It is a revealing story that took courage and strength to tell. It is a story of the triumph of the human spirit over adversity at its finest.

Introduction

There are three questions we are always asked:
1. What was it like growing up on *The Waltons*?
2. Were you all as close as you seemed on the show?
3. How did you grow up to be so normal?

The short answers are:
1. Terrific and hard.
2. Yes.
3. Who knows?

Seriously, I've also wondered how we got through it all. I've always thought of writing a book about what it was like to grow up on the show, and joked it should be titled *I Haven't Robbed a Convenience Store . . . Yet!*

My friend Paul Petersen, who grew up playing Jeff Stone on *The Donna Reed Show*, said to be honest and tell it all. "The life of Hollywood kid actors was hard then, is hard now—and the more people know about it, the better."

Oh, but to tell the truth, the hard truth. Would anyone really want to know? Or, are they more comfortable believing the show and its cast of characters were in real life as they were on TV? If that's true for you, put this book down. The show does deserve its beautiful memories.

This book is about the kooky, wonderful, different, loving, harsh, confusing, fascinating, otherworldly way I grew up as Erin Walton, and how I came out the other side *not* having robbed a convenience store. Despite my lack of criminal activity, I did not escape totally unscathed, either.

The decision to write didn't come easily for several reasons. When people ask me why we haven't written a book about *The Waltons*, I joke that if anyone did and told the whole truth, the rest of us would get together and kill them. So, if I disappear soon after this book is published, consider *The Waltons* family members key suspects.

Seriously, I hesitated to write in deference to my beloved cast mates. We have always regarded each other as family. There's a huge amount of respect for each other's privacy. We are dear friends this many years later; we love each other, and no one will ever break our bond. You don't grow up with ten extra family members over the course of nine seasons and *not* have a lot of life together. They are also why I believe we grew up, well, fairly "normal." But I'm ahead of myself.

I've learned the Universe has a way of confirming our paths to us, and one day the "book" messages pushed me to complete this book. I was at work on *The New Adventures of Old Christine,* where I had a recurring role as Mrs. Wilhoite. I found myself in a conversation with Blair Underwood. (Yes, of all people! And yes, he is the nicest ever. And yes, the most handsome!) I was telling Blair, who played Mr. Harris, my funny stories of Walton-hood and being a mom, and now a "step*monster,*" and he said, "Mary, you have to write these experiences and tips in a book."

Then, later on the set, Tricia O'Kelley (Marly) and Alex Kapp-Horner (Lindsay) were asking me about *The Waltons* and my years growing up in the business. They shared how much they loved the show and thought my stories were great.

"You should write a book! Look at us! Seriously, our mouths are hanging open wanting to hear more," Alex said.

Tricia agreed and said, "You have to write this."

Julia Louis-Dreyfus (who, yes, is the funniest, nicest, most talented, and most gracious woman) joined us and shared some of her own fond memories of *The Waltons,* and talked about how she and her sister, Lauren Bowles, used to "play Waltons" when they were kids.

The timing of these conversations, along with my desire to share my story and offer encouragement to others, confirmed I should write.

So, back I go, to my foundation, my friends, my Walton family. Back to her, the girl I tried to crawl out from under for years. The girl I had sealed away in a Tupperware container somewhere. Yeah, *her.* What a mixed bag for me, being Erin.

Establishing myself as Mary McDonough, separate from Erin Walton, had become important to me, as it is for any actor or performer, whether they are associated with a particular character or just a public persona. I've been taught and had no trouble appreciating fans; yet I yearn for a sense of self, to be loved and understood for who I am, not the image of any character I've portrayed.

Rosemary Clooney, the beautiful singer and actress, was like a mentor-mother to me. She taught me about separating what's important from what can be let go. I met Rosemary in 1982 after meeting her sons and nephew in Kentucky while shooting a movie. More about that later.

She embraced me and treated me like a daughter when I dated her son. I, like many, called her "Mama." She had knowledge about the business that my mother didn't. Rosemary knew better than most celebrities how to separate her private life from her public persona, without disappointing either one. I remember one year we were in a Christmas tree lot and the owner asked her to sing "White Christmas." There, in the middle of the pine trees and fir, reminiscent of that fabulous setting for the movie, she graciously obliged. I know she made his holiday, as she does mine to this very day. I still cherish the Christmas cassettes she sent each year with a personal message to me.

One night after a PR event, she told me it was time to "take the singer off and hang her in the closet." She described it as metaphorically taking off that persona, hanging the girl singer on a hanger, putting on a comfy robe, and surrounding herself with family. She literally knew how to "be" Rosemary, without feeling conflicted with who the world thought she was from the public image.

It would take me years to understand how to do that, but her example helped me learn to put Erin on a hanger and "be" Mary. Eventually I learned it was okay to be both—I didn't have to get rid of Erin; I just needed to know when to wear Erin and when to hang her up.

I had been away from Erin for years, trying to leave her in that "closet." Writing this book, I faced her again as I headed back to Warner Brothers Stage 26 in the shadow of the Cahuenga Pass, the familiar backdrop now recognizable as Walton's Mountain.

At the age of ten, I had no way of knowing how that mountain would change my life. Nor would I know until decades later how the show, scripts, and the people would mold me forever. It became more than a place where I struggled to grow up in a world of contradictions, required to be a working "adult," but treated like a child. I had good times and bad, and one of the most unique and amazing experiences a kid can have.

The mountain became a symbol of my life. My life had been trying to move my mountains of emotion, fear, pain, experiences, failures, and feelings. I believed if I could just plow through my mountains of life's "stuff," I could get to the top and be accomplished, successful, happy, and healed. If I worked hard enough, it would pay off. If I had enough indulgences, I'd get to heaven. (My Irish-Catholic upbringing rearing its head.)

Over the years, I've hiked, run away from, cursed, climbed, screamed, and thrown my rage at my mountain. I've given up a hundred times and felt defeated by my life's mountains. I've brought in huge earthmovers to drill through it. I've assessed and talked it to death and let others tell me how to move it. I've examined every rock, boulder, and pebble, and even had soil samples run on the bloody thing—thinking if I understood it, I could conquer it. Hell, I would have eaten it if I felt that would do the trick. I just wanted to be better, whole, and done with it!

Then one day, exhausted, I sat down and decided . . . maybe . . . just maybe I could enjoy the view. In the stillness, a peace came over me as I realized I didn't have to move the mountain at all; I could just walk around it. I could even sit on my butt and slide down. I finally learned that embracing and accepting my mountain, and all its molehills, made all the difference.

These are my memories of forty-nine years of joy, struggle, loss, love, illness, pain, and pleasure. My fears and tears are just like everyone else's. All right, my experiences are a bit different. Once, when friends were sharing high-school stories, someone commented, "Mary, you can't even share a high-school memory because you weren't a real high schooler." Ouch.

But I grew up, too. I just happened to do it on television in front of millions of people. My solution then was to hide my struggles, thinking if I could be little Mary Walton, I would please all of you. So I kept my secrets until it almost killed me. I've always written, so this book seems a natural way to express my journey as I share the mountain of lessons I learned from the people I loved and the life I led on Walton's Mountain and beyond.

When I found this poem, I realized I must have known my life was changing when I got the show. This poem represents faith to me. Knowing that even though life may be hard, you should always trust and never give up.

The caterpillar symbolized me separating my reality from a kid's dreamworld. At a very young age, I had profound sadness and empathy that often made me cry for strangers, animals, war, starving children, and even snails my dad killed in the yard. I told him it was a mortal sin to kill and he would go to hell for killing the snails. He said, "But these are just snails." They weren't just snails, to me. I guess my Buddhist leanings began early. I think that empathy ultimately saved me and is what makes me good at what I do.

"Caterpillar"

By Mary Beth McDonough (age 10)

One day as I was lying in the grass,
A caterpillar crawled in my ear.
He traveled through the thoughts in my mind
To see what he could find
There were so many roads to take
He didn't know where to go
Up, down, to or fro
So he decided to go down.
There he found grey colors and
In this world was not a sound
No feeling or maybe it was all feelings
He didn't know, so he went up
There he found flowers and sunshine days
And a lot of happy things in many ways
He found experiences good and bad, but
Something about this happy world
Was sad
This place was nice but he had to leave
For soon he figured out it was all a dream
It just wasn't as real as it all seemed
Then he went to and fro
There he saw dreams that could never come true
This made him sad and blue, but realized
This was a reality world
How sad but happy he became, so that
All the dreams seemed the same
Yet, there was still hope
He told me "not to give up, to try and cope."
Because everyone's dreams can come true in life
Although sometimes they may seem stifled and small
Always try and keep building your wall

Hold it together and don't let it fall
After he had been up, down, to and fro
There was something he knew that I
Didn't know
Then he crawled out of my other ear
But he was a BUTTERFLY . . . and
He flew away with all my hopes dreams and cries.

1

IRISH LUCK

I am the middle daughter of a working-class family. My parents were poor growing up, and both came to the "City of Angels" to find their gold. My father's brother, Jimmy, was ill with what we now suspect was cystic fibrosis. His doctor suggested a warmer climate, so the whole family left the farm in Beemer, a *very* small town in Nebraska, and headed west to California.

My father Lawrence McDonough taught us all about life on the farm, devotion to family, God, loyalty to our Irish roots, and the Cornhuskers, of course. Once he told me about how the well-to-do in Beemer treated the less fortunate. Years later, after *The Waltons* was a huge hit, we visited Beemer. He was so happy to be invited to dinner at the homes of those who had shunned him as a kid. I wanted to be mean right back to them, reject them. I said, "Daddy, just tell them *no*. They weren't nice to you when you were a kid." I have a real sense of justice, and knowing my father had been rejected as a kid hit my fairness nerve, made me protective. Okay, if I tell on myself, maybe I wanted just deserts, comeuppance, to level the playing field, or even a little revenge.

He just smiled and said, "Now, Mary B., we'll go and you'll be nice." I begrudgingly ate more fried chicken dinners on that trip than I could digest. As I watched him at all those dinners, I saw his integrity and learned lessons in dignity, grace, and respect. He was a true role model for me. To this day, I strive not to be negative and resentful. But I am only his daughter, I am not my father.

My daddy was my hero, and all I wanted was to make him smile and receive his adoring approval.

Early on in his California experience, he worked as a valet in Hollywood. He vowed that someday he would be successful enough to have someone park his car. He was employed at Lockheed before entering the navy. After his discharge, he worked for several companies before realizing he could help his family more with his own business, so he started an automatic transmission service shop with his brothers. So you can imagine how a television show for one of his kids would be *a dream never imagined.* My dad did get his car parked on more than one occasion, and later even escorted me to the Emmy Awards.

My father is the first layer of my mountain. This boy from the farm rose to every challenge. He instilled in me a rock-solid foundation of love, protection, political involvement, right from wrong, Catholicism, a fierce work ethic, and intense self-scrutiny, all essential foundations for life. He was demanding, but a hard worker who expected as much from me and everyone around him as he did himself. He started the transmission business with his brothers and eventually developed other investment properties. He was tireless in his work ethic and dedication to his family. He strove to raise our standard of living above his own poor beginnings. My brothers and I still talk about how we became who we are through his strength and personality.

A Kennedy Catholic, he instilled in us a political foundation based on our faith. If he had only known then that his little girl would grow up and meet a few Kennedys, it would have seemed impossible to him. I remember political debates he had with my friend Caren's dad, our Republican assemblyman. I couldn't believe he'd argue with my friend's dad, but they did every time they sat down for a chat. I don't think he could help himself. He was a man dedicated to change, even if it was just to change someone else's mind.

Everyone loved him and the personal attention he paid anyone he met. He taught us all to drive, and then a few years ago at a reunion, at least seven people told me he had also taught them to drive. He must have been driving an awful lot. I had no idea.

Dad took all the kids in the neighborhood to ride horses, drive go-carts, fishing, camping, to the beach, and to ethnic restaurants. Anywhere he could, to give us an adventure. He'd load up the car and take whoever jumped in.

He always wanted us to try new things. At one time, he had heard about a restaurant where they made drinks in pineapples and coconuts. We got all dressed up and he drove us to a Polynesian-themed restaurant, complete with palm trees, torches, and Tiki carvings. I had never seen anything like it, so exotic, so different from Northridge, where we lived. Years later, I realized he had taken us to Trader Vic's—all the way to Beverly Hills for a drink! Such fun. My adventurous spirit was born in those excursions.

So, obviously, I was born and raised a daddy's girl. He used to sing "You Are My Sunshine," touch my red hair, and say it was the only gold he owned. Because of who he was, I adored him and desperately wanted his acceptance.

Leaving La Junta

My mother Elizabeth Murray McDonough is the second strata of my mountain. She was beautiful, always. She had a flair for fashion and wore the gloves, hat, and matching purse to prove it. She owned wonderful sets of jewelry from the fifties and sixties, with the coordinating necklace, bracelet, and earrings. Looking back at her in old photographs, I find it hard to believe how well she pulled herself and all of us kids together, picture perfect every time. She also came from a hardworking family, but she had a tougher childhood than Daddy did.

Mother's family was poor. She had escaped her abusive, alcoholic father from the small town of La Junta, Colorado, and came to California. She was kind and sweet. After all the horror stories we heard about her childhood, I couldn't believe she would still visit her father, and take us all back to Colorado so we would know our grandparents.

I once asked her why she was so nice to someone who was so mean to her. She said, "Grandpa was in the war, and he was never the same when he came back. Something happened to him over there." She took a moment and then continued. "I think that's why he beat us."

As a young girl, I remember her sense of forgiveness for her father. She had a sense of duty as a daughter that was passed on and had a lasting impression on me. She hated arguments and disappeared at the first sight of a confrontation. We were not allowed to yell in our house. I never heard my parents argue, and we never really learned how to fight as a result. Disagreements of any kind were too uncomfortable for her. She would say, "Like snow, I've had enough of that to last me a lifetime." She found Catholicism and my father in the same church in Highland Park, and created a new life for herself.

She is the first "feminist" I ever met. She hated that term, because she somehow thought it meant giving up being feminine and a lady. No matter how much I told her she could be a feminist *and* a lady, she would say, "I still like to have doors opened for me and my arm through your father's." But she was truly the first person who taught me to be independent and to create my own life.

"Mary, play the field," she would say when I was little. "Then go to college, and play the field, then have a career, and play the field, then travel the world, and then *maybe* think about settling down."

Perhaps because she had to be dependent on my father, she wanted me to learn not to rely on a man for things. She told me I could do anything the boys could do, "and probably better than they can, too. I always did." I think she was better at sports than some boys, when she was young, but was teased for being a tomboy. She didn't want me held back because I was female. She had survived adversity and wanted to instill independence in me. It worked.

Once, when she was still living at home, Mother got fed up with the beatings and my grandfather's mood swings. She packed a suitcase and took it to school with her, intending to run away to a girlfriend's house. When my grandfather realized she was gone, he hunted her down and banged on her girlfriend's door and threatened—and no doubt also frightened—everyone inside. Her friend's mother let her go. My grandfather tied her to his truck with a rope, shoved her suitcase in her arms, and made her run behind the truck the four miles home. This is only one of the stories my mother shared with me after my grandfather died.

My mother wanted our childhoods to be different from hers in so many ways. She gave all of us the dance lessons she wanted for herself, and sat through more classes than I can count, to give me her dreams.

Her dreams became mine, and I soon found something I was good at. I don't remember my first dance class—it seems I always danced. I loved the pink tights, the black leotard, and wearing my hair in a bun. I loved my dance classes because I could express myself. My active little body loved to keep moving, and dance gave me an outlet combined with structure and discipline.

I went to Marge Patka's Dance Studio on Tampa Avenue and Sherman Way in Reseda. There were other dance studios with live piano players and fancier rooms, but for me, the simplicity of those hardwood floors, barres on the wall, and mirrors were enough. The record player sang out every tune we needed. I learned ballet, jazz, acrobatics, Hawaiian, Polynesian, and tap. I was never great at tap, which I attribute to my poor math skills. Ballet was it for me.

My favorite teacher was Stephanie—"a prima ballerina," my mother constantly called her. I didn't know what that meant. I just knew I loved Stephanie and was so happy to see her at every class. She gave me her joy of dance. Dancing felt natural to me, and gave me a sense of accomplishment and acceptance. It taught me discipline, which would help me later on the set.

Learning toe was a marker of growth for me. I struggled with the blisters, cramps, learning to stuff the perfect amount of lamb's wool in the shoes. I remember, once we had two shows at a recital and were told not to take our toe shoes off before the next show or our feet would swell. I didn't, but my feet swelled, anyway. When I finally took them off, my feet were bleeding into my toe shoes, which were forever stained with my discipline and hard work. Those shoes became a tangible sign of inner strength that helped me all through my life. Mind over matter, the show must go on, rise above it, pull yourself above the pain . . . all those lessons.

Stephanie gave me solos in the recitals, and I felt special. My daddy took home movies and snapped pictures of me in my costumes. I loved my costumes and that we got to wear makeup and false eyelashes at the performances. I sensed my dad loved my dancing, so I worked hard to be even better. When I felt his approval and love, I wanted more. Dance brought me the attention and acknowledgment I craved from both my parents.

I still keep those toe shoes in my hope chest, and am still proud of my ugly feet. I tell people I earned them "when I was a dancer."

Both of my parents wanted us to have it better than they did. They worked for the American dream to give us everything they didn't have. Sound familiar? Yes, the parallel of my Walton family and my own is the foundation so much of my life is cemented on.

SIBLINGS

Several years of marriage later, they fulfilled their own dream of a home in the San Fernando Valley, with children to fill that home. First, my brothers arrived; a few years later, I was born on May 4, 1961.

After I was checked over and cleaned up, the nurse brought me to my mother and said, "Here's Mary."

"How did you know her name?"

"We didn't. We give all the newborns nursery names until the parents make their final decision. She looks like a Mary." So I guess it was meant to be.

They brought me home to meet my brothers, Michael and John. Michael was six years old, John three. When I was three, my sister, Elaine, was born, making me a middle child, just like Erin.

Raised on a farm, my father had learned construction, and he could build or repair just about anything. He designed and built for his bride and young children a dream house at the end of a cul-de-sac, within walking distance of our new church and school in Northridge, California. Near completion, there were still some finishing touches after we moved in.

They were laying the new floor in our foyer and I was in the kitchen with my mom. She told me, "Mary, now stay here and don't walk on the floor. No matter what you do, *don't* walk on the new floor." She carefully took me to the back of the house and put me down, only to turn around a few minutes later to find me in the kitchen again.

"Mary, how did you get in here?"

"Don't worry, Mommy," I said. "I didn't walk. I tippy-toed." Ah, always a literal thinker. My footprints were in that floor until it was remodeled years later.

VALLEY GIRL

Northridge is a small community in the San Fernando Valley, about twenty-five miles northwest of Los Angeles. It's perhaps most famous for the 1994 earthquake, which was really centered in Reseda, but once named, always associated. I can relate to that.

So yes, I'm a born and raised "Valley Girl." In the 1960s and 1970s, Northridge was still filled with orange groves and empty fields, and we could ride our bikes through the parks and down the streets surrounded by the mountains. It was a great place to grow up. Our roller skates made their way around the school parking lot at the end of our street and kids roamed around the community.

There was a freedom and sense of safety for me in our little town. The Vietnam War was on the news, but it was on the other side of the world. I would run past the round television screen, unless one of my favorite shows—*Sea Hunt* reruns, *Get Smart, Bewitched, Family Affair, The Courtship of Eddie's Father,* or *Laugh-In*—was on. The political unrest on the other coast in Washington D.C. never slowed me down, although I remember my father "discussing" the country's future with the neighbors.

Most of our neighbors went to our church, and the community was tight. We spent many family nights at home or eating out along the "main street," Reseda Boulevard, in family-owned shops and mom-and-pop restaurants. We'd ride our bikes to My Hero, a famous sub-sandwich shop, or Dad would take us to a family-style Italian dinner at Morigi's, or for a "with six, you get egg roll" Chinese dinner. We'd also go to San Fernando to have authentic Mexican food. It was there I learned not to trust your brothers and let them put the "it's not hot, Mary" hot sauce in your mouth.

My father made a lot of friends and contacts through his business. As I mentioned, he was a generous man, and I'm certain many of the meals we ate were trades for the work he did at his car repair shop. He once brought home half a cow. Mom said, "Larry, what are we gonna do with all this?" They bought a freezer for the garage and we had beef for dinner for what felt like years.

Our new house was next door to the Reynolds family—eleven kids, their parents, and Granny and Gramps. This was heaven for a kid, and a precursor for my future. For every McDonough kid, there were two Reynolds kids to play with. My Reynolds family member was Connie. I met her when I was three. We were the same age and in the same grade at Our Lady of Lourdes.

When the show started, I was already used to a large, extended family living under one roof. Mrs. Reynolds would watch us when our mother worked at the family business, and often took us on impromptu trips to the beach, which we loved. You've heard the expression "it takes a village to raise a child"—well, I learned about the "village" early on.

EARLY THEATER

I had never really acted before, unless you count the plays I wrote and forced Connie, Claire, and Danny Reynolds to perform in our backyard.

These backyard theatrical productions always involved a Reynolds or two. Poor Danny had to play all the boy parts because we needed him, even though I suspect he would much rather have been playing with the older boys. But he was the youngest, so we dressed him up and told him where to stand.

Our plays were a mishmash of themes I can barely remember. Lots of "weddings" were performed. Usually, a little dance thrown in, since Connie and younger sister Claire took classes at Marge's as well. The girls would dress up in elaborate outfits from our moms' closets and our dance recital costumes. I had learned that art from my cousins Curlie and Patty Hearne, who dressed me up, along with my cousins Bobby and Billy.

We would set up chairs from our dining room on the back porch and use sheets for curtains (my mom loved that, her clean sheets on the patio). Our stage was the patio with entrances and exits from the back door. It was great to have so many choices of actors for our plays. We had a built-in audience with my parents, Granny and Gramps, Mrs. Reynolds, and a few big brothers who heckled us from their seats on the lawn furniture.

As I grew up, I was kept real and humbled by the kids on our street. The open-door policy of families helping each other and being there for community is a big part of who I am. Many rocks in my mountain have the name Reynolds etched on them.

Rosary and Mala Beads

The rosary was a big part of my upbringing. When my parents were dating, my dad would end a date with a decade (a set of ten Hail Mary prayers) or two before dropping my mom safely at her doorstep. We often visited our cousins on weekends, and on our drive home those Sunday nights, we said the rosary as a family. Each of us would lead a decade. My brothers, of course, would poke me and each other to try to break us up, and we would get in trouble.

When each of us was born, my parents had our whole name engraved on the back of a special rosary cross. I still keep mine on my nightstand next to my mala beads. The rosary was modeled after mala prayer beads, so it's all come full circle in meaning. For me, it's about intention and focus, and connecting to Love and the Source.

Saying the rosary is a staple to Catholics. The prayer is a series of the Hail Mary bookended by the Our Father, with a few of what my father called the "Glory Be's" as well. My father loved saying the rosary, and his beads were all he asked for in his last days. I understand now how the repetition of prayers calms the mind. I used to say it when I couldn't sleep. Now my spiritual practices have evolved. While I don't consider myself a religious person, I am spiritual. Today I use mala beads and chant different prayers, but my spiritual practices sprouted their roots during all those years of saying the rosary as a kid. Even today, when I pray for my Catholic family, I use my rosary.

With this prayer and my namesake, I joined the Legion of Mary at my school. We met each week, got on the floor on bended knee, and said the rosary. I wanted to be a nun and walked to school early every morning to go to mass before school. I'm not sure why I wanted to be a nun, since my experiences in Catholic school were tough. I went to a Catholic school until I graduated from high school. My cousins had a very different experience in their school; they learned about a loving God. That was not my takeaway from school.

I felt God was unyielding and unforgiving. Catholic school started the perfection issues I still deal with today. It seemed no matter how "good" I was, I would never be enough for God. I would never have enough indulgences to get anywhere, forget heaven. I was scared all the time. One teacher in particular made me feel imperfect. I felt shamed by her about my appearance, that I was not enough as I was. It was the beginning of trying to change myself to please others. Even then, I wanted to fit in and do the right dance.

MISS PERFECTLY PULLED-TOGETHER

I felt judged by this second-grade teacher. The story is as vivid for me today as it was then. "Miss Perfectly Pulled-Together" had not a hair out of place. She was tightly wound, from her clenched fists to her underlying anger. No yelling, no raised voice, but she used the passive-aggressive noise of her high heels hitting the metal podium to control unruly seven-year-olds and instill mental fear as we waited for her punishment. She would stomp and wait. We would turn to look at her smiling face. She would wait until she had everyone's attention, staring back at us. One day, the perfect bow decorating her shoe fell off from the force of her stomping.

As it lay powerless on the floor, we laughed; then the punishment came. Scolding, shame, and even more *Baltimore Catechism* questions for us to memorize.

She was responsible for one of the horrors that set me up for years of hypersensitivity to disapproval, letting me know I was not enough, not okay as I was. It's the hair. I've always had stringy hair. Every morning, I loved being in the bathroom with my mother. I brushed my hair; then she would pull it back as tight as she could into a ponytail. She would tuck in all the loose ends but by the time I walked to school, the "fly-aways" had already begun to escape. Then, at recess and lunch, I would go outside and play so hard, my face would get beet red—and my hair. . . well, some of it was still in the ponytail. Back inside, we would put our faces down on the desk to rest. I could feel my heart beating into my hot face against the cool desktop.

One day, Miss Perfectly Pulled-Together handed out personal-hygiene pie charts with arrows that spun around pointing to each piece. One slice was marked for *shoes polished and clean;* others were for a clean face, brushed teeth, clean fingernails and hands, neat hair, or clean clothes. If you were especially neat and clean, you might get a star or two to put on your chart.

Another day after lunch, Miss Perfectly Pulled-Together decided to drive the pie chart lessons home. She started at the first row and, desk by desk, addressed each kid and how they were doing with their pie chart. "Carol, you have beautiful hair and already have so many stars on your chart in each category, very nice. Sam, your shoes are always clean, but maybe you could do a little better washing those hands after dodge ball. Adrian, you have lovely curly hair and you always wear a pretty bow in it. Patrick, your uniform is always ironed." She went through row two, then onto row three with more compliments.

Nick sat in front of me. I often stared at his scalp through his buzz cut, wondering if his skin got cold without any hair. "Well, Nicholas," Perfectly Pulled said, "you don't really have any hair, so your hair is always neat." She smiled. I couldn't wait to get my compliments. After all, I did wash my hands after recess and lunch, and I knew my mom always cleaned my uniform, and I had a few stars on my pie chart to prove my success. My ankles were crossed perfectly, my hands folded on my desk, and as she approached me, I sat up a bit straighter.

"Now, Mary. Well, your hair . . . I don't know what to say. And as we all know, if you don't have anything nice to say, you shouldn't say anything at all, so I'm just going to skip you."

I felt the red blush of embarrassment heat my freckled face. I reached to smooth the fly-aways back into the ponytail, but I could feel the stares. I froze in my guilt and imperfection. It devastated me, and it obviously still does, because here I am decades later, and it still makes me sad as I write this. I'm so outraged I allowed this idiot teacher to hurt me so much.

For years, when I went into her class with a note, or saw her on the playground, she'd pull me closer and straighten my uniform. She would tighten my belt, tuck my tag in, push my hair down, pull on my collar, and smooth my skirt. She was a constant reminder that I was not okay; I needed changing and straightening. Her disapproval weighed me down like rocks of shame in my young mountain. Early on, I knew I wasn't enough. I felt I needed to change to please my father, my second-grade teacher, and eventually the wardrobe department.

TICKET TO THE IRISH SWEEPSTAKES

Dance classes brought me to my first audition. Many of the other moms told my mother she should get me into acting. But we didn't have the first clue how to start. My mom thought I would lose interest, so she waited. Several months later, I saw a girl on a Kool-Aid commercial doing a cartwheel and I said, "Hey, I can do that. Why can't I be on TV?" Never thinking about the acting element, I just wanted to be doing gymnastics in a commercial. To this day, I've never done a Kool-Aid commercial, my first dream of being on television.

I bugged my mom so much, she turned to the best place she knew to find a business: the phone book. She called some "agents" and "managers," and we met with them. They turned out to be phonies, wanting money or a seven-year contract before they would "represent" me. My dad would have none of that. Eventually we found a legitimate agent named Mitzy MacGreggor. With a name like that, any Irishman would have liked her.

My first audition ever was a cattle call for redheaded kids. That's how I slipped in. The hair, always the hair. It was for *The Homecoming: A Christmas Story*, based on Earl Hamner's own life and family. We read with lines from the walnut-cracking scene.

My mom held my hands and told me I had my first audition, and we jumped up and down, screaming with excitement. When we got to the audition, I remember seeing a lot of kid actors whom I recognized from TV waiting their turn. I was starstruck and couldn't believe I was in the same room with these kids. I didn't know them, but I *knew* them from TV. Lots of kids all over the country want to act, but I was lucky. I just happened to be living in Los Angeles, in the right place at the right time, with famous kids auditioning for a movie. Unbelievable.

After the original interview, I was called back several times to be paired with different combinations of kids. My mom wanted to cushion the blow, so she told me how lucky I was to get to come back so many times. She reminded me not to be disappointed if I didn't get it. After all, it was my first audition. She took me back for several more callbacks, and we just enjoyed the wonder of it all.

Then I was called in with Jon Walmsley (Jason), Judy Norton (Mary Ellen), Eric Scott (Ben), Kami Cotler (Elizabeth), and David Harper (Jim Bob). We did the same scene one more time. Then Fielder Cook, the director, started talking to us. I don't remember everything he said, but he explained that we would be working with Patricia Neal and we needed to be careful around her.

I didn't understand, but I still listened. They dismissed us and we got up to leave, as we had many times before. But this time, it did seem a little different. As I walked out of the room, it finally dawned on me, and I turned to Eric. "Does that mean we got the part?" I think he laughed. He was a veteran.

This would not be the last time I didn't "get it" about the business, left to figure out what was going on in this wild world I was about to step into. I was ten years old when I was cast as Erin Walton. My dad said it was like winning the Irish Sweepstakes after buying one ticket. Turns out winning the sweepstakes, like getting cast in a movie, will change your life, and your family's, forever.

NO RUBBER BOOTS

We filmed the interior scenes on the CBS Studios Radford lot in the autumn of 1971. It was so wonderful for me, yet scary at the same time. I had never really acted before, unless you count the plays performed in our backyard.

One of the first things I remember was being measured for our depression-era garb we wore while filming in L.A. Since all the action took place in one day, we had the same clothes for all the scenes. I had a dark blue wool dress with a maroon sweater, and for the outdoors, a hat, coat, and scarf. We would run to a post on the wall, grab our coats, and out we'd go into the L.A. sunshine.

Judy wore boots, and some of the other kids did, too. I thought, *I'm so glad I have these little leather shoes. It's so hot and I don't have to clunk around in big ole ugly boots.*

Cut to: Wyoming, late October 1971. When we finished the interior shots at CBS, we flew to Jackson Hole, Wyoming, to shoot the exteriors for the snow. It was thrilling to go with everyone on a chartered plane to a small-town location. I loved that my parents took me shopping for warm clothes. I got a new coat, a snazzy plaid number—it was blue and bright yellow, with yellow trim around the hood.

We stayed in Jackson Hole at a small motor lodge that had a pool in the middle of the common. Judy, Eric, and Jon were having snow fights and daring each other to walk on the frozen pool. Kami and I were less adventurous and made snow angels on the ground. We have home movies of it all. Such a great adventure.

Picture: The end of the walnut-cracking scene. We all leave the barn and traipse through *snow* to the house with the lovely smoke curling from the chimney. So cozy and warm-looking, right?

Well, I'm in the wool dress, tights, and those little leather shoes. After each take, they sent us inside to warm up. The snow caking on my shoes melted, and my shoes were soaked through. Another take was called, out we'd go, and my feet would refreeze.

There's a lovely scene where we followed John-Boy leading the cow across the pasture. You get the picture—my feet were frozen. I'm looking around and everyone else has boots on. Hey, how did that happen? Why can't I wear boots now? Lesson learned: What's worn for the inside scenes must match what's worn for the outside scenes. "Live and learn," as my mom would say.

My mom and Betsy Cox, the costume designer, took me in the honey wagon (the specialized trailer used for dressing rooms and bathrooms on location) and rubbed my feet in front of a coiled heater. My feet were so cold, they ached.

We still had to film the scene in front of the store where a missionary gives out presents to the kids who correctly recite Bible verses. My mom put so many pairs of socks on me that night, I barely fit into those shoes. If you watch closely as we walk past the broken doll Elizabeth gets, you can see my very thick ankles.

ROCKING EDGAR

Next time you watch *The Homecoming*, notice how we kids run everywhere. We jump up and sprint to the door when Charlie Snead, played by William Windom, arrives. We run to see if Daddy's home; we dash to the barn. When we're all gathered around the radio and Claudie (Donald Livingston) comes in to tell us about the missionary, we practically take out Edgar Bergen, who played Grandpa. Watch it in the final cut, his rocking chair goes all the way back, and he's left scrambling in our dust. Fielder had warned us to be careful around Patricia Neal, who had just recovered from her stroke. But he didn't say anything about Edgar.

I'll never forget something that happened when we got to Wyoming. Edgar Bergen realized we'd missed trick-or-treating, so he called everyone to the lobby and we gathered in front of a crackling fire in the huge stone fireplace. He carried in a small suitcase; I couldn't imagine what was in it. My mom fidgeted and winked knowingly, her eyebrows raised in a "just wait and see" look. I was clueless. The anticipation grew until he snapped open the locks, lifted the top, and pulled out Charlie McCarthy. Right there, Edgar gave us our own private show. Watching him in awe, I knew this was a treat other kids wouldn't get for Halloween.

After the lobby performance, my mom urged me to ask for his autograph. I was so shy and felt dumb, but I brought out my little orange corduroy autograph book. Boy, am I glad I did. He drew a picture of Charlie in that little book, and he and Charlie both signed the page. It's a treasure I still have.

Years later, I was working on *Boston Legal* and told Candice Bergen this story about her dad, and how we stampeded him. I shared how he was one of my fondest memories of filming *The Homecoming*. Although I'm sure she'd heard a million of them, she graciously listened to my stories of her father.

Whenever the Waltons listen to the radio—when the broadcast wasn't part of the script, they often listened to the Charlie McCarthy radio show.

LITTLE (CITY) GIRL WITH BIG (COUNTRY) BARN ALLERGIES

I have animal, grass, hay, and dust allergies. You can imagine what the barn scene was like for me before the days of Claritin. Oh, my eyes itched, my nose ran, and I tried to stifle sneezes. Later, we filmed a scene where we're all standing on the stairwell, and the camera pans up. I remember laying my hand on the railing, and then hearing Fielder tell the cameraman to follow my arm. I felt so special in that moment, like I had done something good and cool as an actress. But my nose itched from my allergies and I kept rubbing it. When I watch the movie now, I laugh at that kid scratching her nose.

The walnut-cracking scene became so familiar to me, I loved it. I didn't understand a reference about Mary Ellen's hormones or the laughter at Elizabeth's "I'm gonna have puppies" remark, but I went along, pretending to get it. I danced around it as best I could and tried to keep up. This became a pattern for me when I didn't know what was going on, and I didn't feel the permission to ask. I'm not sure why I felt so unsure and unable to ask, but there's a story my parents told about me from when I was a small child. My dad had the radio on, and I was dancing and dancing, and finally, out of breath, I said, "Daddy"—huff-puff—"can you please turn off the radio so I can stop dancing?"

For years, I kept dancing, never knowing when to stop.

YOU MEAN NOT EVERYONE IS CATHOLIC?

One of my first wake-up calls that I was not in Northridge anymore came in the schoolroom on the set of *The Homecoming*. All the kids were with our studio teacher, Betty King. I was memorizing my *Baltimore Catechism* questions, and she asked about my beliefs. (As Jon Walmsley observed recently, I was so young, I had a hard time defending myself.) The teacher told me she was Jewish, and about the differences in our religions. Eric weighed in, saying he was also Jewish, and someone talked about the "Big Bang" theory. I got so flustered. I had never known anyone who believed differently than I did. They asked me why I believed what I did; I had no answer of my own. I was raised in my church, Catholic school, and parish. I hadn't gotten out much.

I kept thinking, *"God is the Supreme Being who made all things." Isn't that the right answer? I get an A for that at home.* I only knew what the *Baltimore Catechism* said was true.

My head raced and I remembered my mother telling me that Jewish people didn't believe in Jesus—imagine the trouble I had with that! They asked me how I knew God made the speck that made the Earth. *Oh no, what if I was wrong?* I started to cry.

Jon, always a dear one, pulled me onto his lap. I settled down and asked him, "Well, what are you?"

Tenderly he said, "I'm a Protestant."

I burst back into tears and sobbed, *"Ohhhhh nooo!* My mother said we don't even *like* each other!" Jon was so sweet; he calmed me down and assured me we could be friends despite our religious differences. My lesson from his gentle nature was one of pure acceptance. In that moment, the first glimmer of embracing the differences in people, instead of judging them, was born in me. Jon's kindness taught me a deep acceptance I would not truly understand for years to come.

2

WELCOME TO THE MOUNTAIN

The Homecoming earned a thirty-nine share in the ratings, which means that of all the people watching television at the same time, thirty-nine percent were watching us, a huge number in the biz. Christmas shows traditionally do well, and the mood in the country lent itself to a nostalgia piece where family values were paramount in a tight-knit community of neighbor helping neighbor. The CEO of CBS, William Paley, learned of the movie's success, and as Earl Hamner described in his book *Goodnight John-Boy*, Paley screened it while on vacation in the Bahamas and ordered it to be developed immediately into a series.

I was ten when *The Homecoming* aired in December of 1971. Connie Reynolds came over with a special gift of Almond Roca and watched the show with me. We ate the whole can as we watched the show. I was unaware of the business decisions, the political climate, or how my life was about to change forever. It was really a time of uncertainty for all of us, a constant in the entertainment field. Other shows, such as *All in the Family,* tackled issues like racism, religious intolerance, and the war in Vietnam, but ours was the first dramatic series to include these progressive topics in weekly storylines. Slotted to air against *The Mod Squad* on ABC and *The Flip Wilson Show* on NBC, the critics predicted we wouldn't last the season.

THE DEVIL OR THE WALTON

No matter how I look at it now, something in my life was about to change, and it had to do with Hollywood. The only other role I auditioned for between *The Homecoming* and the series starting was *The Exorcist.*

Before they went to New York to find Linda Blair, I was one of six girls narrowed down in Los Angeles. My agent called my mom and told her there was going to be a hypnotist at the audition, asking if that was all right with her. My mother told me years later she anonymously called the hypnotist and asked him what he was going to do. She thought it odd that he was going to an acting audition. He told her they might want to use hypnosis during the movie, and he, too, thought it odd that she was the only mother who called him. This made my mom nervous. She sent me and my dad to the store to buy the book. As a Catholic woman, she needed to know what *The Exorcist* was, before I auditioned.

We'd ask, "Do you have *The Exorcist?*"

They would say, "*Exodus?* Yes, we do."

We told them about the book by William Peter Blatty, and suggested they might want to stock it, as they were about to make a big movie based on it. We finally found a copy, and my mom read the entire thing the night before my audition. When I woke up, she was trembling and pale. She said, "You are *not* doing this movie."

She called the agent, who assured her I would never get the part, but I should just go on the audition so we wouldn't upset them.

I went and all of us girls pretended to be hypnotized. At least, I did. It was acting, right? He told us to hold hands and that we couldn't let go, so we didn't. Then he told me I couldn't pick up a dollar bill off the floor. He placed it there, telling me it was glued and there was a million pounds on top of it. I told him I thought I could. He told me again how I couldn't, and we went back and forth. He said I could have the dollar if I could pick it up, but that I wouldn't be able to because it was stuck and weighted to the floor. Then he egged me on, "Try and pick it up, let's see. There's no way you can do it." I walked over and picked it up. I was escorted out of the room, and I never even got the dollar.

Years later, I met "Blair," as I call her. She became a close friend. She was so supportive when I started In the Know, a resource for women seeking information on body image issues. She bravely told her own implant story for a congressional education video I made.

She is a great girl, whose laugh I can hear as I write this. I am not the only girl with a cackle. The two of us could make people crazy with our laughter. Our laughs even cracked us up. She was not like most people assumed. She stayed home making cookies while I was out on dates. She was the tame older sister—nothing like the image people have of her. We became roommates, and she brought rescued animals into my animal-free house. Her passion to save animals is honorable and unavoidable. Just ask my pink chaise, or what was left of it. At an animal show recently, my girls worked in her booth and helped with the dogs for adoption. She is a rare combination of being funny, beautiful, and passionate.

WALTON, IT IS

To my mother's relief, I didn't book the movie, but I was asked to return and play Erin on the show that would be called *The Waltons*.

It was a time filled with excitement and energy. Everything was changing for this little Valley girl. I'm sure my parents had no idea just how much all our lives were about to change, but the flurry of activity was electrifying.

I remember when they took me to Our Lady of Lourdes to pick up my textbooks, all fourteen of them, to bring to studio school. California entertainment laws require working children to log at least three hours of school every weekday during the school year.

My life was about to explode into two lives, lived simultaneously, yet worlds apart. My own McDonough family was about to collide with the Walton family. One set didn't supplant the other, but the Walton siblings were immediately more present in my day-to-day life.

BACKLOT BABY

People often ask me where the show was filmed. I tell them "Burbank," and watch their eyes widen, since it looked so much like rural Virginia. The exterior house set was on the backlot of Warner Brothers. Ike Godsey's store was literally down the road from the house set. The back roads and Drucilla's Pond were there, too. If you went a bit farther, you would be on Western Street.

To this day, whenever I visit the backlot, it's still a sensorial experience for me. The roads, overgrown bushes, and divots on the path return me to hot summer days, rainy winters, beloved crew members, refreshing lemonade from the craft service wagon, and us kids running around the barn and mill.

The earthy aroma from the eucalyptus and pine trees overwhelm and instantly remind me of walking barefoot on the dirt roads, wearing depression-era clothes often held together with duct tape. I especially remember one dress whose seams came apart one hot summer day. Sweat dripped down my back and the tape stuck, ripping my skin when I moved. I hated that dress and was so glad when that episode was over, so it could be "retired."

No such luck. They just sewed it with a patch and put it back in my wardrobe stall. My favorite was a pink dress with a smocked bodice. It was a shift, so at least it was cool; it seems like I wore it all summer that first season. I also remember carrying prop lunch boxes everywhere. We were always taking them from the house, carrying them to school, using them in the school scenes, and then back home again. We lugged those antique metal boxes everywhere.

With the freedom of summer and no school requirements, we had a great time and got to know each other better. We ran all around the backlot, exploring our new home and "neighborhood." We met all our cast animals and wandered the back road to Ike Godsey's store. It was such an adventure, always something new.

We explored the sets on Western Street, one of my favorites was used as Shangri-La in *Lost Horizon*. This enormous outside set would soon be reshaped into a Shaolin Temple for the television series *Kung Fu*. It was huge, probably three stories tall. I had never seen anything like it before. We ran up and down its steps and hid in the rocks. I tried to imagine what the fountains looked like with water and flowers. It was an imaginary playground turned real life—well, not really. It was amazing to me and so different from Northridge. What better playground could a kid ask for?

EDUCATING MARY

Every script brought something new. We learned some sign language for "The Foundling," about a little deaf girl left on our doorstep. Then there was "The Hunt," where John-Boy doesn't want to kill an animal, but he saves Pa when he shoots an attacking bear. It wasn't scary, because the "bear" was actually a costume we got to see and touch. It was so much fun for me. I mean, what kid gets to be exposed to this kind of stuff?

We were working with the best. They brought in Russell Metty, the Oscar-winning director of photography, to create the look of the show. When I went to film school, I realized he was an icon. He worked with Orson Welles to shoot the famous opening scene for *A Touch of Evil*. As a kid, I didn't know, of course. He was just a man who sat in a chair and chewed a green cigar. He would wave his best boy over and mumble something to him. The lighting changed and the show had an incredible look and feel for the era. Magic. We were surrounded with talent.

There was so much to learn about acting and sets and all the equipment and terminology, I felt like I didn't have a clue what was going on. I knew how to follow directions because of my dance training, so I did that, and I watched the other kids to see what they did, because they had all worked before. It was a thrilling, wild ride and I was glad to be on it. I felt I was part of something special.

KID IN A CANDY STORE

When we weren't working, the interior sets were another place we explored and poked around. First we explored our new "home." The interior of the house was in Soundstage 26, the exteriors were filmed in the backlot. The house was modeled after Earl Hamner's childhood home in Schuyler, Virginia—a common structure in the area because of its practical design, usually a two-story, with three windows across the top floor. For the Hamners, the upstairs was divided into bedrooms for all the kids, but the Waltons had to squeeze the girls in one room, the boys in another, Olivia and John in theirs, and another one for John-Boy, who had his own room. And with the bathroom, that made . . . too many rooms for the facade. To make it work, the furniture for all our different rooms would have to be removed and replaced each week depending on the script.

The girls' room and the parents' room were actually the same set. So, when we filmed a hallway scene, we didn't have enough doors. Whenever we ran out of the room into the hallway, we'd have to "appear" from our room. To make it look believable, Kami, Judy, and I squished together, hugging the wall. At "action," we would walk out of the "wall," like it was a door.

We loved exploring Ike's store, with its antique props from the 1930s. It was like a museum. I looked in awe at all the toys, the bolts of old fabric in gingham and heavy ticking, the vintage clothes and the canned goods with nostalgic labels. The candy counter was our favorite. When we filmed, the props department filled it with licorice, hard candies, and all kinds of tempting treats. We were warned not to touch anything, but we snuck a few here and there, when nobody was looking.

Eric, David, and I once went into the store set when we weren't filming. It was dark and all the counters were covered with sheets. We peeked under the protective cloths, hoping they'd left some candy behind, but no such luck. One of us did find some ancient tobacco leaves for roll-your-own cigarettes. Eric dared us to try it. He took a small piece, David took a chunk, and then they looked at me. The good girl in me was challenged; I knew we shouldn't, but I didn't want to be left out. I broke off a small corner and we all put a taste onto our tongues. We stared at each other, trying to be cool, but the tobacco was old and tasted like acid. We spit it out, but tiny pieces stuck to our tongues. We frantically searched for somewhere to wipe off the foul taste, but we were in wardrobe, so no using our sleeves! We ran to the craft service cart and threw back glasses of the very welcome, ever-present lemonade to wash the disgusting taste out of our mouths. We laughed and realized how old those tobacco leaves must have been. Lesson learned: don't eat antique props.

We used Frazier Park for location shooting a few times a year. Now, that was a great time. We were in a beautiful setting, with mountains and trees, and would spend the night at a hotel in Gorman, California. This was the high life to me. Imagine us kids running around the hotel, enjoying ourselves. Jon Walmsley once jumped into the pool in his pj's. It was all harmless, but so much fun.

We ran around the hotel, and one night we saw Richard Thomas in the bar with some crew members. We wanted to be with everyone, so we went in for a visit in our pj's. I remember watching the bartender make a drink they called a Cardinal's Cap. In a small glass, he floated a thin slice of lemon on top of the liquid. He carefully placed a clove-dipped sugar cube on top of the slice. Then he lit it on fire. Amazing to me. I had never seen anything like that before . . . or since, now that I think of it. This was incredible for a ten-year-old. My memories are so vivid, and each new experience touched me. Suddenly I was a part of a new life and family that made me feel unique, to say the least.

The first episodes were incredible—so many memorable stories. When I saw the amazement on my mom's face and realized how different this new life was, I became as enchanted as she was to meet and work with Hollywood legends. In "The Carnival," Billy Barty, who had been acting since 1925, played Tommy Trimble. Once again, I took out my orange corduroy autograph book. He signed it for me and was so nice; we were all enthralled with him. I can be as starstruck as anyone, and every time we saw him on TV after that, my mom and I would say, "Oh, look, there's Billy," like we were his best friends. I still jump when I see someone I have met or worked with on TV. The magic is never lost on me.

An Acting Lesson from Bob Butler

On the set, I was just a kid, and a bit lost when it came to the acting part. They wanted us to be kids and act like kids, so not a lot was said about our technique. Without formal training, I made mistakes. I wanted to be so good and perfect (I equated perfection with grace, like memorizing the answers in the *Baltimore Catechism;*

if I followed the Catholic Church's rules, I was good. To me, a mistake was a sin, something bad to be ashamed of. Every time I made one, I felt evil inside. It took me years to learn it was a *miss*-take, not a sin.) I didn't really know what I was doing; so the more mistakes I made, the worse I felt about myself. I started hearing whispering and mumbling, "She keeps looking . . . ruining the shot. . . ." I knew they meant me.

Robert Butler, God bless him, directed many episodes of the show, and he gave me my first acting lesson—a huge one I am so grateful for. One day, he said, "Mary Beth, come over here, I want to show you something." We headed to the sweeping pepper tree that held the swing in the front yard of the Walton house.

"Watch this," he said. "I'm going to catch a snake that's asleep under the swing, but I have to be very careful not to scare it away." He slowly approached the "snake," his eyes glued to the target. He moved at a snail's pace, his hands raised, the tension mounting the closer he got to grabbing the snake.

I was mesmerized. He was so focused and intent on the invisible snake, I believed it was really there. He moved in slow motion, closer and closer. Suddenly his eyes darted away and he looked straight at me. He broke the moment. It was ruined. The magic was gone.

He showed me how losing focus and looking at the camera destroyed the whole scene. I got it. I never looked at the camera again. I was always a visual learner, and he showed me in a way I could understand. I was relieved to know what I'd been doing wrong. He treated me with respect, and I am still grateful for Bob Butler's lesson under the pepper tree that summer day.

THE HORRIBLE SECRET

The school scenes were fun because there were lots of other kids around. Our real-life siblings and some of the producers' and some crew members' kids came in to fill up the Walton's Mountain schoolroom. It was a fun time to have all our families with us, most of the time.

Early in the first season—I was almost eleven by then—one of the kids told me something that rocked my world and set me up for humiliation, insecurity, and constant fear.

We were sitting outside the school set, and she sauntered up to me and said, "I know something you don't know."

"What?" I said.

"It's a secret, and I'm not supposed to tell you."

"Tell me," I pleaded. I watched satisfaction literally spread across her face.

"I heard"—she paused, either for dramatic effect or because she enjoyed the attention—". . . I heard something about you."

Now she had my complete attention. "What did you hear?" My stomach turned.

"I heard you weren't very good in *The Homecoming*, and they didn't want you back when they picked up the series. The casting director didn't like you and wanted a new Erin. You were lucky you even got to come back."

I crumbled inside. My mind raced back to when we were first cast and Earl Hamner's remarks about how I reminded him of his real sister. So that was it. The only reason I got to be on the show was because I reminded Earl of Audrey. Not because I was talented or good. I thought about that stupid nose-rubbing incident in *The Homecoming*. I wanted to cry, but I held it in, numb, barely able to make it through the rest of the day.

I cried for days, but not in front of anyone, of course. That secret became a gray cloud that lived deep inside me, reminding me I was out of my league. I wasn't liked, I wasn't wanted, and I'd never been good enough. I could be replaced. I lived in fear that this wonderful ride would end at any moment. So much valuable energy was wasted on this fear.

This was a boulder on my mountain I would face over and over again, never feeling I was talented enough. And it set up a pattern: I learned to hide my sadness during the day and cried alone at night. I couldn't tell anyone, because I feared what she said might be true. I didn't want to remind anyone how awful I was. I never even told my parents what the girl said. I was afraid to be a disappointment to them if I was let go. I felt I would have ruined the most special thing about me. There would go all the attention and love that I craved.

I'll never know what caused that schoolyard bully to say what she did to me. Jealousy? Attention? I do know that if I had only felt safe enough and asked my parents, or Earl, or even my schoolteacher back then, I would have saved myself a lot of pain, and my life might have been different. I would have known the truth, instead of hiding a terrible secret, which wasn't true at all. Over thirty years later, I finally got up the nerve to ask Earl. He said he had no recollection of any discussion about replacing any of us kids when it went to series. I also asked Claylene Jones, one of our producers. She said the same thing and wished I had told someone. Me too!

Expressing my own voice has been one of the best lessons of my life. It took many years of running headlong against that boulder to learn how.

SCHOOL DAZE

People often ask what it was like to go to school on the set. It was great on a lot of levels, but unusual and different for me. Our first schoolroom on Stage 26 was an old train car left over from some show. I always thought it was probably left over from an old *Bonanza* episode. Stuck in the back of the soundstage behind the painted backdrops, this boxcar still came complete with a sliding cargo door. We had to lift the lever, then slide the door open, but not while filming, because it was too loud. We had to be really quiet since the ceiling was chicken wire covered with a sheet of cotton. They even hung a red light over us, and when it turned on, we would look at each other and say, "Shhh, they're filming!"

Our teacher, Mrs. Deeney, lobbied for a better classroom situation, which we eventually got.

The law required at least three hours of school a day, but that didn't mean we only went to school that long—at least, I didn't. On our set, we were able to add school hours with a system called "banked time." It's usually used when you are working so many hours, you don't get your three hours in one day. You can make up for that time on slower filming days. The studio teachers keep track of the time kids spend doing schoolwork, and log the extra "banked" time. It's a standard practice for most studio kids. I had to get my assignments completed for my school's requirements, three hours or not. Because I had so much schoolwork, I had over a hundred hours of banked time.

In the early years, we had different studio teachers, usually two at a time, one for us younger kids and one for the older three. Once when Eric needed a teacher who could teach him German, we got a teacher for that requirement.

One of our teachers early on was Thordis Burkhardt. Her husband was the famous abstract expressionist artist, Hans Burkhardt. One year, her Christmas card was a print of one of his sketches, a treasure I still have.

There was one teacher we did not like. She wanted us all to sit in cubicles facing the wall so we wouldn't waste time talking and distracting each other. Well, let's just say she wasn't there very long.

Catherine Deeney was with us a long time, though. She was a special woman. She had taught everyone, even Shirley Temple. I remember thinking that was the coolest.

Mrs. Deeney taught me moderation. I ate a lot of candy as a kid, and she asked me to cut back and eat only one piece a week. It was a huge request for me at the time. No one had ever taken an interest in me like that before. I felt cared for, with her special attention and lesson. She educated me to the why and how about candy. She told me why sugar was bad for me and my teeth, and I agreed with her idea. I decided if I had to wait a week for a piece of candy, I would pick something that would last longer than one bite, so I chose one of those red cinnamon square lollipops, which were popular. I brought it to class and Mrs. Deeney kept it on her desk until the given day. I really enjoyed that lollipop and learned about delayed gratification, patience, my teeth, sugar, and moderation. I know this lesson affected me later in life, too. When I learned a moderate way of dieting later on, I applied this early lesson from Mrs. Deeney.

When they are old enough to do so, Roman Catholics reconfirm the faith their parents baptized them into. When it was time to choose a confirmation name, I chose Saint Catherine in honor of Mrs. Deeney, who was Catholic. I added "Catherine" to my already long name. Now I was Mary Elizabeth Catherine Murray McDonough, a proud Irish lassie.

One of the hardest parts of being a kid actor for me was going back and forth from the set to school. I would be in the middle of a math problem, and they would call for us with "ready on the set." We needed to go to the set, even if the math problem or chapter was not finished. Then it was time to change gears, put on a different thinking cap, remember blocking and lines, and get into the Erin character again. I wished I could just finish the problem instead of having to start all over when we got back to school. Heavy emotional scenes were even harder.

Some days, being on the set was so much fun, we never wanted to leave to go back to school. Think about it. Stay on the set with the activity, the cameras and lights being set up, and all the grown-up actors talking and laughing . . . or go back to school and find "x." No comparison. I remember Jon would often start talking to someone and never make it back to school; sometimes they'd have to send someone to bring him back.

When Jon and Judy graduated, I was jealous, and our class size got even smaller when Eric graduated. I hated to be in school while they were having fun on the set. I knew I was missing out. I was so glad when I graduated and could focus on the work and feel like a real participant.

BUCKTEETH AND BRACES

There is vulnerability in growing up in front of so many people. The entire country sees every aspect of your childhood. In my case, it started during my youth, lasted through the awkward teenage years, then into my early twenties.

When it wasn't the hair, it was the teeth.

When I was younger, my teeth were really crooked. I inherited my mom's small jaw and my dad's big teeth. For the show, it was perfect. A farm girl in the depression with irregular teeth fit the part. One of the aspects that made the show real was that we were not perfect-looking.

I suffered through as many teeth-straightening procedures as I could for a better smile. I had baby teeth pulled, and then some permanent ones were taken out. I felt like I lived at the orthodontist's office. I wore headgear every day and when my mouth wasn't visible to the camera. After years of orthodontia, it became clear that I would need braces. The Waltons were a poor family in the depression, so my having braces was out of the question, according to the production company.

Cut to: A few years later, *Little House on the Prairie* started. *Little House* was set in an even earlier time than *The Waltons*. So imagine how chapped my hide was when I saw Melissa Gilbert, as Laura Ingalls, wearing braces in the late-nineteenth-century American West. I couldn't believe it. I think they were clear and on the back of her teeth, but there they were. My dad lobbied again, but the answer was still no.

Despite the orthodontic jealousies, Melissa and I met a few years later at a *Tiger Beat* party, and we became good friends. We saw each other at different promotional events, and had a lot in common and many mutual friends. One friend used to rent a cabin up in San Bernardino every year for his birthday and invited us to ski with him. A bunch of us went and had a great time. Melissa and I would usually do the shopping, play house, and cook for everyone. Spaghetti, if you're wondering.

When she started to date the young actor Rob Lowe, he joined us on those ski trips. It was interesting hanging out with actors before they got their big breaks, and then seeing their careers take off. Rob's certainly did. It was fun for me to follow their success and remember a simpler time when we all skied and just hung out at my house. I was a bit older and owned my own home by then, so I had parties. Not wild or Hollywood parties, I lived in the Valley. But I did have a Jacuzzi, and we would fill it up with Mr. Bubble and everyone would jump in. All good clean fun, but a bit odd to think of how our parents let us do all that stuff. Years later, when I did a small role on *The West Wing*, Rob and I laughed about those parties.

Another perk of hanging out with kids from other shows was meeting Alison Arngrim, who played Nellie Oleson on *Little House*. She is a hoot and a half. With her wit and personality, it's no wonder she went into stand-up. Over the years, we became friends, and she came to my Christmas Eve brunch every year. When I made my short film, *For the Love of May*, Alison was perfect to play the sarcastic Jude. She is wonderful in the film. I feel lucky to have had Alison and Melissa's friendship over the years. We have a common bond, having lived through growing up on television.

Years later, I told Melissa of my jealousy that she got to wear braces and I didn't, and we had a laugh. I still have not had braces, but I do wear retainers every night.

MISSING McDONOUGH

Being plucked from my "Valley" life and dropped into "Walton" life felt like I was running up the mountain to get by in this completely new world. Adjusting was tough for me. I didn't see my family as much, and different guardians took me to the set, because my mother was working. We lived about an hour from the studio; Northridge is about eighteen miles from Warner Brothers, so I was in the car constantly. It was a long drive for a ten-year-old.

As much fun as I was having at studio school, I still missed my friends at my regular one, especially my best friend. When I started working, she stopped being my friend. I never understood why she didn't want to know me anymore. My mom told me one day some people didn't like or approve of "the business." Even my aunt warned my parents that I would "go to hell" if they let me work in show business: "Nothing good can come from that." She warned that this "terrible" place I was going every day was bound to corrupt me. It just wasn't very "Catholic." I heard a rumor that was also why my best friend wasn't my friend anymore; her parents felt the same way.

I was torn between enjoying my new world, and letting go of my life as I knew it. I didn't complain, because all I heard was "You're so lucky, you're so lucky." I knew I was. I was having a blast, after all. However, now I had not only lost friends, I had received scorn from family members, and that gray cloud of self-doubt hovered over me like a shadow across my happiness.

PROMOTION AND BEYOND

Soon we were booked almost every weekend to promote the show. We did more parades than Carter has little liver pills, as my mother would say. I even made an appearance for Toys for Tots. Again, I didn't know what to expect, and no one told me ahead of time what I would be doing.

So picture me. I am about eleven or twelve, standing at the edge of a holiday set clutching a toy my father has handed me. A stranger gives me a microphone and says, "Walk up to that marine, offer him your toy, and *don't blow it.* This is live television, kid."

Don't blow what? What was I supposed to say into this mic? My mind raced and my hands started to shake. I could feel my dad's eyes from off stage. I didn't want to sin; I wanted him to be proud of me. *Don't drop the toy, Mary! Wait, what's a marine, anyway?* I trembled as I walked up to a very large man in a uniform. He took the toy from me, and I knew I should say something. I put the microphone to my mouth . . . and the rest is a blackout. I have no idea what happened.

I still wish someone would have told me what to do or say. After so many of these experiences of having no clue—I still think of it as dancing to a tune I couldn't hear—I developed a fear of trying anything new, afraid I wouldn't perform as perfectly as expected. How could I if no one taught me the steps?

I was afraid of the unknown, the not knowing what was coming next in the performance arena. In the physical arena, I'm actually quite the daredevil—Bob Stivers, who created *Circus of the Stars,* invited me to perform on his show. I did an aerial act thirty feet in the air with Scott Baio.

I also guest starred on Bob's show *Celebrity Daredevils.* I had to transfer from water skis to a helicopter skid, and then the chopper flew up and over the lake, down onto the beach, where I stepped off onto the sand to join Bert Convy, who was waiting for me on the shore. In my private life, I've skydived, and bungee jumped off a 250-foot bridge in New Zealand. But those were physical feats I chose to take. It was an entirely different challenge learning how to speak in public. So I failed, and felt miserable.

I eventually learned to dance, even when there was no music. I accessed my daredevil nature to help me through my fears and learned to find my voice, but it was a gradual process that took years before I worked past those feelings of shame and self-penance.

THE SINNER

In one of our first-season episodes, a young minister came to the mountain and preached "fire and brimstone," then spent the afternoon with the Baldwins, had a little too much recipe, and got drunk. In "The Sinner," John Ritter joined our cast as Reverend Fordwick. I vividly remember one of his first scenes. John-Boy pulled up in his car and John, or "Ritter" as we called him, got out of the passenger side, only to pratfall, hit the car door, then tumble to the ground, over and over. I was amazed how he could play drunk and do his own physical work. I was so afraid he'd hurt himself. He was great in that scene, and on the show.

He told me once that he thought some of his best work was on *The Waltons.* I agree. His work was some of the most memorable, and so different from his famous comedy. Little did I know this funnyman would someday help save my life, but more on that later.

DADDY DIRECTOR

"The Fawn" was an episode I'd rather forget. Talk about the embarrassment of a lifetime. This episode is where Erin wants to adopt a deer, Lancelot, but has to send it back to the forest where he belongs. There is a parallel storyline where a boy—who, I'm sure, was very nice in real life—is interested in Erin. For instance, he brings flowers to her at school. I was so mortified by the crew teasing me, I could barely breathe.

Ralph directed this episode, and I'd asked him to cast a cute boy. He picked who *he* thought was cute. I remember being so resistant to the scenes we had together, I was pretty impossible to work with. I think I frustrated Ralph tremendously. When you are playing out in front of millions what you have never been through in real life, it freaks you out. At least, it did for me. Sorry, Ralph.

One of the reasons I had a hard time with that episode was because I arrived at the show fearful of boys. When I was eight, I was the victim of inappropriate physical experimentation by neighborhood boys. This set me up with another secret I gave no voice to.

These "boys on the block" told me I was the bad one, I was to blame, and if I ever told anyone what they did to me, I would be in big trouble. Their threats silenced me: I carried that with me until I went into therapy years later and finally started to deal with the toll their actions took on my body, mind, and soul.

I was guarded and scared, unsure what was expected of me. I hated feeling obligated to men and authority figures. The pull between getting approval from them and doing what they wanted tore me apart inside. There were so many authority figures at work to cater to, I betrayed myself in deference to them. Only once did I tell my mom about a crew member who insisted I kiss him every day behind a backdrop.

I was about twelve and I'd bought a trendy outfit to wear to the first day back at work for a new season. It was a cute crop top and a pair of hip-hugger jeans. As we got closer to the studio, I got scared. I knew the crewman would want his kiss. I was maturing, and I sensed my new outfit would get me into more "trouble." I didn't want to touch him ever again.

My mom was very quiet about "girl things." She was prim and proper and didn't like to talk about what she perceived as the darker side of life, maybe because of her abusive upbringing. Right until the day she died, I never heard her say the words "tampon" and "gynecologist" . . . ever. So I had to choose my words carefully.

"Mom, I'm afraid I wore the wrong outfit."

She glanced over at me. "Why, Mary? You picked it out yourself. I thought you liked that one."

"I do, but I'm afraid of how the crew will react."

"What? Why?"

I spilled the beans about the daily kiss, the crew guy who coaxed and teased me into doing it all last season. She was furious. She told me that I never had to kiss him, in the first place. I was so relieved. She finally gave me permission to say no to someone in authority. For the first time, I felt I wouldn't get in trouble for disagreeing with someone. I was grateful my mom was on my side. It was nerve-wracking when I got to the set, but I did tell him on that day that I wasn't giving him the obligatory kiss *ever again.*

As big a step as that was, other obligations hovered in my confused little-girl brain.

I still couldn't talk to anyone about the whole truth, why I felt this way, so I withdrew. As Erin grew older, there were many love stories for her to play, but Mary didn't want to play these at all.

This was the case a few years later when, at age fourteen, I had to kiss a boy. One of the many kisses Erin received, usually followed by tears and a broken heart. Imagine having to kiss someone in front of thirty of your big brothers, sisters, and crew members, all who consider themselves your extra parents. Oh, I hated those scenes.

I looked for reasons not to like the guys I played opposite. Okay, one of them burped, spat, and farted before scenes, so I think that one was fair game for my disapproval. One of them tried to get close to me, probably trying to make light of a tense situation, and picked me up from behind by my pants, giving me a wedgie. I thought I would die. I swung at him, but he wouldn't put me down. My guardian, Cori Cook, rescued me from him, saving me from the humiliation.

Cori became my full-time guardian, and she is another person I credit with helping to save my life. She was a fierce protector, and would actually "body block" assistant directors who wanted to overwork me and say, "Not with my kid, you don't." She came to my aid, defending and teaching me things my own mother couldn't. She was a friend, guard dog, big sister, aunt, cool chick, and substitute parent all rolled into one. She accepted me for who I was and helped me grow into who I am today. She cemented in me the belief that it was important to stand up for yourself and okay to say no. If I developed a spine at all, it was because of Cori's care and example.

IT FLOATS, IT FLOATS

Among the tough days, there were many times that reminded me not to take it all too seriously, and Will was usually a part of the antics. A figurine that Grandpa won in "The Statue" annoyed

Grandma so much, it set the two to fighting. She said it resembled one of his old girlfriends, but Grandpa was like a kid with a new toy, and he set up the statue in the front yard, reciting lines from Edgar Allan Poe's romantic love poem "Annabel Lee" to her. After she caused so much marital discord, Daddy and John-Boy gave him a stern talking-to, and Grandpa finally decided to send the home wrecker to her resting place at the bottom of Drucilla's Pond.

This was an enjoyable episode to shoot, and I'll never forget Will leading the way, and we kids following merrily behind him, pushing and pulling the offensive statue in a wheelbarrow to the center of the bridge. We acted like it was a somber funeral procession, with Kami carrying wildflowers, bringing up the rear. Ralph, who directed the episode, had told Grandpa they would cut just before he gave us the go-ahead to push the statue into the water. Ralph warned us, "Make sure you don't push it over in this take. We only have one statue."

We shot the scene, up until the figurine perches precariously on the top of the railing. Ralph yelled "Cut," and shooting stopped. As they reset the camera for the big moment, we all waited patiently. Finally, we took our places again and heard "Action." Will said a few lines from the poem in a loving farewell, and someone pushed "Annabel Lee" into the depths of her watery grave.

It was very dramatic; the water rippled out in circles from the sacrificial plunge. A few moments went by and with a . . . *plop* and a . . . *splash* . . . she popped back up to the surface, bobbing and floating. Will, of course, without missing a beat, said, "Hello, you've come back to me." We all cracked up; the shot was ruined.

We had another long break, waiting for the property department to figure out a way to sink the pesky statue. When you watch the final, you can see the statue fall; then they cut to the closer shot as we bend over, watching dramatic bubbles rise to the surface. "Annabel Lee" never did sink, and they had to shoot from above because we couldn't get through another take without laughing. I loved when these funny things would happen while filming. For me, it's part of the magic: *For the moon never beams without bringing me dreams of the beautiful Annabel Lee. . . .*

COOL GUEST STARS

"The Gypsies" was another fun episode. Barry Miller played the Gypsy's son. He gave me a belt, and wrote a line from the show, *Craska gives,* on the enclosure card. That was the first time a boy gave me a gift. I was nervous and asked my mom what to do. She told me I could keep the belt. It was hard for me to accept the gift; I felt like I had to do something to deserve it somehow. I still find it hard to receive; I feel obligated to give something back in return.

I saw Barry in the Neil Simon play *Biloxi Blues* years later. When I spoke with him backstage after the show, he didn't seem to remember the belt, or me. This used to happen to me a lot as I grew up. I know now it could be because I had literally changed—I grew up. But back then, I felt forgettable.

"The Ceremony," written by Nigel McKeand, is one of many episodes where I sensed the show was special. Even as young as I was, its importance affected me deeply. Radames Pera (later of *Kung Fu* fame) played Paul, a young Jewish boy nearing his thirteenth birthday. His family had come to the mountain to escape Nazis in Germany.

In the story, Grandpa invites the Mann family to celebrate Paul's Bar Mitzvah in the Walton home. Radames was inspiring to watch. I thought he was so good with the Hebrew as he read from the Torah. I realized this episode would have deep relevance. People hadn't often seen in a television series this important social statement about embracing others' beliefs.

In the episode, Ellen Geer, Will's real-life daughter, played Paul's mom, Eva. Her hair was in braids, wrapped over the top of her head, very German. I loved that hairdo in real life, and Erin adopted that style in many episodes after we filmed "The Ceremony."

We all became friends with Radames, and when he started on *Kung Fu* as Young Kwai, we would sneak over to each other's sets as often as we could. It was fun to leave 1930s Virginia and travel a few soundstages away to the exotic Shaolin Temple. The massive set was lit with candles and burning incense. How cool is that?

We did a *Tiger Beat* magazine article with Radames about the kids working on the WB lot. He wore his skullcap and black costume with the high collar and frog buttons; we wore our vintage clothes. We could not have been more different; yet we were the same. Kid actors, bonding over work.

Radames and I have stayed in touch and I consider him a dear friend to this day. He has helped me sift through the dirt of my childhood to find nuggets of positive memories. I'm so grateful the show brought me his friendship.

In another pioneering television moment, John-Boy teaches Verdie Grant, played by Lynn Hamilton, how to read and write. John McGreevey's Emmy Award–winning script portrayed the struggle of this brave black woman to overcome her lack of education in "The Scholar."

I am proud to have been a part of this groundbreaking series, and to have it become a part of Americana. How many times in life does a person end up in the encyclopedia and *MAD* magazine? It's still astonishing to me.

I'LL CRY IF I WANT TO

I was twelve when we filmed the "The Easter Story," in which I had a larger than normal part. It was a special that was aired like a movie of the week and was at the end of the first season. It was two hours long, and had two titles. (It was also called "The Waltons' Crisis.") Earl Hamner Jr. and John McGreevey crafted the story around a scary time in our country. Leaving church one day, Olivia collapses, and the doctor diagnoses the dreaded polio. After the initial shock, everyone seems to take it in stride, business as usual. All the action moves to Mama's bedside so she can supervise and be a part of their lives. All except Erin, who is so afraid to see her mama sick, she hides in the barn.

This was my first crying scene, and I was terrified. My stomach was in knots all day as I waited in anticipation and dread. They scheduled the scene for the end of the day, because it needed to be dark. It was such a big deal for me as an actress, my dad even came down to the set to watch us film. With each hour that drew closer, the more scared I got. The producers had no idea if I could cry, and I knew it was in the script, so I better come up with the goods. Pressure on, and not just in my stomach.

The barn was on the backlot, where the exterior of the house was located. That night, it was full of crew members, equipment, and hay. As I prepared for the scene, I watched the dust particles rising up into the lights they'd set up all around me. They were so calm and peaceful, just rising to the light, backlit and glowing. I simply wanted that calm, to be floating effortlessly in the light, peaceful, almost still. I huddled on the floor and pulled my knees to my chest. We rehearsed for the camera, and Richard was so sweet. I didn't cry for the rehearsal. I had been revving up all day—and come hell or high water, I was going to cry, but there was still time. I didn't know how yet, but I set my mind to figure out how to cry as we waited for the lights and camera angles to be adjusted.

I heard our director, the wonderful Philip Leacock, tell Richard not to bring out a handkerchief in case I didn't cry. He didn't know if I would be able. Richard nodded and stuffed the handkerchief in his pocket. I thought, *Of course, I'm going to cry. I'm just waiting until we shoot.*

I used that pressure to get to it. My pride wouldn't let me *not* do the scene as written. I had been watching the best and brightest all year. I had a little training from Lois Auer, an acting teacher who seemed to teach everyone in those days. I still wasn't trained *how* to get myself to cry, but I longed to be good in that scene.

I waited while they set the lights. I was so anxious. I walked away, seeking a quiet place to be alone for a few minutes. Then I heard "We're ready," and my stomach turned. I felt like I was about to walk the plank, the sword was in my back forcing me into the depths.

I climbed into position, and waited for the announcement of "quiet on the set."

Then I heard "Roll camera."

"Sound speeding!" Bill Flannery called out.

And I went to the edge of the plank, thinking of the dust particles, the stillness.

"Action!"

I looked up at Richard and allowed myself to release my pent-up emotions. There was so much inside me, my tears fell. Richard said his line, dug in his pocket, and handed me the handkerchief. Oh, the connection and then the release.

Philip looked pleased and a little relieved. After that, they wrote many tearful scenes into Erin's life, so I cried all the time. Then when I got older, I kissed a lot, too. I always say Erin kissed and cried a lot through nine seasons.

My stomach knots relaxed and I could finally eat something. My dad scooped me into a great big hug, and told me how proud he was. That alone was worth the entire day of trauma. *My daddy is proud of me.* For a born-and-raised daddy's girl, it doesn't get much better than that.

It took me years to realize the sadness and release in stillness. A lesson I would later learn from Buddhist teachings. When I first started to meditate and get still, I often found tears in the quiet. My friend Jeanie told me, "The Buddha said that 'in meditation, every tear is a diamond.' " Sadness was often a struggle for me. For this night, anyway, the struggle paid off. I felt I had attained my goal.

A MILLION DEGREES

At least it seemed like it. One day, I was in the Waltons' green truck, sitting between Michael and Ralph, and we were filming a winter scene. These are always shot in the blistering heat of summer to be ready for broadcast in the proper season. I had on a coat, mittens, and a hat. We had to keep the window shut for the takes, it being "winter" and all. As I sat there, I could feel sweat dripping down my back. It was so strange. I was broiling, and yet I had chills and got dizzy at one point.

I was so well behaved, I never would have complained. I just got quiet and focused on the sweat running down my back. This wasn't the last time I felt sick or uncomfortable and didn't speak up— that situation became rote for me.

I'm sure they didn't want me to suffer, but somehow I needed to be the quiet martyr. After all, I could be replaced. The feeling I had no right to say anything would someday burn me in a worse way than roasting in this car.

SANTA AND MORE

To promote the show, we rode in a lot of parades on weekends, so we found ways to make them interesting. One game we played was to wave a certain way to see if people would copy us and wave back the same. Eric and Jon would call to people holding those plastic trumpets to see if they'd blow them. Sometimes we'd jump off our float and walk around in the crowd. I always liked watching moms waving their babies' arms for them. Like the baby knew who we were. Cracked me up.

One special occasion was the Hollywood Christmas Parade. A tradition since 1928, now over a million people line up along the route to watch celebrities on elaborate floats and in fancy cars. Marching bands and animals, such as horses, camels, and dog acts, pass by. Originally called the Santa Claus Lane Parade, it inspired Gene Autry to cowrite "Here Comes Santa Claus." (It was also once called Hollywood's Santa Parade; who can keep up?) Whatever they called it, I had watched for years on TV. Now I was actually *in* it! I was so starstruck, and I loved to see all the familiar faces from TV right there, in person. What a thrill for a kid!

We rode in that parade for years. We were on a float once with the *Barnaby Jones* cast, and Buddy Ebsen (Barnaby) had brought his own method for staying warm. The next year, Eric copied the tradition, and it kept us all warm. Can you say "recipe"?

The first seasons were like Mr. Toad's Wild Ride. Working all week and appearances on weekends kept me away from my friends and birth siblings. I had a new family to get to know and deal with. Just finding my place among them was a challenge. I was the middle child, too young to play with the older kids (Judy, Jon, and Eric), yet too old to play with Kami and David, who quickly bonded. All the responsibilities of being a kid actress—like crying on cue, learning lines, and balancing school and work and my family—weighed on me.

But there were perks—one was when I was sixteen. Along with the rest of the cast, I appeared on *CBS: On the Air—A Celebration of 50 Years*. It was a nine-and-a-half-hour miniseries that aired every evening for a week in 1978. After a look back to its roots in radio on Sunday night, each evening featured the primetime shows that were currently airing. Our night, Thursday, was called "Join the Family." Richard Thomas hosted, and we all joined him.

I still remember all of us gathered to tape the special and take the now-famous picture. Talk about starstruck! Everyone—even Lassie—was there. The picture is a framed treasure I still keep. Only the amazing Don Knotts stands between me and Lucille Ball! There I was, little Mary, with all the stars. I mean, think of it. Imagine being in a room watching Dick Van Dyke and Danny Kaye telling jokes and "shuffling off to Buffalo."

My favorite lesson ever in staying comfortable on set came from Vivian Vance that day. We were told to wear black dresses. I had on high heels and my feet were killing me. I limped to the back, and there was Vivian Vance, sitting on the edge of the set. I sat down to rest my feet, but I was too afraid to remove my shoes, for fear my feet would swell like they did whenever I took off my toe shoes. Ms. Vance looked at me and said, "Honey, let me give you a little tip. . . . They never see your feet." I looked down and saw she was wearing black Chinese slippers. She looked as comfortable as can be.

I have quoted her a million times since then and used her wisdom to confirm my "comfort before beauty" motto. "Vivian Vance told me one day . . ." Like Billy Barty, she, too, was added to my "best friend" list.

Throughout these incredible experiences, I worked hard to live up to the expectations as I made them up to be. There wasn't a lot of explaining, so I ran and jumped and climbed as best I could. When I fell, I took it hard—privately and personally. Overnight my life had changed beyond recognition. I loved so much of it, even though I missed my first life. I was lucky; I was on a show learning from the best ensemble a kid could hope for.

3

AMERICA'S FAMILY

There would be no Walton's Mountain or Walton family without its creator, Earl Hamner Jr. The mountain grew from Earl's own memories of his family living through the depression in Schuyler, Virginia.

His voice has a melody of its own, as heard in his soft, Southern lilt narrating the show's opening and closing in each episode. He is a gentle and kind man. He always has been. From my first experience of meeting him for *The Homecoming* to today, he has always been as supportive and encouraging as the day I met him.

We have all traveled to Schuyler to see where he was born and the real home of the Hamners. I love going there in the fall, my favorite time of year. There's something so special about his family and that town. It's no wonder thousands of visitors are drawn there every year. One gets a sense of the quality of the people and how Earl's experiences growing up there made the show so special.

One Christmas when I was about twelve, Earl sent us all Virginia hams as presents. My dad was so excited about that classic smoked ham, I thought he would eat it right out of the paper, until he saw the directions said you had to cook it first.

There is an Erin because of Earl and his sister Audrey, for which I am grateful. I would not be writing this book if not for his brilliant example of sharing a memory, a story, and a family's love. He is the real John–Boy, and a big brother to us all.

ADDING GRANDPARENTS

From the beginning, each one of the actors I worked with left his or her own unique stamp on my personality. After *The Homecoming*, Will Geer replaced Edgar Bergen as Zeb Walton and quickly became "Grandpa" to America, and to us. If you thought he was a character on TV, well, he was an even bigger one in life. His booming voice, large presence, his jokes, and the way he would ramble while saying grace during the famous dinner-table scenes were his trademarks. (Listen carefully, and you'll hear him listing plant names. The "trailing arbutus" was our favorite.)

In our first seasons, we filmed many of the mountain scenes in Frazier Park, north of Los Angeles. We would ride in the back of that familiar green pickup truck, or just walk along, and Grandpa would stop and break a small branch from a nearby shrub or plant. Then he would pull off a few leaves and say, "Kids, open up, try this" as he shoved the plant in our mouths.

One day, he chose small ferny leaves for our day's lesson. "Here, taste these," he said, his face lit up with his familiar, mischievous grin.

"Not me!" "What is it?" and "I'm not eating weeds, not this time, Grandpa!" we protested at once.

"Oh, go on." He winked, chewing on a stem while we watched.

Finally one of us tried it. "It's licorice!" the brave taster announced.

"That's anise. It's what licorice is made from." Grandpa beamed and the rest of us couldn't wait to try this "candy."

At first, we were hesitant. As time went on, though, we knew Grandpa wouldn't hurt us, so we usually opened our traps and got a good lesson on some herb and how to survive on it. Will had a master's degree in botany, and he loved sharing his love of nature with us kids. He tried to teach us volumes of information about plants: what their Latin names were, or the medicinal and dietary uses the Native Americans found for them. Honestly, I can't say I retained it all. The whole thing still makes me laugh.

I can still picture him in those overalls, always one shoulder unhooked, one hanging down his sleeve. He'd sniff the plant's aroma with a huge inhale, like he was snorting it, and make some yummy sound on the exhale. That only made me want to try it more. Sometimes he would take a little taste himself, but usually not before we did. Seemed he wanted to see our reaction.

Now, you might think this an odd thing for a kid to do, or a parent to allow. My dad had been a farmer and my parents thought all of this quite normal. Given their own upbringings, my parents were so thrilled by my new life, I think they appreciated the experience I was having more than I did back then. Besides, they never wanted to rock the boat on this great job I had. They never said not to try his earthy morsels, so I always did, and usually willingly. Sometimes I didn't like the taste of the tidbit at all, but I was so drawn to his energy, and how alive he was, I couldn't resist.

Honeysuckle grew behind the Walton house, and by Ike Godsey's store. Grandpa taught us to pluck off the green end of the flower gently and then suck the blossoms for their sweet drops of nectar. You had to work really hard to get those drops. Sometimes you could pull out the center, and a nice drop would be there for the licking. Other times, we had to squeeze a little to get the tiny drop. We loved doing this as kids. Kami and I would hunt for honeysuckle nectar all the time on the Warner Brothers backlot. Years later, when I bought my first house, I planted honeysuckle in the backyard, a loving tribute to Grandpa Walton. He "ate life" with gusto, and passed his enthusiasm for nature, and people, on to us as well.

Will Geer had been blacklisted during the McCarthy years. He hadn't been found guilty of anything worse than refusing to testify in front of the House Un-American Activities Committee (HUAC), but he, nonetheless, couldn't find work acting. During the years he was considered unemployable, he founded the Theatricum Botanicum for himself and other blacklisted actors. Times were hard for everyone then, and he traded admission for items such as eggs, homemade bread, or canned goods. He had cut his acting chops in Virginia's Barter Theatre and never wanted anyone turned away if they couldn't afford a ticket. Another similarity in my two "families," for my dad would also take trades for services in his auto mechanic shop.

The Theatricum (now the Will Geer Theatricum Botanicum) was, and still is, known for its excellent theatrical productions. Will coached, acted, and led folk singing in this still-popular venue. Pete Seeger, Arlo Guthrie, Della Reese, Burl Ives, and many others performed there at one time or another.

Will loved his Shakespeare and made sure that every plant mentioned in his works would be planted at the theater. He tried to teach us about the Bard, and we even did a show at the Hollywood Bowl with him. Kami, David, and I were the three witches in *Macbeth*. I still remember bending over the imaginary pot. "Double, double, toil and . . ."

I never really understood why I was so reluctant, but I dutifully learned the lines, even though I resisted. I wish now that I wasn't such a typical teenager and learned *more* from him. The reason I didn't might have been because of what happened during one particular play.

Grandpa always wanted more Shakespeare for us. He asked me to perform the role of Ariel in *The Tempest* . . . in the nude. He tried to tell me how "natural" it was, and that I could climb up and down the trees and it would be fun.

Well, I certainly wasn't comfortable appearing in the nude, and I'm sure *The Waltons* publicists would have freaked if I had, but we did go to watch. I sat in the amphitheater's hillside seats with my mother, watching as a man, not one of the actors, came out . . . and he was completely naked. It was the 1970s, of course, and streaking was popular. This man, I must say, barely streaked. Not a lot of running going on. It was a nude saunter, more of a bobbing across the stage and off into the woods. Well, it *was* very "natural," wasn't it? Just like Grandpa had promised. After all, it was very crunchy-granola-hippie living out there in Topanga Canyon.

I stared; people were laughing; my mother screamed and tried to cover my eyes. That's hard to do while yanking your thirteen-year-old daughter's arm out of its socket while dragging her to the car. He was my first naked man, after all. I was quite frightened; yet, at the same time, I was a bit interested in the different parts, as it were. I tried to get a better look without my mother noticing, and a bubble of laughter gurgled up in me. Then I saw my mother's face and I "got it." This wasn't a laughing matter—at least not to her. Bubble burst.

Then the audience started to laugh at *us!* Oh, the mortification, the embarrassment! Yikes! Isn't this "education" supposed to happen in the streets or at school with your friends? Oh yeah, I didn't really go to regular school like the other kids. I wasn't normal. Oops. I forgot.

So, instead of what I'd imagined, that warm, bonding, girl-friends-huddling-giggling-pointing-gasping-with-amazement over a man's body in some hot picture from *Playgirl,* I got my first glimpse of a naked man—with my mother! Yes, I was not raised like other girls my age. My life was different. My work life gave me wild Will that day. So different from the life my mother was trying to take me home to. To my teenaged embarrassment, we left in a huff, made a scene, and almost upstaged the streaker.

This whole evening at the theater and the difference between Will's attitude and my parents' became a pivotal moment in my whole approach to body image. I hadn't thought much about the way my two worlds collided and intermixed, but they had been, ever since the beginning. When I landed the role as Erin in *The Homecoming,* my mom had insisted that I wear a longish camisole with a training-bra-type undergarment so when I had to change in front of the others, I was discreetly covered. Now, mind you, I was ten years old at the time. But to uncover in front of the other girls, and possibly the wardrobe ladies, had been too scary for my mom. But it also sent a message to me: your body isn't good.

Compare that to the free-stylin' attitude of the rest of the country, Grandpa included, that bodies are to be admired as art in their freest form, and it was no wonder I was confused. On one end of the spectrum, I should be ashamed of being seen. On the other end, Will represented that I should be accepting and free with my body. Will was a hippie and could cast off any inhibitions through his art. While learning to be more accepting of myself and my body would have helped me in my struggles, I think something in the middle ground of my two experiences may have been better for me.

Because of Will's sometimes wild ways later that year, Grandpa gave me an extra Christmas gift. He led me away from the others, and with a wink, he whispered, "I think you're not learning about the beauty of nature at your house. Here, I got this for you, but don't show it to your parents." Thus, I became the proud owner of my first—and still only—book of nudes. (Yes, I still have it.)

Grandpa tried to encourage me to move toward being comfortable in my own skin and not ashamed. Even if it was just in my mind, I took a tiny step toward accepting myself with his unorthodox ways. My parents wanted me to be a lady, discreet and modest, but often I misinterpreted that as being bad or ashamed. Grandpa was trying to provide a balance, which would take me years to comprehend fully.

Grandpa would be glad to know I used the book of nudes to educate my own daughter about the beauty of the human body, breaking the cycle of shame. Today I use those lessons in my Body Branding workshops to empower others to make peace with their bodies—sharing my lessons of embracing and not judging yourself, and getting comfortable with the skin you're in.

He gave me other books, all of which he signed. One was on Bob Dylan and another on the Rolling Stones. He signed Mick Jagger's picture with an arrow pointing to Mick and wrote: *Mary Beth, WE adore you.* Like Mick knew who I was. What a sense of humor he had! (Oh, by the way, the only book he *didn't* sign was the book of nudes.)

Will was just so full of life, as if he was making up for being blacklisted. The irony was not lost on him that he had missed several years of his career to this horrible movement of suspicion and distrust, but now he played America's most beloved grandpa. He was so appreciative to be playing Zeb Walton, it seemed he got back a little of what he had lost so long ago.

He carried no bitterness, that I know of. He came to work every day with an upbeat, positive attitude. He made a point to meet new people every day, and is quoted as saying, "For well over half a century, I have never gone a day without getting acquainted with some other person, and in those times, I've only had my face slapped once and been called a few names."

He taught us to stand up for what we thought was right, especially when he thought someone was not being treated well. This applied to all people, even entire races. When a script once called for a Native American character, Will and Ralph Waite protested when they cast a Caucasian, instead. They made such a stink, the original actor was let go and the role was cast with a Native American ("The Warrior," Season 6). This act of defiance left a lasting impression on me.

I learned by their example how important it is to stand up and fight for what you believe in and live by your beliefs. They shone light on what they felt was an unjust practice and gave a voice to those who were speechless. This was unheard of for that time in television. These remarkable role models left a lasting mark that empowered me to do the same thing years later.

A LIGHT LESSON

When I was sixteen, my brother John served as guardian on my first trip to New York. The trip was an incredible gift. It was great to have my Walton and McDonough family members together on a special trip to a place that neither John nor I had ever been to before. Aside from parades in California, there weren't a lot of events my brother could go to. I was thrilled to take him with me and have a little bit of the fairy dust land on him, too.

We were accustomed to flying because our dad was a private pilot. He bartered his mechanic skills in trade to a group of doctors who owned a plane. In exchange for his work, they let him borrow it to take us on vacations. Imagine six people crammed into a small Beechcraft Bonanza.

So flying to New York for John and me was an adventure we cherished. We flew first class, a huge treat, especially since my brother is six feet five inches tall. He had never been in a plane where his legs didn't bump the seat in front of him, let alone one large enough to walk around in. The upstairs of 747s were lounges in those days. And I was so glad to be able to share my good fortune with him; I loved seeing him so happy and amazed.

All the Walton kids, and Will, were invited to be the honored guests for a Daughters of the American Revolution gala at the Waldorf-Astoria. Such a beautiful hotel, we felt like royalty. Once again, I had no idea what was going to happen, or what was expected of me. I don't remember any program or agenda, just the order to show up.

The dinner was a very fancy affair. Will addressed the large crowd on our behalf, and then sat down with us at the table. The presentation began. The lights dimmed, and doors at the back of the room opened. In walked a long line of women in single file carrying candles, chanting, "Walk in the light, walk in the light."

We didn't know if we were supposed to chant with them, or watch, bow our heads, put our hands over our hearts . . . what? They just kept marching to "walk in the light."

By this time, we were all pretty uncomfortable. We knew it was a reverent event. However, it became one of those moments, like when you're in church or another solemn occasion and you know you're not supposed to laugh, but you get the urge to giggle.

At the time, *Young Frankenstein* was popular. Will leaned over, and in unison with the women, whispered a famous line from the movie, "Put the candle back." That did it; we lost it. I started to chuckle first; then my shoulders rose and fell. Eric started to chant with Will; then Jon joined in; and we all dissolved into stitches. We were horribly behaved at this very proper function—I still feel ashamed about it—but we couldn't stop laughing. Those gracious women were marching in their procession and we acted like . . . well . . . teenagers.

Will regained control of himself first and indicated with a nod we should leave the table. One by one, every few minutes, one of us would stifle our laughter, get up, and make our way out the door. We finally gathered in the hallway, and with Will as our merry leader, we left the giggle fest holding our sides.

Grandpa was really a kid at heart. He had a good-natured habit of grabbing you with one arm and pulling you close to his chest.

One day, he swept me into a headlock. As he clutched me against his warm flannel shirt, I could smell the spicy aroma of his . . . uh . . . earthiness. That's a good way to put it. Will was very earthy.

He pointed to a group of people sitting at the other end of the kitchen table and whispered in my ear. "Mary Beth, Mary Beth, do you see those people over there?"

"Yes, Grandpa."

Leaning his grizzled face next to my ear, he said, "Right there is dissatisfaction."

"What do you mean, Grandpa?"

"They're looking for ways out of here. They're dissatisfied. I've been waiting all my life to play this part, and I will never leave. They'll have to carry me off this set on a stretcher. Mary Beth, you've gotta be grateful for what you've been given. What they don't know is that this is the best gig they'll ever have. Every day I realize this is the best part I'll ever have, and I'll never leave. Someday they'll look back and see this show is the best thing that ever happened to them."

Grandpa died a year later. His ashes were buried in a corner of his beloved Theatricum Botanicum.

Our sense of family manifested itself in many ways on the set, and we demonstrated it soon after his passing. In our dinner scenes, he customarily took the patriarchal seat at the end of the table opposite Daddy. When a director innocently tried to place someone else in Grandpa's seat, we protested so much that he gave in and left it empty.

In a sweet moment almost a year after that, we felt enough time had passed. The next person we allowed to sit in this place of honor was Erin's beau, Ashley Longworth Jr. in "The Legacy." (Ashley was played by Jonathan Frakes, whom I adore. More on "Number One" later.)

Will Geer planted in me the seeds of gratitude. He showed me how to appreciate life, the positive and even the negative things. He modeled how to "eat" life, to love nature and people, and to stand up for the things I believe in. In the years to come, I would remember his words, "Mary Beth, be grateful for what you've been given," and I would appreciate whatever gig I was blessed to have.

As we grew older and people left the show, I did appreciate the show and all it brought to me. He might have been America's grandpa on the screen, but he was a real "grandpa" in my life.

A New Grandma

I only knew my father's mother, whom we called "Nanny," because she lived in California. My mom's parents lived in Colorado, so we didn't see them often. Ellen Corby didn't have children of her own, so she adopted us, and even gave us presents for our birthdays. Ellen was an incredible woman. She was strict like a real grandmother, similar to how she was on the show. She laughed more than her character Esther. We called her "Grandma."

She taught me one of the most important elements of acting for film, which I still use to this day. It made me a better director, and I used it in all aspects of my filmmaking years later.

Before she became an actress, Ellen was a script supervisor for Laurel and Hardy, where she learned about the technical importance of a scene. She was impeccable at matching. Our dinner table scenes were a good example of her lessons: when to sip milk, when to butter your toast, pour a cup of coffee, or when to shovel in that forkful of peas. She taught us to remember exactly what line we did things on, then to match it on every take. This was important because for every close-up, or two shot as they call it, you must be doing the same thing you were doing in the master, or the wide establishing shot. I'm sure it was a huge relief for her not to be script supervisor with so many mouths to watch. Her instruction made us look natural, and we didn't ruin the coverage.

Years later, I was in *Midnight Offerings*, and in the master take, my purse fell off my shoulder. When we did the close-up, I made my purse fall exactly at the same moment. Someone asked me how I did that. I answered in two words, "Ellen Corby."

Some people don't know about another side of Ellen. She studied Eastern philosophies, and was so limber from yoga, she could bend forward, legs straight, and place her palms flat on the floor. People were surprised to see someone her age so limber. She loved seeing their shocked expression.

She was the first person to teach me visualization, to focus on the best, most positive outcomes for my life—a technique I later learned more about from Shakti Gawain's book *Creative Visualization*. She asked me once to hold her Emmy statue and really feel it as my own, to "see" myself winning one. She said, "That's what I did, and look, you're holding it now. You have to see it and believe it. Create it as true for yourself." Years later, on my own spiritual journey, I realized how much Ellen demonstrated "seeing and speaking" my own positive attitude into reality.

As a grandma, she was way ahead of her time.

THE BABY BLOOOOS

Ralph is our Pa Walton, our daddy. We always called him Ralph, never Mr. Waite. Whenever I hear someone mention Ralph, the first thing that pops into my mind and immediately makes me laugh is the "I Shot the Sheriff" story, but I'll tell you that one later.

He must have looked too young, because I have many memories of the makeup man touching him up to make him gray. He used what looked like a small toothbrush to sweep through his sideburns. I thought it was so cool to see his hair and appearance change before my eyes.

Ralph has *very* penetrating blue eyes. With one look, he can scare you, make you laugh, or cause you to burst into tears. One day, he sat at the head of the table, and before his close-up, he bent down, looked at his reflection in the camera, fixed his hair, and then straightened up. He looked at us and said, "How are the baby bloooos?" He got a big laugh, and this became a Ralphism. Many followed over the years.

As you know, we spent about half our lives at that kitchen table. Whenever we got bored or needed a break from a tense moment, he would jump in with the "Ralph" version of a song or joke. He added his own twist so they'd have an even funnier replay value. He would wait until the crucial moment, then crack us all up, get the energy moving again and shift our focus to the work. These moments are so distinctive that years later, one of us can begin a

Ralphism, and everyone else knows where we are headed . . . usually to loud laughter. Ralph always had the knack, and he still does.

When we started the show, Ralph had a hard time remembering our names. Here he was, playing the head of the household, with this litter of kids and a lineup of confusing names. There was me, Mary Elizabeth, playing Erin, not to be confused with the character Elizabeth. Mary Ellen was played by Judy, John–Boy was Richard, Ralph himself played John, and Jon was Jason. So he had a struggle to get the names right.

He poked fun at himself for that a lot. We were doing a reunion show years later, and he turned to Jon and said, "Now I know you, you're Eric, right?" Still makes me smile.

What we didn't know as kids was that he was struggling with alcoholism. He later told me that looking into our faces, realizing we looked up to him for guidance and as a surrogate father, had actually jolted him into getting help. He got sober and has been helping others do the same ever since. He is remarkable in his strength.

When he ran for the U.S. Congress in 1990 and 1998, we all supported him because we knew he wanted the best for his community. Ralph has always wanted the best for people. I love him for that, and for the continued smiles and laughter he still brings me . . . even as I write this.

A GIRL NAMED MICHAEL

I had a brother named Michael, but this was new to me. She was so beautiful and always so nice to us kids, maybe because she had sons of her own. What a nice mom, friend, and an example she set for me. Michael Learned became like a mother to me during the show, but through our years of friendship, she has become more like a sister. She was supportive like a parent, but without the scorn or disapproval a parent often brings.

One year, I wanted my ears pierced so badly, I begged and begged. The producers wouldn't let me because of the show. All my friends were getting pierced ears, and I wanted to be like them.

I even argued that Olivia had pierced ears, so why couldn't Erin? The answer was still no.

Michael heard about it and came up with an idea. She suggested writing it into a script. It didn't happen, but I loved her for going to bat for me. It's important to have someone in your corner, speaking up with a voice you yourself don't have . . . yet.

I'll never forget the scent Michael wore, a beautiful lily perfume, I think from France. I kept asking her the name, but could never remember it when I went to tell my mom. (I still don't speak French well.) Years later, Michael gave me my own bottle, and I still wear lily-scented perfumes to this day.

One year on the night of the Emmys, I had a scene with her and we worked late. They gave us a dressing room on the lot to get ready. (That would never happen these days.) Now all the actors go to the Emmys and walk the red carpet. When a show wins, the cast goes onstage. Back then, we sat at home and watched on TV along with everyone else. We kids did get to go once; we sat in the nosebleed section. When Will won his award, he dedicated it to us, and it sat on a shelf in our schoolroom until he passed away and we returned it to his daughter Ellen.

So there we were—Michael was trying to get ready for the Emmys, and she looked over at me and said, "I should show up in my Olivia hair and depression-era frock, and if I win, I'll thank the producers for giving me so much time to get ready for tonight." (Over the years, she won three Emmys as Olivia Walton.) When she did show up that night, she was stunning and beautiful in an elegant and stylish gown.

Michael influenced me in so many ways. She taught me to be considerate and to have a backbone, while keeping a sense of humor. She would fight for me and people she never even met.

She is a caregiver who taught me generosity and even a little chutzpah. I loved that in her; I had never seen a woman like her before. Michael added shale—a solid foundation, yet still soft to the touch—to my mountain, and built in me an inner strength I wouldn't realize I had until years later.

SISTER, SISTER

I was the older sister in my family, so having a big sister was also a new experience. Judy Norton was hip and sassy, and a little like Mary Ellen in her athletic ways. She had this long, lovely hair; she knew how to talk to boys; she wasn't afraid like me. I admired her and wanted to follow her around. At first, I think I was a pipsqueak to her, but we became friends as we got older. Older Erin and Mary Ellen had more story lines together, too. We hung out, had lunch, gossiped, and even vacationed together.

We cruised the Caribbean together one hiatus when I was nineteen. Somehow we never got any of those pictures they take of you when you're on board, because other tourists would buy them before we could get to them. A strange thing happened on that cruise that increased my awareness of the outside world and the impact we'd had in America's living rooms.

Judy and I decided we should have some fun before the next season began. Whenever we went out, we never told people who we were; we were raised not to draw extra attention to ourselves. Besides, it seemed obnoxious to expect people to make a big deal over us. There was a handful of people on the cruise we were having fun with, hanging out and enjoying the activities like normal people do.

Then someone must have recognized us, because the identity of the characters we played on TV spread throughout the ship. A few people we had been enjoying became angry at us for not telling them who we were. We were stunned. We had no idea it was our duty to inform people who we were on TV. We just thought it was okay to be us, two sisters taking a holiday, no pretenses, no bragging. We finished the cruise by staying with those not offended. It wasn't the same after that.

Judy became like a big sister. We shared girl talk, the boys we liked, had some sibling jealousies, made up, and then went back to telling each other about all our boyfriend troubles. Now we share wife and mothering experiences. Having a big sister has been something I never would have known without the show.

SISTER-IN-LAW

When Leslie Winston joined the show to play Cindy, Ben's wife, she joined the sisterhood and we earned the nickname "The Three Musketeers." We hung out together and had more fun than we probably should have. I was a bridesmaid to both of them, just like real sisters. When Leslie married her husband, Bob Yannetti (who directed me in *Boston Legal*), Eric and I were in their wedding. I remember watching how in love Leslie and Bob were. How they looked into each other's eyes during the ceremony. Their eyes were filled with such love and joy. I had never seen or felt anything like that in my own life. When Erin got married, I pulled from Bob and Leslie's love to use for Erin's wedding to Paul.

A few years ago, Eric and I helped Leslie and Bob celebrate their twenty-fifth anniversary. The close bonds are one of the reasons I think the cast was successful; we really were like a family. Actually, we really *are* a family.

BABY SISTER

The youngest Walton, Elizabeth, was played by Kami Cotler. Kami became my baby sister. I still treat her like one. I was very protective of her from the start. There's home movie footage of us in Wyoming where I am "helping" her walk across the snowy meadow. I have my protective arm around her, leading the way until I trip and take her to the ground with me. Ah, big sisters who are not so big themselves.

Kami is the smartest one of all of us. She may be the baby, but she was always way ahead of her time. She taught me many things my own parents didn't know how to teach me. Her parents, Barbara and Ken, were younger and "with it," as I would have said then.

While we waited around at the first *TV Guide* cover we shot, Kami had brought along a book to read called *How Babies Are Made*. She was about six; I was ten. I was a little shocked seeing her read it. I asked what it was about, and, in detail, she clearly explained the biology. Out loud. I was embarrassed; we never spoke about such things in Northridge . . . at least not in my house. I glanced over at my parents; my dad didn't say a word, and my mother stared at the floor. It's a good thing I had Kami to educate me, or I may never have had my daughter, Sydnee. Oh, wait—I had Judy and Leslie to give me a clue.

That first *TV Guide* photo shoot was shot with all of us in costume. I remember we were taken to the photographer's home, where he had a studio in his garage. We all changed into our wardrobe and sat on a backdrop. This was the first time we were all arranged as a "family." Every year after that, we had a "family" cast shot done. They were usually done on the set. In those shots, you can see us gathered around the kitchen table, the radio, the stairs, and the front stoop of the house. I like seeing how we all grow each year. The last *TV Guide* shot we did, we were gathered on the truck during the Thanksgiving reunion special in 1993.

BABY BROTHER(S)

David Harper was Jim Bob. David played my baby brother, but we are actually less than a year apart in age. He was a natural. He had such an ease and calm about him. He went with the flow and was fun to be around. He brought such a "real boy" feeling to his portrayal of Jim Bob, it's no wonder people felt so close to him.

Eric Scott, as Ben, actually started out older than Erin. Then as I grew taller, we became the same age. I think we may have been twins for a while, or maybe that was our joke. When I grew taller, I think he was no longer a big brother, but then a younger one. Eric and I had a particularly close relationship. Judy, Kami, and I were his first sisters, as he only had brothers when we started the show. So he had some getting used to with us girls, but I was already a younger sister to two boys and felt comfortable with him as a brother.

SWOLLEN HEARTS AND TEARSTAINED FACES

I often arrived at personal appearances and events upset for one reason or another. Eric would talk me down. He understood my sensitivity, my parents, and the pressure. He would always know when I'd been crying on the drive over.

Once I'd had a fight with my mom before an autograph signing at Universal Studios. Eric saw me, put his arm around me, and walked away from the eyes on us. He said, "What happened?"

"My mom wanted me to wear the outfit she picked out, and I didn't want to," I cried. "I wanted this and she said, 'No Walton girl should look like that, and no one will want your autograph.' "

Eric's listening ear and soothing comments would calm me down. He was a good big brother—he still is. Eric has talked me off more cliffs than I can count. His empathy and understanding are incredible. To this day, Eric calls all of us to see how we are.

I've always admired Eric's ability to view his acting years as being part talent and a lot of luck. "There is a lot of talent you never see, because of the luck of the business," he told me.

Years later, his advice to me as a new mother was to remember that our real job is to be there for our kids, and our work is to pay the rent. Whenever I've yearned to "be successful," he reminded me my success as a parent to my beautiful Sydnee is testament to my success, not the dollars I bring in.

One great thing that did come out of that day at Universal Studios was that we got tickets to my favorites, James Taylor and Joni Mitchell, in concert at the Universal Amphitheatre. Looking forward to seeing "Sweet Baby James" made up for those tears.

About this time of my battle for independence, I started to battle my weight and body image. I was fourteen, so I was growing up and naturally out. I begged my mom to stop taking dance classes. She resisted. She couldn't understand how I could possibly want to give up something she had always wanted. Hadn't she given me everything she never had, everything she dreamed of as a child? It made no sense to her. We fought about it, until she realized taking dance classes, piano and singing lessons, practicing for all of them, working full-time, being a cheerleader and on the volleyball team was a bit much for me. Why wasn't what I was doing enough? Ballet was first to be cut loose.

I quit ballet in defiance, an act of independence I regret to this day. I loved ballet, but I needed to separate from my mother and doing what *she* wanted, so I quit all dance. It was probably the worst time to quit something so familiar and good for me, and certainly didn't help with my growing body and curvy changes. I had always been rail thin and now I had curves. Something natural and normal in a woman's growth, but not accepted easily in my industry.

BIG BROTHERS

Richard Thomas, the central character of *The Waltons*, defined the role of John-Boy. Richard was already a respected actor, and he came from a dancing family. His parents were professional dancers, so I was especially in awe of him, and wanted his approval. I admired his talent and hoped to be as good an actor someday. His sister was also a beautiful dancer, and when their company, U.S. Terpsichore, came to Los Angeles, we all went to see the performance. I felt ballet was something that bonded me to Richard. I remember one day I had my hair in a bun and he liked it. I think it reminded him of a dancer. I was pleased.

Richard became a big brother and we all grew to adore him. He'd talk to us in character as John-Boy when we were filming. Then when the cameras weren't rolling, he would become Richard and tell a joke or story that would have us cracking up until the moment we heard "Action!" He was a big brother to me, but it was more than that, he was the figurehead of our show. I sensed that what he did and thought was important, so I wanted him to adore and accept me, just like a real sister. He was an authority figure of sorts. I added him to my list of people I wanted approval and attention from. If he liked me, then it meant I was doing a good job, I was accepted.

Jon, who played Jason, was always as loving to me as he was during our discussion about faith while filming *The Homecoming*, and his music carried us into song, dance, and laughter. I loved his "Ironing Board Blues," which he wrote for "The Easter Story." As Jason, he played it in a scene while Grandma ironed. I was a true little sister (okay, a pesky brat) because I would pester him to play that song all the time. It's so peppy and happy. Jon played and composed for many of our shows, and his story lines usually included his talent and passion for music in some way.

Jon also had a band, and would play in local clubs in Los Angeles. We always went to see him, and sometimes he would invite us to join him on the stage for a song. He is so musically gifted and talented, I asked him to score my short film *For the Love of May* years later.

I am a lucky girl to have so many wonderful brothers.

GODSEYS AND BALDWINS

We had so many other "family" members on the show, all of whom were an integral part of the show's success. Joe Conley was Ike Godsey, the storekeeper. He was always so nice to all of us kids and treated us the same way off and on camera. Joe has a wonderful singing voice and used to sing to me a made-up song, "Mary Elizabeth Is Her Name." I would get embarrassed. He'd wink at me and smile that dazzling smile of his. He was such a part of our Walton lives. Seems we were always at Ike's store.

A few seasons later, Ronnie Claire Edwards came in to play Ike's wife, Corabeth, and they created a dynamic duo whom fans still talk about today. Ronnie Claire is hilarious and always intrigued me with her dramatic flair and exaggerated Southern drawl. She was always fascinating to listen to, telling a yarn of a story. Once, Judy and I gave out awards at our wrap party, and Ronnie Claire got the very dramatic "ennui" award.

The Baldwin sisters, Emily and Mamie, were played by the incredible Mary Jackson and Helen Kleeb. I loved their elegance and charm. I got to work with them alone in a few different episodes. They were a treat to watch. Two accomplished actresses playing off each other so well and with perfect rhythm. They danced with each other as those characters. I sat in awe of their work.

Another pro was our own Yancy Tucker, with Bob Donner playing him to the hilt. Bob was such a funny man, both while acting and behind the scenes. When he played Mork's dad in *Mork & Mindy*, my mom and I had another celebrity moment of pride as we watched. Bob was a deserving actor, with a heart of gold.

There were so many great character actors around us and we were lucky to be embraced by the best.

I am blessed to have all my family members. Each one of them brought a unique sensibility to the show and to my life. From widely different backgrounds, we united to become real siblings, family members, and neighbors—and even more important to me, true friends.

4

WHAT'S A "DINAH"?

When the show became more popular, so did we. We were dragged to appearances on weekends. I was just trying to keep up. My parents were also new at being the parent of a kid in show business, and besides being there for my brothers and sister, they wanted to help me with my added obligations. My dad tried to help us with our homework, but he was a tough teacher. He would sit with us at the kitchen table and diligently explain science or math until we understood. I was a different type of learner than he was and it frustrated him because I couldn't understand it the way he explained it. I really tried his patience once when I couldn't get a concept having to do with fractions. Finally he filled several glasses and started pouring water back and forth so I could visualize the equations. I hated his disapproval and would usually end up crying with frustration.

MERV AND THE CHRISTMAS KIDS

Later that year, Eric and I were "Christmas Kids" on the *Merv Griffin and the Christmas Kids* special. Yes, the little Irish-Catholic girl and the nice Jewish boy were asked to read the classic poem "A

Child's Christmas in Wales," trading off verses. Here was another time I tried my daddy's patience.

I can barely read this poem aloud today, let alone when I was twelve. I just couldn't get it. Didn't understand what it was about. My dad took on the job, as he assumed he should, to help me memorize it, but I struggled. I had a mental block against it.

I didn't understand the poem and what the hell a celluloid duck was and why it mattered, anyway. This was new to me. Learning lines for a character who was my age was very different from learning a world-class poem and trying to perform it with the class it deserved. I was out of my league, with no training to speak of. No one took the time to explain it to me, and the more I tried to learn it, the more blocked I got. My friends were going out that night and I wanted to go with them. My dad said, "You can not go anywhere until you memorize the poem. When you can recite it to me, then you can go."

I was so pressured and angry about my mental prison; my emotions shut me in more. While I sat in my room staring at this nonsense, my dad would come in and say, "Okay, now, do the poem." He took the script away to make sure I was word perfect. I stumbled and couldn't get it all out. He shut me in my room again and forbade me to leave until I learned it perfectly.

I was frustrated about the unfairness of it all. I hated my dad for that. He was so strict and disapproving of me. The more I tried, the less I retained. I missed the time to go with my friends and take a break from the stupid duck of a poem, which made me more frustrated. My dad was not sympathetic at all. He yelled at me and I was banished to my room until I learned the poem.

My father was tough in that way. Unyielding. He believed practice made perfect. He worked hard and long hours to get things done, so why shouldn't I? He was hard on us to teach us lessons he felt important. His anger at me only fueled my insecurities and reach for perfection. When he was angry, he closed me off. With his silence, I felt utterly unlovable. I thought he'd love me more if I was perfect, which, to me, meant do it his way.

My father understood the incredible opportunity I'd been given. He had so little when he was growing up, he didn't want me to lose any part of the gifts. I didn't see any of this. I just felt the pressure to hold and keep it all, which made me come to a breaking point. While it was difficult at the time, and took many years of therapy to sort through, I know my work ethic, high standards, get-it-done attitude, and competence came from those difficult times with him.

"Doing Merv" became another drama for me—a terrifying situation where I thought I had to be flawless, but my gray cloud informed me I wasn't. I knew I was no good and was faking it.

What happened when I got to the set not knowing the poem by heart? I was scared to reveal my failure to memorize the poem, and I had a stomachache all through the taping of the opening number. I wore a red-and-white-striped dress—yes, like a candy cane.

Eric and I were to open a door and step onto the winter set, complete with snow. Fake snow, that is. The music played, our cue came, and we opened the door, revealing our bright faces amazed at the scene. The plastic "snow" floated down and one flake landed right in my eye. I tried to cover and not ruin the shot, but it hurt and I couldn't see. Just one more thing added to my mixed bag of nerves. I knew the dreaded poem would be worse than a snowflake in the eye.

Eric and I took our marks and they gave us the go-ahead; a teleprompter was set up. We read every word as they rolled by, no memorization required. Why didn't someone tell me I didn't have to memorize every line? So much fighting for no reason.

Recently I found the original script in a folder with Merv's smiling face embossed in red on the cover. A letter from the producer referred to the "enclosed Merv album," in which side two, track five, contained the poem, which might "help with the reading." What? What album? Why had my dad never played me track five? Maybe I could have had a clue. I don't know if the company forgot to send it, and my dad felt he couldn't ask, or what—but, boy, that sure would have helped!

Eric and I were paired together a lot. We traveled on a tour to promote the show, four cities in four days. We visited children's hospitals every day. Burn units, cancer wards. Eric was strong and had a great sense of what was right. We cheerfully signed pictures and visited with the kids; then we would be off to the next city. On the way to the airport, I was sad because I knew a lot of those kids would never leave the hospital. Eric always looked at the positive. He reminded me how the kids were happy to see us, and as hard as it was, it was a good thing we were there. He, too, was raised with the importance of mitzvah, giving back. Eric's a mensch and I learned a lot from him.

DINAH AND THE TOADS

One day, someone on the set asked what I was wearing for "doing *Dinah*." I panicked. I didn't know what "doing Dinah" was. I asked my mother, but she was so excited, all she said was, "Oh, honey, yes, you're doing *Dinah*, but what will you wear? We'll have to get you an outfit."

She took me to a store called Stardusters, of all things, that catered to mothers and their shopping needs. While she sat in a nice chair, I was put in a fitting room and dressed by a clerk, then paraded out to model for her. I hated the place—they didn't have anything hip to wear—but my mother liked the whole charade. I felt like a fourteen-year-old doll being dressed up and taken out for display. But I had to have something to wear to "do Dinah."

Everyone talked about it as the date grew closer. I didn't want to admit to anyone I didn't know—again—what was going on, so I kept my mouth shut, listening to that familiar music reminding me to dance. Before I knew it, we were on our way and the pressure was on.

But what's a "Dinah"? Help!

We arrived at the studio, and production assistants showed us to a green room. As the moments ticked closer, I felt the familiar cloud of the unknown darken inside me. Eventually a man came and led me away from my parents. I dutifully followed him, and we walked down the hallway and stopped behind a big black curtain. He looked at me and said, "When you hear your name, go out to the couch and sit down."

I knew this was important, so I better figure it out . . . and fast. He patted me on the back and said, "Go! Go to Dinah." Someone pulled the curtains apart and I could see onto the stage.

Oh! Dinah's a person! We were being interviewed on one of

television's most popular talk shows. You must have already figured it out—it was *Dinah!* Since I was either in school or on the set every day, I'd never heard of the woman introducing me to the audience. I was relieved to see that Ellen Corby was already out there on the couch.

Dinah Shore was as nice as can be. I took my place next to Ellen, and Dinah flashed her beautiful smile. Then, with five innocent words, she said something that would plague me for years. "I hear you collect frogs."

Oh no, no, I thought. *I don't collect frogs.* My mind raced. *What do I say? I can't lie . . . can I? On TV? Can I contradict Dinah in front of America?*

Ellen Corby was famous for collecting ladybugs. One day, she asked me what I liked. I said frogs, because I liked to draw them, and I drew a pretty good frog in my day. The next thing I know, Grandma started to give me frogs. She liked collections, and it was a good hobby, I guess. So for the show prep, she told the *Dinah* people she started my frog collection with me.

What could I do? I sat there and thought, *I'm "doing Dinah" and all I get to talk about is frogs? Why am I being asked such a stupid question?* So I did what any good Catholic girl would do, I lied. I lied to protect Grandma, the show, and Dinah. I said I liked frogs very much.

After *Dinah!* was aired, people sent me frogs . . . lots of frogs. For years, people thought I collected frogs, and because of that, I guess I did. I had ceramic, cloth, plastic, and crystal ones; large, small, whimsical—every kind of frog that people could make or buy and mail to me. I kept them all in my room, until I moved out many years later. Letting that frog collection go was a step toward living in my own truth and my own desires, not what I thought others expected of me.

Years later, I found out Ellen urged Eric to start an owl collection. He laughingly said it took years to get rid of all those owls.

BEATING THE BRADYS . . . NEVER!

Eric and I did an episode of *Celebrity Bowling* and lost to Bobby and Cindy Brady (Mike Lookinland and Susan Olsen). My dad took me bowling in preparation, but I'll spare you (no pun intended, really!) the gory details of my dad helping me train for that gig. Here was another mountain I didn't have time to climb before we taped.

Eric and I were a team, and Mike and Susan were the other team. We lost horribly, and it was just humiliating. I saw Mike Lookinland—like, a million years later—and the first thing he said to me was "Hey, remember when we beat you in bowling?"

WOULD MAN SEE IF . . .

When Mrs. Deeney retired, we went through a few teachers before a more permanent replacement could be found. I heard many teachers who were approached declined. They didn't want to deal with the pressures—or was it just the extra work—from the production company that often wanted to work us overtime. Our life required a balance of work and school; then factoring in our varying ages and diverse curriculums proved a challenge for a teacher.

We finally found a teacher who rocked our world. He was new to the studio system, plus he had the energy and creativity to deal with all our needs. Glen Woodmansee was a breath of fresh air, and he became one of my favorite teachers. He had long hair and wore a three-piece green suit to work on his first day. I think he was trying to look professional, but we told him he could lose the suit and we'd still have respect for him. He did, and we were off to the races.

Glen was incredibly smart and a little mysterious. He drove an old VW van with a piece of wood he'd wired on as the back bumper. I thought that was wild. I wondered if he was a hippie, a surfer, or an alternative thinker.

He was not a hippie, but he was brilliant and accepting. He loved taking classes himself; at one time, he carried twenty units at UCLA, while teaching us full-time. I was amazed. He showed me college was something you could always do; and education just keeps on, no matter how old you are.

Glen was also a scuba instructor. When I was sixteen, Jon and I took his incredible class, and we were certified by NAUI and PADI. We did our beach dive near Malibu at Zuma Beach, with a clambake afterward on the beach.

We took our certification dive off Catalina Island. The Garibaldi fish swam right up to my mask. The feeling of being able to breathe underwater is still amazing to me. I still dive whenever I travel in the tropics.

Glen counted down the days until lobster season, and told us funny stories about trying to lure them onto his dinner plate. For me, being underwater was a privilege. I didn't want to upset it in any way, and I would never take anything.

Whenever I dive, I hear the lyrics from America's "Horse with No Name." The lyric "The ocean is a desert with its life underground" reminds me exactly how true that is. It looked like the desert with water added. The peace of the sea life made me feel invisible in a foreign land. So different for me, I felt like a pioneer, given a privilege that lasted as long as the air in my oxygen tank allowed.

In those days of unease, it grounded me to be part of nature and escape to the quiet peace under the sea. There was unfounded calm in buoyancy, floating with the tide, the sound of my own breath, the regulator releasing my old breaths to the surface to rejoin the air that sustains. The stillness of it took me to a place I would later recall in meditations. *Return to nature, then you'll see, how fun it is to be set free*, I wrote in my poem book. I still return to nature when I feel off my path. Water, air, and fire return me to myself.

I Beg to Differ

When I was in high school, my own school required biology lab, including dissecting a frog. It wasn't a requirement for the other cast kids, but I had to have it to graduate. During a hiatus, my mother drove me to the studio to get special permission from the producers, and ask them to cover the expense of the frog dissection.

I was nervous because I had to take this class or not graduate from my school. I thought my mom was going into the meeting also, but when the assistant came for us, she only asked for me. Mom nudged me to go in. I had no idea I was going to do this alone. I felt abandoned and unprepared; I didn't understand why I had to beg for a class.

The lights were dim in the office, shutting out the bright California sunshine. Two overstuffed leather chairs sat across from the executive producer's massive desk. He motioned for me to sit. I did, but I looked at the empty chair and wished someone were there with me.

"So, Mary Beth, why are you here today?" He knew why I was there, and this game made me uneasy and angry, but I explained why I needed biology. It was like playing Monopoly when the other player owns all the real estate you land on:

"Can I have Park Place?" she squeaked.

"You cannot pass go. You cannot collect one hundred dollars. Go to jail! No 'get out of jail for free' here."

It felt horrible. To me, all our negotiations with the company were like that. Every year, I hated contract negotiations, and now this.

"The other kids didn't have a biology lab."

"Yes, but my school is different," I squeaked. "May I graduate from high school, please?"

"No!" the big voice of authority rang out in my head.

In the end, I did take biology. Kami and David were part of the lab experience when I dissected the frog. I did graduate from high school, but to this day, I don't play Monopoly.

BROOM DANCE

Whenever I was going through troubled times, Glen would just let me rip. One day, I'd had it with a math problem. We had a knife in the classroom for cutting fruit, and I picked up the weapon and aimed all my frustration and anger at the math book. I eyed Glen, and he calmly watched as I got closer to my victim. Algebra was going down, unless he interceded, but he patiently waited, passively giving me his okay. I stabbed the textbook right through its linear equations.

I felt a bit crazy, but once I started to let it out, a deep rage took over. Glen stepped in and created a safe way for me to vent. He made a dartboard out of the book's cover and pasted some of the torturous problems on it as a target.

It was more than frustration toward an assignment. The pressure to be on top of all of my activities oozed from me, making me feel like I was about to burst at the seams. I couldn't seem to fit it all in. By this time, I was on the cheerleading squad at my high school, played on their volleyball team, and maintained a 4.0. Add to this the worries about my weight and—oh yeah—the work. Oh, that.

Glen's acceptance of my need to vent my frustrations made me feel safe to be me, to be weird and angry, and he was one of the first people I didn't feel judged by. I could let my pent-up energy and frustrations, growing pains, teenage angst, and hormones scatter around the schoolroom. Yet, I knew there were boundaries, that I was safe.

A natural outlet for me was to dance. One day, in one of my more spirited exhibitions, I began a kooky tap dance around the classroom. Glen, as usual, sat calmly watching me—I think he even had a bit of a smile on his lips, and that did it. I took off from there. I grabbed a broom, and "Fred Astaire" and I impromptu danced. I incorporated desks and anything in my way. The door was open and I tapped my way down the stairs, then back up, stomping, jumping, and pounding until I was exhausted.

Kami was there and thought it was funny. And it was. At some point, my outburst played out, the anger vanished, and I was ready for schoolwork. I didn't realize it at the time, but I was learning to give in to my feelings, instead of avoiding them. Since then, I've often tapped into my creativity to escape the tornadoes of my emotions safely. Glen's acceptance of a very confused little Mary chipped a crack in the iceberg, and I began to embrace the weird me and find a way back to self.

Walton's Mountain News

One of the most fun times for me was when a new kid arrived on the lot. Finally someone else to play with. Set hopping became a favorite pastime. When the dramatic series *Apple's Way* came along, we went over to hang with Patti Cohoon (Cathy Apple) and Vince Van Patten (Paul Apple).

Since I was new to the industry, it was so cool to meet people and get to know them outside the image. When *Eight Is Enough* filmed a few soundstages over, we'd borrow bikes and go visit. Willie Aames (Tommy Bradford) came over to our schoolroom and we all hung out. Willie was into photography, and Glen had set up a darkroom and taught us photography so we could learn how to shoot and develop photos for our newspaper.

Then Willie suddenly became a huge teen idol. It cracked me up. Here was this guy who had lunch with us, developed photos with us, and was shorter than I was. But he became a teen heartthrob. Girls were crazy about him. When we went to an event, he couldn't walk to his car without being mobbed. Willie and I once had to run from a gang of screaming girls. We hid until we could jump in the car and lose them. It was weird to think of my friend that way. To me, he was just Willie, even a little geeky. Oh, the power of fan magazines!

The same thing happened with Vince Van Patten. Vince was a reserved and not-too-talkative guy, who had a grape-colored MG. I saw the Van Pattens recently and we still joke and laugh about that car. But the girls went wild. For me, it was a lesson in who people really were as opposed to who people thought they were. While Richard had his girl followers, my Walton brothers never became heartthrobs; so what Vince and Willie went through was comical to me.

Glen was always finding new things. He was terrific at teaching us using hands-on activities. One project I'll never forget was the *Walton's Mountain News*. Ironic, since John-Boy would soon write the *Blue Ridge Chronicle*. We wrote articles, interviewed crew members, and wrote poems. We drew pictures for the cover art, and Glen helped us publish our "paper." We usually printed one near a holiday. Halloween was our favorite. Bats are so fun and easy to draw.

We even invited kids working on nearby sets to write articles and stories. Some of the *Eight Is Enough* kids have bylines in one or two issues. I still have a few of these treasured editions. And while I don't think she had enough time in her schedule to contribute to our paper, we met another friend on the lot I'll never forget.

One day, we heard the beautiful actress Brooke Shields was filming *Just You and Me, Kid* on a nearby stage. Kami and I went over to her school trailer, knocked on the door, and asked her if she wanted to write an article. We left one of our past issues for her to read. I've wondered if she and her tutor thought we were crazy or just intrusive, but we really wanted all the studio lot kids to be a part of our paper, no matter how famous.

Years later, Brooke and I were on *Circus of the Stars* together. We worked really hard to learn the acts. Brooke did an incredible performance, hanging by her ankle upside down on a rope, elegantly working "the web." When she finished her routine, she asked the rest of us, "How did I do?"

Everyone told her, "It was beautiful. You looked great."

Then she said, "But how did I *do*?"

"Oh, it was so pretty. The costume looked great, and so did you."

And she asked yet again, "But how did it look? Was my toe pointed enough?"

"You were beautiful."

Not what she was asking. I understood she really wanted to know how the routine was, not how pretty people thought she was. So I told her she did a really good job, and yes, that toe could have been more pointed, but it was a solid performance.

She seemed relieved, and was so sweet and unassuming. Her mom seemed to trust me and we hung out all weekend. I understood her on the beauty vs. performance comparison. I realized I was not alone in wanting to perform well.

After raising all of us, Glen went on to teach kids on other shows. He continued the newspaper when he moved over to tutor on *Full House*. Glen sent me a few editions of their papers. I was glad to see the tradition continue.

PORCELAIN TEARS

As I grew, my insecurities got the best of me. I wanted to be what everyone wanted me to be, so I did what I was told. If someone didn't like me, I would work harder. I needed approval from everyone so desperately, I would mold myself, trying to fit what they expected me to be so I could feel accepted.

I felt so much pressure, I wanted to escape. I wanted *happy*. I read Harlequin romances every day, wishing for romance and a happy ending. Unlike most of my friends, I didn't have a boyfriend and had not been asked out. I sat at home on prom and home-coming nights and cried, wishing I were pretty so someone would like me.

My brother Michael saw me slipping into myself and tried to get me to stop reading and just talk, but I would have none of it. I wanted to hide. He took my book away from me once. You would have thought he cut off my air supply. I panicked and scrambled desperately to get the book back.

When I was thirteen, I developed a severe case of insomnia. I played the part of "Little Mary Sunshine" during the day, and when I was alone at night, I became depressed, hormonal, and stressed. I fell into a pattern of worry, fear, and sadness. Often I stayed up all night. I went to the bathroom and started the shower. I would lie in the tub and cry. Alone, I felt it was safe to let it all out. Over the years, I shed many tears onto the porcelain, hidden from the world, secret. Until one day, my body betrayed me and I developed a rash.

It was a red, itchy rash on my scalp. I pretended nothing was wrong, but my parents took me to a local dermatologist, who diagnosed seborrhea dermatitis. He gave us a prescription, but he expressed curiosity about the possible underlying causes of this condition.

He wondered if I was under any stress, and without even asking me, my parents answered, "No, nothing unusual."

Did I speak up? No.

Did my parents really think my life was "usual"? No, they thought it was a dream come true. Did they think I was coping? I hid it well, I guess. Years later, a doctor described me as "stoic." I was taken aback. I'm an emotional person, so I would never describe myself that way. I washed my feelings down the drain, thinking I had tricked them all.

I find it ironic that I only developed the rash on my scalp, not on my face or arms or anywhere else. Outwardly, I was still perfect. Could I have somehow willed the rash not to be where it would be visible on camera or obvious to the world? I only allowed imperfection where it didn't hold up production.

I managed to keep the rash in place, but I couldn't convince my body to fall into a peaceful sleep. So my father—God love his Irish ways—offered me gin gimlets at night. "Here, drink this," he'd say. "It'll help you sleep."

"Larry, you're gonna make that girl an alcoholic," I remember my mother saying.

My brother Michael—God love his hippie ways—knocked on my window one night. He climbed in carrying a lovely cloisonné pipe filled with pot. He said, "Forget the gimlet, try this."

So I became a pot smoker, and finally started to sleep. I reveled in the blissful escape, the relaxation. I reconnected with myself. I was lucky. I had some kind of shut-off mechanism, and I could set boundaries on my smoking. It wasn't a party drug for me. I was young, only in middle school.

Michael and his friends would take me to a beautiful place outside to walk, hike, and enjoy nature. I really connected with the outdoors during that time, and I feel it grounded me and gave me the escape I needed. I could calm down, get out of my head, and—in a beautiful canyon—enjoy the trees, rocks, and mountains. I never worked stoned; I was too disciplined for that. I knew my responsibilities. I did, though, finish a few term papers in a smoky haze.

My dad caught me once and we had a huge fight. By now, I was in the ninth grade. He grounded me and threatened to limit my time with friends and take away my privileges. I threatened to move out. We came to an impasse right in the middle of the Northridge Mall. I walked away in a dramatic huff and didn't speak to him for days.

While I was asserting my independence, the fight was still unsettling. I felt horribly guilty and knew I had hurt my father. I never told my dad, but I stopped smoking pot that day. He never asked or followed through on his threats, and we never spoke of it again. It's unfinished business. There were so many things left unspoken between us before he died.

I put so much pressure on myself to get it right, to be perfect for everyone. From my desire to be a good cheerleader and make it to every game so I wouldn't let the team down, to being a good actress, to earning good grades and fulfilling all of my activities. I had to be the good daughter to get my parents' approval; I didn't have time to get sick, but I often did.

I really wanted to be "normal," but the show didn't leave much room for that. Even though I was busy working all day, as I said before, I had tried out for the cheerleading squad for my high school and was busy with that in the evenings after work. My dad was so dedicated to my having that experience; he came to work and waited while I changed into my uniform, then drove me to the games.

When we performed our "hello" cheer for the other team, I was often recognized, and it ruined the whole thing for me. I just wanted to be a regular girl. It was embarrassing when people called out my character's name, or, even worse, my famous brother's name. I wanted to fit in, but instead I felt like a sore thumb. So much for being "normal."

I yelled at the games and stressed my vocal cords, and I was also susceptible to colds. I remember I couldn't breathe on the set once, so they called in the studio doctor and he gave me a shot of adrenaline to clear up my lungs. I finished the scene. Then I was sent home with a fever and another prescription. I would often work until I got so sick, I needed a few days off to recover. I would push myself and work until I dropped from exhaustion. When I was about fifteen, I started to have stomach issues. I kept it to myself, thinking it was because of nerves. I didn't want to bring any attention to myself. I thought it would go away.

TEEN BEAT

There were some gigs I really enjoyed, though. It was the *Tiger Beat* magazine era and all the heartthrobs were in the articles and on the covers. We started to be in them as well. I started going to parties with Willie Aames, Vince Van Patten, Valerie Bertinelli, Melissa Gilbert, Lance Kerwin, and other kids who were on shows.

I even went on an arranged "date" with Leif Garrett. I had never met him. Imagine my surprise when we got a call from his manager "asking" me out! We went to an awards show in a limo. It was wild. I wasn't allowed to date yet, but I was allowed to get in a limo with Leif that night. Anything for publicity, I guess.

The *Tiger Beat* parties were fun. It was like seeing all your TV friends. I met Jimmy Van Patten, Vince's brother. He was a good guy and became my "date" for many public events. Because he was from a Hollywood family and knew the business, I could take him anywhere. He usually knew more people than I did. I took him to a CBS affiliate dinner, and when they whisked me away to do something, he was fine. Jimmy also satisfied the press's curiosity about what boy I might be dating.

Scott Baio was another kid magazines made into a heartthrob. I didn't get to know him until we did *Circus of the Stars* together. Ours was an aerial act thirty feet up called "Pirates in the Sky." It was a terribly disappointing experience for me.

My inner daredevil and dance background made me crave doing *Circus*, as we all called it. Judy did *Circus;* everyone did. I wanted to as well. It was a great show and I was excited when Bob Stivers asked me to perform.

The shows had great costumes, with sequins, feathers, and elaborate trimmings. My first wardrobe fitting was to take my measurements. I went to work dieting after that session. They made the costumes on a sewing dummy expanded to your measurements. When I returned for my next fitting, the costumer looked at the rather square dummy and said, "I hope you've lost weight." Holding the skimpy costume up, it looked like a cube. More like Fred Flintstone than glamorous circus performer. Was my body that square? Someone said, "The body that would fill out this costume might not look so good in it." My starvation had paid off, and when the costume had to be taken in inches, the costumer was relieved. To tell the truth, so was I, one hurdle down.

I drove myself out to Bob Yerkes's house in the Valley, where he had a training yard. Scott's dad, Mario, was there checking out the rigging. Anyway, we started learning the act on the ground first. Two men who performed for the professional circus were there to train us. Mario looked at the rig and didn't know if he wanted Scott doing it. He said, "Get the girl up there and let's see how it goes." So I got up on the rig and was fine. I am a natural monkey, as my mom used to tell me. I climbed the jungle gym in our backyard before I could walk, and I scared my mother half to death. This was not too tough for me. Mario still seemed unsure about Scott on the apparatus. The trepidation transferred to us all and it went downhill from there.

I still don't fully understand how something so fun could get so weird, but I do know Scott and I never connected. One of the reasons was because we each trained separately with our professionals; so when we were alone, it was scary and a little odd. I tried to be encouraging, but I think Scott felt really nervous and pressured. I tried to joke and tease him into relaxing, but he pulled away and the act suffered.

During a rehearsal, he made a verbal call I was supposed to make. I wasn't ready. So when he called for the rig to be moved, it hit me in the head, and the anchor rope pulled across my wrist, burning me. I was mad and hurt, and, of course, didn't say anything. I felt unsafe with him as my partner and the act suffered, which can be dangerous thirty feet in the air. I made one last attempt to lighten things up and joke around when we got to Vegas, but Scott was into his own thing. I was disappointed but not surprised when it didn't go well for the taping. I felt like Brooke did when she finished her act for *Circus,* but I knew better than to ask how it went. As a trained dancer, I knew I could do better and felt embarrassed at how it turned out. I was so used to a family atmosphere when I worked, I innocently expected all other sets to be the same. Lesson learned: not all actors are committed to the ensemble; found out more than once later on that was true.

The fashion shoots, *Tiger Beat* photo sessions, and commercials were a mixture of fun and famished fatigue. I dieted to look good in the clothes. I loved to work away from the show, to do something different and wear modern clothes.

One gig, a Sea Breeze ad, was so much fun I remember it well.

The theme was "Clean is a Feeling," and I was familiar with the product because our makeup man used it as a staple on the set. My guardian, Cori, and I went to Laguna Beach and stayed in the Surf and Sand Resort so we could be at the location early in the morning. The chilly morning air, the sea gulls, and the sand were so different from the normal days' filming, and I was excited to be having an adventure, even if it was for just one day.

I thought I'd left Erin behind for just a little while, but even on the Sea Breeze ad I couldn't get away from Erin. They brought out a piece of my wardrobe from the show. Yuck, not that one! Clean is a feeling, not an old, dirty dress. They arranged it to look like I was on the *Waltons'* set, and I wore the dress in the shoot. Very clever, I'll give them that. I also sat in a chair with my name on it. That was nice since we kids didn't have chairs with our names on them. (I am grateful Michael Learned changed that for us one Christmas a few years later.)

I rode a horse through a freshly mown grass field, the salty ocean breezes blowing through my hair. Back and forth, take after take, the gelding's legs cantered, I felt so free and was having a great time. I was a good rider. Besides all those hours riding Blue, the Waltons' mule, on the backlot, my dad took us horseback riding a lot. Then my allergies kicked in. That grass and hay thing again. If it was just the horse, crew, and Cori, it wouldn't have been a big deal. But still to come? I had to shoot a dinner scene with a male model playing my date in the ad. The glamour, the attention . . . the tissues.

So with the grass and horse dander, and hard work, I got sick again. I remember Cori driving me back up to L.A. I was bundled up, shivering. I looked up, and all the windows on my side of the car were steamed up with the heat from my fever. I spent the next few days in bed.

MILK, MAALOX, AND DONNATAL

After I recovered from the allergies, a new crack began to open in my façade. I could no longer hide some stomach pains I'd begun having. Cori took good care of me and when the pain got worse, she noticed. Off to the doctor I went. It was right before the airing of one of my first expanded storylines for an episode.

Diagnosis: I had the beginnings of an ulcer. The doctor prescribed Donnatal, and told me to drink milk and Maalox. He put me on a restricted diet so my stomach could heal.

When I returned to the soundstage, I saw Claire Whitaker and Rod Peterson, our producers, approaching me with a carton of milk and a big box of crackers. Something was up. Claire handed me the box of saltines.

"Here, Mary Beth, eat these," she told me, watching my face.

"What? Why?" I could see the worry in her face.

"Your episode's preempted, but only in California because of a political debate. The rest of the country will see it."

I didn't get to see my special episode. I ate the saltines, instead. I should have known politics were in my future somehow.

CAN YOU FIT IN ...

So here's the truth. During this time, I started yo-yo dieting. In the episode where I was "the Jefferson County Cutie," remember when Ben takes a picture of Erin in short shorts and a tie top with midriff showing and submits it to a newspaper contest? Knowing I was going to do that photo shoot for the picture, I starved myself. In a photograph of me at the time, I'm sucking in my stomach and looking a bit crazed in the eyes as I tried to look thin.

Being called the "pretty one" had been part of my entire body image struggle. Early on, someone had whispered in my ear, "You know, you're the pretty one, but don't tell anyone I said that, because it would hurt the other girls' feelings." Why would anyone say that? Imagine a grown-up telling a kid that. I wanted to believe it was true, but why would it be a secret? I wasn't able to separate the fact they were whispering something that sounded nice, but telling me not to repeat it to anyone, which made it bad. The only logical conclusion was that being "pretty" must be a bad thing, not a compliment. Yet, it was something people said to me. Can you say "mixed message"?

Another body image rock I tripped over happened when I had gone in before a new season to get fitted. I was fourteen, and when I got the call for the fitting, the wardrobe woman asked, "So, can you still fit into last season's clothes, or have you gained more weight?" I knew I wasn't the same as I was at the end of the last season, so I started another diet.

With that comment etched across my mind, the standard became: "Pretty equals thin."

This remark sent me into a panic. I couldn't believe it. If *she* was wondering, then everyone else must be talking about me. They must think I was fat, too. I wondered, was this an inquiry sent from the producers down to the wardrobe department? Or worse, the network? Were they mad at me? Would they fire me? I went from panic to starving for perfection again.

Saran Wrap and M&M's

I tried so many diets, I can't remember them all. One season after we wrapped filming, I remember sitting in a hot car with Claire Reynolds, my neighbor, our bodies covered in Saran wrap. We'd seen the infomercial for fat suits that helped you sweat off the pounds. We made our own version. We rolled up the windows to heat the interior of the car and even put on our coats. Somewhere inside me, that safety valve that protected me from really harming myself opened, and while we sat there, puddles of sweat forming, we started to talk about one of my favorite things: warm M&M cookies right out of the oven, usually how I broke a diet.

The more we talked, the more we realized we'd had enough. We went inside, made the cookies, and ate them all. My rebellious side was a saving grace at times. While not the most reliable, it did keep me in some kind of balance.

I followed the Atkins diet for a long time. I was so strict on it, I would not eat anything not on the plan. In a lunch scene one day, our director asked me to take a big bite of an apple. I refused, because it wasn't "allowed." He argued that I had to, because it was lunchtime in the script and Erin would eat.

"No," I said. "Erin's not eating the apple."

I was so angry that they had encouraged me to lose weight, and now they were pressuring me to blow my diet. It made no sense to me at all. I was only thinking of being thin, not of my character, or acting, or even what mattered to me the most: to be good on the show. I was stubborn and stood by the diet. Either they wanted me thin or fat. Somebody, somewhere, choose already!

When my bullheadedness spurred me to extreme measures, my teenage resistance kicked in and I would diet—or not—depending on my mood. In the beauty contest episode, they put Erin in a pink crepe dress with lace. It was a period piece out of the wardrobe department, so it couldn't be altered. I needed to fit into it.

I went on another abusive diet until it was time to shoot the episode. Then, the closer we came to the last shot, the more I ate. Toward the end of the day, I went over to craft services and stood right next to the donuts. I said loudly, "How many scenes do we have left?"

"Three!"

Back to work on the scenes, then it became: "How many shots? Only three more? Well, I think I'll have a donut."

And then after every shot, I ate another one, right in front of wardrobe and everybody.

This set up a pattern of unhealthy eating that lasted years. My fad diets included going to a doctor who gave me injections of a hormone to lose weight, and another who overprescribed thyroid medication to speed up my metabolism. I fasted, and then I tried predigested protein drinks. I even tried sticking my fingers down my throat to rid myself of the evil food I loved so much. Extreme measures again—anything to get to be thin, to be accepted. My friends lost weight, but I didn't. Then I found out they were vomiting six times a day. I'd never tried that and couldn't bring myself to do it every day, but I did binge and purge, which was a horrible cycle to be pinned under. Once again, I was lucky; my survival mechanism kicked in. I was fortunate I wasn't successful purging, and I never lost weight this way. It is such a dangerous practice, that years later I had to deal with the emotional aftereffects. I did anything for beauty, praying it would get me approval. After all, wasn't I the "pretty" one? Wasn't that my value, what I had to offer?

The stupid thing is that during this time, I wrote a magazine advice column on diet and healthy living for teen girls. Here I was, dispensing advice, and I couldn't live up to that image without abusing myself. I couldn't be what they wanted without a diet, a pill, a doctor, shots, or starving myself. Or so I thought.

I hated myself, my body, and my urge to make and eat cookies. I had a rebellious love-hate relationship with food. Since I stuffed my emotions, I started stuffing food for comfort, and to rebel. It created the illusion I had control.

Feeling so beaten by the boulders of body image, I called myself "Hog Body." I drew a self-portrait: an ugly, lumpy body, with the face of a pig. She is how I felt I looked, how I thought the world saw me. Every time I got dressed, Hog Body was there to remind me how crappy I looked, how fat I was. The voice inside my head would scream at me with distaste and hatred. *"See how 'pretty' you are now, you fat pig? You look terrible in that, if only you would have stayed on that diet. When are you going to learn, Hog Body?"* I berated and punished myself for my body.

When my brother asked me if I wanted to go to the beach with him, I would say "Let me ask Hog Body if she feels like putting on a bathing suit today." Hog Body became my alter ego for years.

It makes me cry today to think I saw myself that way. I look at pictures of me then, when I let Hog Body run my life, and I can't believe I felt that way. I still carry her with me at all times, but I have learned to love her and care for her.

Now if I am getting ready for something, and her voice starts nattering at me, I close my eyes, put my hands on her face, and love her. I let her know she was, and is, beautiful inside, and I am so sorry she was hurt back then. Now I embrace her as part of me—my lessons and my journey.

5

LESSONS IN LAUGHTER

Almost as famous as the good-nights were our dinner table scenes. From the family scrambling into their seats, saying grace, the cold food we had to "eat" right after lunch—you can watch us whirling peas or some other unappetizing pile around on our plates—we spent many hours at that wooden table. Every episode had at least one dinner table scene, and they were the focus of our time together on the set. We were all there, every time. There are many dinner table stories, and they still bring a smile to my face, or make me laugh out loud. I can still hear Will rambling on, often unscripted, as he had a tendency to do. When he thanked the trailing arbutus, we smiled, knowing another long dinner scene had begun.

On every show I've worked on, there is always at least one set that is tough, for one reason or another. Either the energy drops, or the type of scenes played there are demanding or take an especially long time to shoot. The kitchen set was ours, specifically the dinner table scenes. If we were in the kitchen shooting a scene, it was fine. The minute we all sat down for a meal, though, we knew we were in for it.

BOREDOM ANTHEM

We spent so many hours at that dinner table, we would get punchy and a bit slaphappy. We often sat in the same places, and my spot was usually between Michael and Jon. One particular day, the energy level was especially low, and to relieve the boredom, Ralph started singing a staccato "I shot the sherrrrrr-iff, but I did not shoot the dep-u-teeeeee. . . ."

Now, Ralph is not a singer that I know of, and his rendition of this Eric Clapton song was so out of tune and oddly inflected, he had us all in stitches. We burst out laughing, but when we eventually calmed down, we suddenly had the energy and focus to continue working. For years, and to this day, Ralph cracks us up when he starts to sing that song. His great sense of humor was perfectly timed to lighten us up so we could move on.

Ralph made those long scenes easier to bear, but sometimes harder, too. I got in trouble for getting the giggles from time to time. Right before a take, Ralph would lean in and whisper something off-the-wall, or nudge Michael underneath the table to get a rise out of her. Well, she was a professional, and once the camera rolled, she would focus and be the ideal Olivia. I did not have such control.

It was usually during grace, and when I sat next to her, she'd squeeze my hand to keep from breaking character. I'd feel her grip tighten, then her arm shaking up and down against mine. I knew she was laughing inside, and I couldn't help myself. I am not one to keep a straight face, which was the fun part, to me. I would start giggling and break up the scene, ruining the shot. I felt awful, but I laughed, anyway. I couldn't help myself.

When we were out of control, usually a stern look from Grandma would get us back in line. Although there were times I'd sneak a peek down to the "grandparent" end to see Ellen laughing and slapping Will on the arm over the hijinks down there.

Ralph had a habit of repeating the same jokes over and over; so eventually all he had to do was say the punch line and we would crack up. One favorite was when he'd put up a hand, lean in, and with that twinkle in his eye, he'd yell, "Not so fast, Ferguson!" It was from a joke he'd told several seasons ago. This resulted in lots of laughter from us. Whenever this happened, new directors would lose total control of the scene as we relived a shared moment from Walton history. We were so bonded because of the time we spent together. I spent more time at this dinner table than I did eating with my own family.

It got naughty at times, too. I heard more dirty jokes around that table than my parents would have a heart for. Some kids learn in the back alley, the streets, or the school yard. I learned from the crew, and on the set, including at that table. I didn't know what many of the jokes meant, but I laughed, anyway, then tried to figure them out later. As I grew up, I got the off-color jokes the crew made in earshot of us kids. As naughty as I knew it was, I felt like I was part of a secret club trying to figure out codes and secret signs. Keeping it all a secret from my parents gave me an even deeper sense of belonging. I knew my dad would blow a gasket if he heard half the things I was exposed to. Years later, my mother admitted she guessed what was going on.

"I know a lot happened to you, but I just didn't want to know it."

"Mom, don't worry," I said. "I would never tell you because you would have a heart attack and die. Besides, I turned out okay."

Yes, the dinner scenes were a wild ride, a joyful combination of acting, shoving coagulated food around our plates, and getting through the scene without falling behind schedule. There was always a professional standard on the show, one I am proud to have learned from Richard, Ralph, Michael, Ellen, and Will. They set the bar high, but somehow at that kitchen table, all bets were off as they taught us that even when you work hard, there's always time for laughter.

EATING MOUNTAINS

Ralph always insisted since we were a starving family in the Depression era, we should eat a *lot!* He made up for the rest of us by eating whatever props served. I think he's a method actor.

I learned the hard way that for consistency, whatever I ate in the master shot, I had to eat in every shot afterward. One day, we started a scene before lunch. I was hungry and ate a lot in the shot.

It was warm and tasted good. Then the assistant director said, "Lunch, one hour."

We went out to lunch, like we did every day, then returned, took our seats at the table, and I realized I had to match what I'd taken in during the master shots. Yuck. I was full already, and worse, everything was cold and gross. It had probably sat on the table while we broke for an hour.

To avoid that happening again, I learned from Michael to look busy by buttering my bread or sipping milk, which was usually safe. A trick I got from Eric was to load a fork full of food and bring it to my mouth. Just before taking the bite, get very interested in the dialogue and lower the fork to listen. The fork never passes the lips. But now, I'm telling secrets.

Later on, I rarely ate, because I was always watching my weight, but I wasn't the only one. Ralph still jokes that Olivia Walton never ate a bite of food through the entirety of the show. Michael says she never ate as she was too busy saying, "More coffee, John?"

After Michael left the show, Ralph was directing an episode and I wasn't eating—as usual. While I sipped coffee, he launched into his argument about why Erin would eat, and that he wouldn't print the shot and move on until I did. I ate more in that one shot than I did in three seasons. It was pretty funny, but Daddy ruled, so I did it.

UNDIGNIFIED DINNER BEHAVIOR

The show won a lot of awards in its day. Several Golden Globes and Emmys, a Peabody, and one special award that was presented to us on the set, at the dinner table of all places. A very nice man came to the kitchen set to present this lovely recognition. No one told us ahead of time what the award was for, but we knew they were going to film his presentation.

He stood at one end of the table, and we were seated at our usual places. On "Action!" with the award in hand, he walked toward the camera and spoke of how special the show was.

As he handed over the award, he said, "And now, to honor *The*

Waltons television show, we are pleased to present you with the Decency Award."

Well, Eric, at that precise moment, had just taken a sip of milk, and upon hearing the word "decency," he spewed the white fountain all the way across the table. The irony was too much for us. We lost it. This poor unsuspecting man was not met with "decency" by the Waltons, but with a bunch of tired actors who were like any other family, and not the characters we portrayed on TV. I think we got a stern talking-to and apologized to him; then we did another take, trying our best this time to live up to the "decent" standard for which he was trying to honor us.

COMPANY FOR DINNER

Shooting "The Boy from the C.C.C." (Season 1) was also cool. I thought Michael Rupert was the cat's meow. He played Gino, a boy who escapes from the children's camp of the Civilian Conservation Corps. John-Boy and Elizabeth find him injured in the woods, and they bring him home.

During the dinner table scene, props served us horrible chipped beef. We'd never had it before, and thank goodness, we never saw it again. It sat on the table waiting for the lights to be set, and by the time we ate, it was cold, coagulated, and tasted awful. Poor Michael was supposed to be starving, so he had to eat a lot of it. We watched him in sympathy, but he never complained.

From then on, when we would have to eat when stuffed or were complaining about the food, Jon would say, "Hey, at least it's not chipped beef," and we'd all laugh. I can't remember if we teased Michael about the meal we served him.

Years later, during that first trip to New York City, I got to go to my first Broadway show. That was a perk, and so exciting for me. Michael Rupert was starring in *Pippin*, and we all went. We went backstage to see him—my first Broadway show *and* I got to go backstage. So cool. The whole time I sat in the theater seat watching, I wondered if Michael would even remember me. He did, and he was so nice.

We have many outtakes that include kitchen mishaps. Michael

Learned was making salad once and she put her hands into the bowl, lifted handfuls of lettuce, and threw them in the air, screaming with each toss. Even the crew cracked up. That one is in the gag reel.

In others, lines were missed, we spilled drinks, broke character, and dropped forks. And we had more than one food fight. One day, Ralph picked up a bowl of biscuits, dumped it upside down on Richard's plate, and said, "Here, boy, eat up!"

The dinner table scenes were a mix of fun and fatigue, but we were all together, and I believe our sense of camaraderie and closeness transmitted to the audience. We liked each other, we had fun, and it showed.

Never Work with . . .

Many of my "costars" were animals: Blue, the mule. Chance, the cow. Reckless, the dog. There was the raccoon, and also the deer. Then there were the chickens. I'll never forget the chickens.

Harry Harris directed more episodes than anyone else—forty episodes and several of the movies. He became a mentor and got to know each of us well. He was like another father on the set. He was always a good sport, with all the Walton goings-on, but he never had much luck with the animals. Seems like he would always get the episodes with an animal story line and had trouble wrangling them. Many times we would hear him say to our AD Ralph Ferrin, "But, Ralph, what are we going to do about the chickens?" If you wonder what I mean, try to direct a chicken to . . . well, do just about anything . . . on cue. For years, we would repeat that to Harry when things on the set got hairy.

I used to ride Blue through the back roads of the studio lot when I had some free time. One day, something spooked him and he tore through the trees. I tried my best to stop him, but he just kept running. I ducked as best I could, until a branch smacked me in the face and knocked me off on my bum. I came to, on the ground, and panicked about what might have happened to the old mule. I was shaken by the fall, but even more scared of getting in trouble for losing or hurting him. Thankfully, there he was, standing near the tree, patiently waiting for me. I took the reins, but he wouldn't budge. I pulled and pulled, crying for him to move. He started munching a branch and I yelled at him to follow me. I finally persuaded him to let me lead him back to the barn. I was hobbling in pain, afraid someone would see me. I hid my scrapes and bumps from everyone, especially the makeup people. My fear of making that mistake kicked in the bad-girl feeling.

Harry had an interesting animal experience that I have never forgotten. I couldn't believe it was true, so I had to go over to the set to see it in the flesh. The scene called for Blue to be frightened and run away. I never knew what had spooked him when he ran away with me in the backlot woods that day, but I know it was not what they'd planned to use in the upcoming sequence.

Apparently, someone had studied American history—remember "Uncle Sam's Camels"? At one point in time, the army had tried to use them; it was a fiasco. It had spawned a legend that camels couldn't get along with horses or mules.

So they brought in a camel, hid it behind the house, and set up for the moment when Blue was supposed to be frightened by something, rear up, and run away. Someone fetched old Blue for his big scene. Off camera, a handler tried to coax the camel out from behind the house, Blue patiently waiting on his mark. That stubborn camel didn't want to come out, and the wrangler pulled and prodded until finally he emerged from behind the corner of the house so the mule could see him. Sure enough, Blue spooked and ran away. Of course, they needed more than one take, and the trouble was that Blue got used to the camel. After that, he didn't run away with the same gusto as in the master.

From then on, we teased him with, "Harry, what are we going to do about that camel?" All the animals could fit into that question from time to time. The animal stories became part of our shared tales as the years went by.

COW FOOT

I was not great around animals. My allergies kept me at a distance from them. As evidenced by the incident with Blue, I should have stayed even farther away. At one point, there was a writer's directive, which I wholeheartedly supported: Don't write anything for Mary Beth with animals. Yet, I couldn't seem to stay away from working with them, and Erin even fell in love with animals in many story lines.

When Yancy Tucker set the barn on fire in "The Sinner" (Season 1), we were all called out of bed into the yard to help put out the fire. We lined up, barefoot and in our nightgowns, passing buckets of water as the animals were led past us to safety from the burning barn. Of course, I was standing nearest to Chance, the cow, when they led her out of harm's way. She came to a stop with her cloven hoof right on top of my instep for a very long take. I heard my bare foot crunch, and tried to shove her off without making a commotion. Cows are very heavy animals, it turns out. I thought I would scream, it hurt so much. I didn't, though, because that would have ruined a very dramatic scene. I was trying to be professional, at all costs. My foot was bruised and badly scraped—but luckily, no bones broke.

The animal wrangler was a salt-of-the-earth kind of guy, who even let me ride Chance one day. Maybe that's why she stepped on my foot, retribution for that ride? As much as I was eager to experience everything, there was one suggestion I didn't take him up on. "It feels great. Do it, Mary Beth," he urged me, pointing to a fresh, warm patty. Even I wasn't dumb enough to take him up on his offer to walk barefoot through cow manure.

MISHAPS ON THE MOUNTAIN

Considering how much we ran around the lot, we were lucky there were no bigger accidents or broken bones. One thing did happen, and my gray cloud of guilt and shame enveloped me for days.

The others were filming down the road at Ike Godsey's store, so David, Kami, and I wandered over to the tree house near the barn. It was a pretty fair climb up that pepper tree. The entrance was a square cut out in the floor, and we climbed in and just sat there, talking and looking around. We hadn't asked permission, and something—the rule follower in me—knew we shouldn't be there. Of course, childhood curiosity won out. It was so fun to be up there with the bird's-eye view of the house, the yard, and the mill.

Then I heard a scream. Kami had stepped back through the hole in the floor, fallen, and hit her head every inch of the way down. I will never forget the sound of her screams. I was horrified, and I don't even remember getting down myself. David ran to get help, and I did the best I could to comfort Kami. She had a lump on her head the size of a lemon.

They took her to the hospital. I was miserable. I was the oldest, and I felt it was entirely my fault. I should have known better, and now my baby sister was hurt. I cried and knew I was wrong to have wanted to go up there. My gray cloud hovered as I tossed and turned all night, waiting for the punishment. No one told me it wasn't my fault. I just knew that after they took care of Kami, I would be in trouble. My cloud didn't dissipate until after I saw Kami the next day and saw she was all right. I didn't get the expected grounding, and no one said a thing to me about it. I vowed to myself to follow the rules. I punished myself by being miserable and said the rosary. I knew I was bad, and bad things happen to bad people. The fall should have happened to me.

I carried this belief around for years, punishing myself for "bad" behavior: from gaining a pound, breaking a diet, not being perfect, speaking my mind, or blowing a line. It was a horrible way to live. I was so hard on myself, which only added to my misery. A wise therapist once said to me, "Mary, you would never talk to or treat anyone as mean as you treat yourself. You would never judge anyone the way you judge yourself. Why are you so hard on yourself?"

The truth hit me like a bolt of lightning. Her words helped me start looking at how I beat myself up constantly, even when no one else did. I saw how I held myself back by being the victim and martyr. Eventually I learned to give up my belief that if I was a good girl, I could make good things happen.

Maybe I was enough as I was. I am still learning forgiveness, especially toward myself. It's hard to get those nuns' harsh lessons out of my head sometimes; yet it would be vital for my survival. But that was another mountain to climb.

THE CORK AND THE PEARL

Some of us had a hard time with dialogue from time to time. Eric had a difficult time saying "Marsha Woolery" in one script. Then there was "practicing basketball," which came out "praking baket-ball." We cracked up so much, we had to do eighteen, or maybe more, takes on that one.

As a result, the producers thought it would be a good idea for us to learn to enunciate properly. The obvious solution was for us to work on it in school. Someone brought in corks and we were supposed to put them in our teeth and read aloud. The idea was that if we could be understood while we held the corks in our mouths, we would articulate even better when they were removed. It was a challenging exercise, for sure.

Glen, as he always did, made it interesting. We had to read *The Pearl* as part of our school curriculum; so there we sat, cork in mouth, taking turns reading John Steinbeck's classic. We had a hoot with that one, because we sounded so funny. I am not sure it ever did any good, because we still muffled lines all the same.

CHURCH ANTICS

There were times when our outtakes were off-color. Actually, a lot of times, but they were all in good fun. Richard is a very funny man. He has a great sense of humor, and you wouldn't think it— for all the sensitivity John-Boy had on the show—but I would say Richard was just as funny as he was dramatic. It's an indication of how special he is as a person, and talented as an actor.

He had us in stitches a lot. I love to laugh, so these moments are still precious to me. There were times when he would flub a line and turn it into a comedy sketch. Sometimes he would limp, or affect an accent, or exit the house with the walk of a completely different character. One time, he hobbled out like the Hunchback of Notre Dame, all hunched over, crippled on one side, and dragging one leg behind him. Our gag reels are full of Richard's hilarious antics.

I remember when he was in his monkey phase. He jumped on

the couch, protruded his lower jaw, squinted like a monkey, and picked through our hair. This always made me crack up. I loved the silliness amidst the seriousness of the hard work.

Richard played pranks, sometimes on us, sometimes on unsuspecting crew members. When Ritter visited the mountain, he and Richard melded like a comedy duo. They were famous for trying to break each other up, usually during takes. They went to great lengths to pull off these pranks, which played out while cameras rolled.

I'll never forget a particular church scene. We were in our Sunday best, and Reverend Fordwick had a huge, very important sermon to give. This was a really difficult speech, and there were a lot of people in the warm, close room; extras filling the pews, the crew, and all the equipment made the hot room even hotter. Picture the Waltons up front, the camera right behind us pointing toward Ritter waiting at the pulpit.

On cue, he stepped up and began. All eyes were on him as he launched into this long-winded sermon. Prepared to be bored through long pages of dialogue, I glanced over at Richard, earnestly staring up at Ritter, a perfect John-Boy look of rapt attention on his face. Then I noticed a huge wad of white, thick, foamy spit seeping from the corner of his mouth. The ooze of drool made Richard look absolutely rabid.

I almost burst out laughing on the spot, but for my amazement at the total focus Richard gave Ritter. I was worried I would be the one to break, and all the while they stayed perfectly in character. Ritter gave Richard his most sincere "Reverend" look, continuing to deliver his powerful sermon. I couldn't believe my eyes. How could he not be laughing? My sides hurt from holding it in.

From behind us, the camera could only see the back of Richard's head, not the drool, so shooting continued. The longer it went on, the more spittle dribbled out of Richard's mouth. I looked at Ritter as Reverend Fordwick, thumping his Bible and pounding the podium, and back at Richard soberly listening, the drool now covering his lips and making its way down his chin. Ritter's performance was fantastic; he never broke character or blew a line. I was amazed and hoped someday I'd be as professional and controlled as these two.

Turns out, this little trick was done with a makeup sponge. The timing had to be perfect and Richard had been working up to just the right consistency and saturation before the scene started. He chewed it like gum until it absorbed enough saliva; then at the perfect moment, a gentle bite on the sponge released its contents. The visual was effective, if not disgusting. I was fascinated and grossed out at the same time.

Everyone, even me, remained professional and focused until Ritter finished his lines, and the director called, "Cut!" Ritter and Richard faced off, screaming wildly with laughter. They hooted and hollered like two boys who had just gotten away with hiding a toad in the teacher's desk, congratulating each other. They were great friends, and we all enjoyed their friendship, pranks and all.

From time to time, we all played practical jokes on each other. I will never count myself to be as clever as Richard and Ritter, but I do remember one fateful day. Cameras rolling, we were gathered around the table, reading letters from the boys at war, passing them to each other, sharing the news our brothers described from their war experiences.

Elizabeth was reading a letter John-Boy had written. The piece of paper had holes cut out as if the war censors had vetted it against security infringements. Kami passed the letter to me, and I noticed she'd written her lines on the prop letter.

After "cut," I gave her grief about not learning her lines. Then, when she wasn't looking, I wrote something naughty—I won't spell it out here, this *is* a family show—in purple pen right below her line.

We set up again, the cameras rolled for the close-up shots, and I passed the letter to her. She scanned the page for her line, and her eyes got big, and she broke. "Mary wrote on the letter!" The shot was ruined, but I felt like a big sister teasing her.

As we got older, the lines blurred between being "the kids" and coworkers. Just as all parents do, my Walton parents let me in on more things as they felt I was old enough to handle the jokes and "adult" material.

One day at the dinner table, Ralph was teasing Michael about a movie he'd seen, and she was laughing and pushing him away. He told her it was in his trailer and she should go watch it. They were having so much fun over whatever movie this was, I couldn't resist and followed them. Ralph set up the video and left, and Michael saw me in the open doorway.

"Come in and keep me company," she said.

Just what I loved, to be included. It was so cool to be invited in, so I jumped at the chance and went in and stood next to her. Maybe I should have been suspicious when she wouldn't even sit down to watch. The first images came on the screen, and I was shocked into silence. Michael was horrified as well, and then we ran out of the trailer, screaming like schoolgirls. She felt horrible, but I assured her I was okay. Truth was, I was a little freaked, but being included in the whole thing made up for having my first glimpse at porn with the notorious *Deep Throat.*

That was the day Michael became more of a big sister than a mom, and she's still a sister, a dear friend, and a close confidante.

MOUNTAIN MOON

My favorite gag reel shots are the naughty ones, of course. Being raised in these two conflicting worlds, I relished pushing the envelope. As the repressed religious girl, I pretended I didn't hear the dirty jokes or off-color language. But I still waited until I was alone and could give in to laughter in secret. Eventually, though, I learned it was all right to laugh out loud, along with everyone else.

In "The Heritage," filmed for the second season, Grandpa pulls his back lifting lumber, and John-Boy volunteers to escort him for a long soak in their hot springs.

Indeed, they make it, but instead of delivering the dialogue as written, at the opportune moment, Richard and Will turned around and lifted up out of the mountain Jacuzzi and shot the moon at the rolling camera. This one scene opened the way for many dropping-trou outtakes.

This was all hilarious to me, even though I had to hide giggles from my parents' stern glances. I longed to be funny and maybe even someday make it into one of the gag reels. It was like a mark of success for me.

FISH KISSES

We Waltons were all very touch-feely and loving with each other. At the McDonough home, public displays of affection were not a common practice. When my dad would wrap his arms around my mom and kiss her in front of us, she would shoo him away with the swat of a hand and say, "Larry, stop it."

Even though I was new to all this demonstrative openness, I wanted to be part of the free-flowing hugs and kisses. I loved the attention and affection. We were always jumping onto John-Boy's bed, and we had to snuggle up close so we'd all fit. We would lie around and just be all over each other. Not in a "Hollywood" way, but like a litter of pups pawing and rolling around together.

The makeup room was another great gathering place. We spent a lot of time in there getting ready; so naturally, everyone talked, gossiped, and caught up. Sometimes we'd run lines in there, too. I loved the makeup room because it was so communal. People coming together and sharing life, everyone talking about their lives before the workday began. I loved the authenticity, the vulnerability. We were who we were *before* we were made up to be who we played.

One morning, when I was about eleven and trying out my new lifestyle, I decided to give Richard a good-morning kiss. As I approached, he started to chuckle. He said I looked like a fish coming at him with my lips puckered and mouth open; then he imitated me. I was embarrassed at first, but everyone else joined in with "fish kisses," and I had to get over myself. This was one of those family moments that can either shut you down or you can just join in and laugh at yourself. This was one time I lightened up and didn't look at my "kisses" as mistakes or doing something wrong. I actually learned something.

He taught me a valuable lesson on what a kiss was not. I'm glad I had this safe place to get "with it." I could have put myself in a truly embarrassing situation later on. That's what big brothers are for, right?

CACKLES

Another makeup room topic was my laugh. One day, we were talking about laughter, and I said, "I giggle all the time." Big brother Richard said, "You don't laugh. You cackle."

I wasn't sure what that meant, but it didn't sound good, like my laugh was wrong. I took it on myself that his comment must have been negative, so I decided to change. I wanted to have a laugh, not a cackle. For the next few weeks, I tried on different laughs. No one seemed to notice how ladylike I was when I giggled now, or, heck, even laughed. No more cackles for me. No way.

I tried a high-pitched, dainty laugh, but I probably sounded more like Betty Rubble. Then I tried not to open my mouth at all, stifling a giggle. Probably sounded like I was drowning. After trying a few more on, I settled on a squeaky, little laugh I thought was adorable. Still, no one noticed. I worked hard to change my laugh so I might fit in better, but no one cared. I was so overly sensitive, I was willing to change myself and my laugh to be accepted. This was just the beginning of a long list of thinking I could change to gain favor. It cost me in the future when it wasn't just my laugh I thought needed to be changed to get recognition.

Then one day, a few weeks after Richard's cackle comment, I laughed so hard—probably at Ralph singing, I had to let go. No one seemed to notice that, either. I looked around to see if I had been caught—or worse—ruined something. Everyone was just going about their business. So the cackle came back, and has been here ever since.

MEN OF THE MOUNTAIN

We had guest stars every week, coming to the mountain. Some of the men were very cute, and we had our share of crushes on them. Okay, Judy and I did; maybe Kami was too young. Okay, maybe I did.

In the fourth season, the very handsome Stephen Collins played Todd Clarke in "The Abdication." I thought he was just the nicest person. Judy and I really liked him, and he paid attention to us, which was even better.

One day, we were working in a scene at the front door of the house, and it was getting late in our day. Judy and I could only work for a little while longer, as our nine-hour day was rapidly coming to an end. There was some chatter about getting an extension for us, unless we could finish in time. If not, they had to bring Stephen back the next day. Well, Judy and I looked at each other and read each other's minds. We smiled and nodded. We thought Stephen for another day was a great idea. The flirting began.

"Wouldn't you like to come back?" I said. (*Of course, he would,* I thought. *What actor wouldn't want another day's work?*)

Judy and I were whispering about how we could help by messing up our lines. We could blow the takes on purpose, or maybe we should have a laughing fit long enough to extend us past our quitting time. Then voilà, we'd get him for another day. The episode's director, Harvey Laidman, caught on to our little plan. We didn't blow any lines on purpose, and Stephen had to go home because we finished the scene.

Years later, I saw him in the lobby at a New York theater. What if this man I adored didn't remember who I was? How embarrassing would that be? I finally worked up the courage to go over and reintroduce myself. We chatted for a moment. . . . He did remember me! Then I really took the plunge and admitted I'd had a huge crush on him back then. He winked and said he had a crush on me, too. I could feel myself blush as I returned to my seat all aflutter. What a classy guy, and what a beautiful way of putting me at ease about my admission. No wonder he is so popular now.

Another visitor to the mountain was Richard Hatch, who played our cousin Wade. He was way too good-looking to be our cousin! Despite being "related," we thought he was cute, anyway. He was always very nice to me, and we really seemed to connect. Years later, we ended up on similar spiritual paths. It's amazing how you feel a connection with someone, and then your paths cross again, confirming a bond that began years ago.

I was often confronted with not being remembered, and I think the following experience had something to do with it. One man who came to the mountain went on to fame in his own hit television series. We found out he was filming on the lot nearby, and we all went over to visit. (As I said before, we liked to set hop.)

He didn't remember us at all—even as we stood there in our wardrobe. That was a rude awakening for me, and I was embarrassed. I took it personally, but Jon knew instinctively what kind of person he was. As we walked away, he said, "What a jerk."

The most famous visitor to the mountain was Elton John. While he was not on the show, he was a fan and visited us on the set. He took Richard and a few of us kids to lunch at the Blue Room, the restaurant side of the commissary. He also invited us to his concert and a big party, set up like an amusement park, at Universal. It was one of the best perks I ever received from being on the show. I got his autograph on the invitation, which I still have. It was so cool to actually meet the man you fall asleep listening to. I swear that the *Goodbye Yellow Brick Road* eight-track melted, I played it so many times.

We all went to the concert, even Ellen. I remember telling her we were going to get a drink. I asked her if she wanted me to bring her one. She just kept smiling and nodding to the music. Then I screamed over the loud music, "Grandma, you didn't answer my question. Do you want one?" She looked at me and nodded again, then reached up and pulled out an earplug.

WACKY WALTON

I do not consider myself a comedian, but there was a point when the producers thought I had a flair for the funny. It started with "The Tailspin" (Season 7), when Mary Ellen sets Erin up on a date she should have gone on herself. Erin is running late, and Mary Ellen is helping her rush to get ready, so she decides to wash Erin's hair in the bathtub to save time. There I was, my head bobbing up and down. It was a funny scene, and Judy and I did a good job.

The producers thought I had great timing and started to write comical things for me after that. In "The Home Front," Erin's male chauvinist boss, J.D. Pickett, refuses to consider her for a position as assistant manager at the defense plant because she's "too pretty and young." So she dresses as a Southern belle, complete with ringlets and a hoopskirt, greets him one morning with a sweet Scarlett O'Hara lilt, and offers him a demitasse and homemade cookies. When she bends over to discard the mail and filing she used to do, but now couldn't bother her "pretty, little head" about, her dress lifts and exposes frilly pantaloons, embarrassing J.D. (Shocking, huh?) While I didn't think I was funny in that scene, Lewis Arquette, who played J.D., was funny. No, he was hilarious.

I smiled whenever I saw Lew was returning for an episode, because I knew it would be a good time. He was professional, interesting, and different for the show. We didn't have a lot of comedy, but Lew made J.D. Pickett a delightfully hateful boss, and he was great to work with.

He told me about his kids, who were close in age to me. He was quite thoughtful about them, and spoke in great detail of their individual qualities. I asked him if they were interested in acting. Looking back, I think, *What a dumb question!* The Arquettes are one of the most successful families in entertainment. Way to go, J.D.

I learned a lot from watching Lew. I wasn't trained in comedy, so I felt fortunate to work with and to watch "funny." I learned timing and how to be a bit out-of-the-box by watching him. His character, J.D., was over-the-top, something Erin could have used a bit more of. I treasure the times I had with him, and the environment that allows you to get to know people while waiting for the lights to be set and "action" to be called.

There were many wonderful lessons in laughter. I'm a lucky girl, so glad to have been a part of the off-camera jokes, silliness, and pranks—and of having the opportunity to work on my own comedic skills, and not be embarrassed to let loose every now and then with a very loud cackle.

By the way, Erin got the job as assistant plant manager.

MOUNTAIN WOMEN

Many women also came to the mountain. Some became famous after they left; some were already quite well known when they arrived.

Beulah Bondi was one of those famous women. Her first episode as Aunt Martha Corinne Walton was "The Conflict" in 1974. She had been acting since 1897 when she was nine years old. She had worked on Broadway, in movies, and on television for seventy-nine years when she did her last performance with us in "The Pony Cart" in 1976. She was so smart and sweet and tiny. She seemed frail to me in her backwoods dress and apron hat, but as soon as she opened her mouth, her strength filled the set. I was amazed she remembered the lines for a very long story she had to tell us in that episode. Her portrayal of our aunt Martha Corinne earned her an Emmy award.

Beulah had never married or had children of her own, but she played Jimmy Stewart's mother in four films, including Ma Bailey in *It's a Wonderful Life,* my favorite movie. Every time I watch it, I say, "There's Martha Corinne." And, of course, when Ellen appears as Miss Davis, I say, "There's Grandma!" There is something so magical about actors that always touches my heart.

Jean Marsh also stood out as a respected actress in our midst. She was beyond accomplished when she visited the mountain to play Hilary Von Kleist in "The Hiding Place."

Toward the end of a long day, there was a scene that required tension, but we were in one of those giggly moods and couldn't stop. This time, lesson learned from Richard that forever changed my view as an actor. He told us we were an ensemble and every actor needed our support. This important message has helped me in numerous life lessons as well. We are all here to support each other. Everyone deserves our respect.

Here was this wonderful actress having to deal with our mountain "qualities." We shaped up, and there wasn't a giggle in the house the rest of the day.

Jean had cocreated and starred as Rose in one of my favorite *Masterpiece Theatre* events, *Upstairs, Downstairs.* My mom and I watched it together, and I think it started my fascination with all things British and proper.

Sissy Spacek guest starred twice as Sarah Jane Simmons, first in "The Odyssey" and then "The Townie." We knew she was special from the moment she walked onto the set. She had a great sense of humor. She and Richard cut up and are in more than a few gag reel shots together.

Sissy even looked like us with her red hair and freckles. It was so fun to watch all of her movies over the years. I liked to think we were a stop on her train to the Oscars. Three years after she was on our show, she was first nominated for the Academy Award for *Carrie,* and then she won in 1981 for *Coal Miner's Daughter.* I remember sitting in my living room in my sweats and eating brownies, watching the ceremony, feeling it made me cool because I knew her.

Kathleen Quinlan appeared in two episodes, "The Thoroughbred" and "The Collision," as Selina Linville. I remember how elegant she was atop the horse, and how my Walton brothers and the crew also thought she was quite spectacular. When her Golden Globe–nominated role as Deborah Blake in *I Never Promised You a Rose Garden* launched her to fame, again I felt proud.

Another actress who had a positive influence on me was Joan Pringle. In "The Illusion," filmed in 1978 (Season 7), Erin and Esther were harassed by J.D. Pickett when they worked together to get Esther a job at his defense plant. After some tough challenges, we succeeded against the male-dominated world.

I so admired Joanie for her grace and class. It was an honor to watch her work. I could see her talent and aspired to be as good an actress someday. She went on to be a regular in *The White Shadow* and many other shows, and I was so happy to see her career flourish.

I learned so much from these women, lessons I've carried with me to every set I've worked on, hoping to someday be as classy as my mentors.

ANOTHER ERIN

In 1975 when I was fourteen, Erin Moran, who played Joanie on *Happy Days,* made Ben jealous in "The Song." She was a hoot, did a terrific job as Sally Ann Harper, and we had a great time with her on the set. She was my age, fit right in, and we all became fast friends. But we got into some trouble with her. Eric, for instance, sped around the lot with her in his sports car. The guards at the gate were always all over Eric for rushing the gate. He didn't like to slow down in his fancy sports car.

We decided to take Erin out to our favorite off-the-lot lunch spot, The Magic Apple, a fabulous place that served organic food. We did something that day I still have the heebie-jeebies about. Picture it. There we were—Jon, Eric, Erin, and I—still in our "homespun" wardrobe, because we only had an hour break. We were sitting at a table waiting for our smoothies, and in walk Donny and Marie Osmond. We knew they were probably on a break from doing their show over at ABC Studios.

They were dressed in these 1970s-era bell-bottom pantsuits, and I want so badly to say they were matching, but memory doesn't serve that well. I just know the hair was big, and the outfits, well, nothing like ours. As they were led past us to their table, someone from our group said, "Nice outfits." I cracked up. There was such a disconnect between our drab clothes and plain hair and their trendy fashions and makeup.

Erin started to sing that she was "a little bit country . . ." and Jon joined in with the rock-and-roll line, and we all burst out laughing. It was another "church moment"; it was rare for us, but we couldn't help acting our age. I still hope they didn't hear us and think we were rude. Sometimes we let loose and had to be kids. Sorry, Donny and Marie, this was one of those times.

Erin and I continued to hang out and became friends. We had so much in common, having been raised in a similar way, and now we were both on TV. I wrote about her and the time we spent together in my journal: *I have been going out with Erin a lot lately. We are kind of the same. We grew up the same way too. I like her a lot.*

We often visited each other's sets. I even got to go to *Happy Days* on taping night, which was a big deal. I met Henry Winkler. Imagine being fifteen and getting to go to the show and meeting "The Fonz," how cool is that? These were the moments that made it all worthwhile, getting to be behind the scenes of America's favorite television shows. I sensed I was part of history, even then.

I enjoyed seeing Ron Howard again. The previous year, 1974, in our second season, Ron had done an incredible performance on our show. As Seth, a friend of Jason's who died of leukemia in "The Gift," he played a dramatic role that was quite different from Richie Cunningham. Ron was so good in that episode, people still talk about it as a favorite. He says it was that performance that landed him the role as Gillom Rogers in John Wayne's last film, *The Shootist.*

Jon also gave a great performance. I'll never forget him sitting on the porch, playing "Beautiful Dreamer" on the recorder Seth made before he died, as Earl's narrative begins: "As time went on, there were other occasions that necessitated our grieving, and I often think that this early brush with total loss made us better able to face those which were to come after."

I cried when I watched it at home: the family facing the death of their friend and standing beside neighbors in their times of need. I believe one of the reasons the show had such an impact, and still does, is because of important story lines written by our wonderful writers, such as this one by Carol Evan McKeand. Being a part of all that was not only another perk, but facing these serious social issues with my Walton family helped strengthen me for the impacts my own family would soon experience.

I went with Erin and her family to Mammoth Mountain to ski, and we went to parties together. We used to go to a diner kind of place called Norm's in Westwood, or Dr. Munchies, another hangout. Erin was older, so she drove us around in her new Volkswagen Scirocco. We smoked cigarettes and drank black coffee (no cream because of the calories) until late at night, talking and laughing. Erin exudes contagious energy. Her laugh is as loud as mine—well, almost, and her eyes could light up the sky. She has a devilish grin and perfect smile: 1976 . . . sometime in the spring I wrote, *Erin and I are going to the People's Choice Awards. Erin is going with Jimmy, I am going alone, as always.*

At the awards that night, we were bold enough to approach Sylvester Stallone and gush to him about how much we liked *Rocky.* Many years later, I reminded Mr. Stallone of what I'd done when I was fifteen, and he got a kick out of it.

Erin was on the cover of the May 1981 issue of *Us* magazine, and I was pictured in one of the sidebar boxes as one of "TV's Sexy Teens." Valerie Bertinelli was pictured, and also Lisa Loring from *The Addams Family* and *As the World Turns.* The cover article's subtitle was, ON THE TUBE THEY PLAY GAWKY TEENS, BUT OFF CAMERA—WOW!

Erin was there for me throughout a difficult teenage time. It was so good for me to have someone to talk to. She was someone I could relate to, as we went through similar experiences: *I am really very jovial, but sometimes I change myself for different people. At work I can never be myself. Richard recently asked me, "Who are you really, Mary McDonough?"*

I felt safe with Erin. I remember talking until we fell asleep; we loved Stevie Nicks's "Landslide," and played it over and over. I felt that song completely related to me and my life. I had been so "afraid of changing, 'cause I've built my life around you." The "you" being the show. What was I without this girl I played for seven years?

Who was I? My journal illustrates the questions I wondered back then: *Who is Mary McDonough? Do I really know? Yes, I do and sometimes I don't. I guess I don't really let people know who I am.*

Erin and I talked about our shows, the casts, and the producers. We even talked about being Catholic. We shared our experiences in the fast world we lived in, and how tough it was to live up to the unrealistic expectations. Like any other teenagers, we shared diets and secrets, and had fun. Erin's strong spirit encouraged me to be bolder: *I have had fun the last few months. I have done things I never thought I would do. It's great. I live a radical life. Here's my latest motto. "Live each day so you have a story to tell tomorrow."*

I am grateful for her friendship. Whenever I see her now, I still think about us running around and staying up late, sharing what it was like to be us. To this day, we still exchange Christmas cards. Even today, "Landslide" is still a special song for me. I now look back to that time of my life and can see my own growth. I was a young girl afraid of changes. Today when I listen to the song it brings tears to my eyes. I think of another girl about the same age I was then. The "you" in the lyric is now my daughter. It's a powerful song whose metaphors still bring me so much growing and learning.

6

MOUNTAINS AND MOLEHILLS

August 1976. It's hot in the Valley. I'm fifteen years old, sitting on the edge of my parents' backyard pool, staring into the clean, clear blue water. That familiar gray cloud that lives inside me is particularly menacing today. A storm rages in my head as tears stream down my face. If only *I* could be clean and clear . . . a solution emerges from the cloud. *"Mary, just exhale, fall into the pool, and inhale. Then you won't be so sad. You won't have to worry about your weight, Hog Body, working, or fitting in."*

My singing teacher had told me about her own near-death experience. She said drowning was "peaceful." I longed for that peace, an escape, to leave all the pain behind.

I watched my feet slowly moving back and forth in the cool water and thought about what people would say. Would anyone have expected it? How many would say, "She had it all. Everything handed to her. What was she so sad about?"

Would my close friends understand?

Then I thought of my parents, how it would hurt them. Besides, suicide was a mortal sin. *A mortal sin? Are you kidding me?* I smiled. That old safety valve kicked in, and I actually found the humor in where my mind took me.

Saved from that round, but there would be many more rounds

to come. Luckily, I had some big angels help me through tough times and teach me powerful lessons.

In those teenage years, life seemed to speed up and so many things happened.

F FOR DRAMA

Back at regular school, I needed to take an elective to fill credit requirements. I think they figured I needed a break, so they put me in drama class.

I was terrified. I had never taken a class like this. All the other kids in my school were doing musical theater and putting on plays all year. I had never taken any classes, especially improv.

I sat and watched. Whenever there might have been a place to jump in and participate, I never did. I was paralyzed, the voices in my head said, *"You've been working in the business for how long? Shouldn't you be better at this? Everyone will laugh at you and you'll be seen as the fraud you are."*

One day, the teacher said, "Mary, you have to start joining the exercises in class, or you won't get a good grade. It wouldn't look very good if I failed *you* in drama, of all things."

That thought touched on my insecurities. Once again, I was magically supposed to know how to do something. Facing literal failure, I put my fears in the backseat and forced myself to participate. My mouth dried up as each day came and went. One day, as I watched the exercise, I knew I had to get up. I tentatively raised my hand and joined in on a simple improvisation exercise, urged on by my peers Perry and Roger. Their gentle encouragement helped. I took a breath and stood before the class, knees trembling. I fought to get past the terror of doing something I didn't think I could do perfectly or even very well.

I was so relieved and even felt a bit proud of myself. I had started to face my fears. By doing this simple improv exercise, I began to face up to a long list of things I would never dare for fear of failing. With my new attitude, no matter how scared, I forced myself to jump in and learned that facing the fears makes them fall away. Once I challenge them to a standoff and look them squarely in the eye, I can see the truth: These situations are never as frightening as they seemed when I hid from them. Not dealing with them kept me immobilized. Taking action always makes me feel better.

I actually began to have fun in the class. I even made a few new friends. Oh, and I did pass.

MARY BETH'S HIPS

My teenage years were a contradiction of messages. Our wonderful producers arranged special Christmas parties with a special presentation or event. They would show us a hilarious gag reel of our goof-ups, put on a skit spoofing something that had happened during the season, or Earl would read a funny poem mentioning each one of us.

One year, Rod Peterson, our producer, sang a tribute to the tune of "Thanks for the Memories." The lyrics about me had a line that went, "Ronnie Claire's lips and Mary Beth's hips." I was horrified. My hips? Oh no, what's wrong with my hips? Instead of taking it as a compliment as intended, I thought it meant something was wrong with me. Feeling so embarrassed that I couldn't ask about the real meaning, I took it upon myself to "fix" the problem. I went back to extreme dieting.

As Erin—and I—grew up, we were always being put into contradicting situations. As Mary, I was told I was "the pretty one." As Erin, I was taught that the pursuit of anything based on looks was wrong.

In "The Fire Storm" (Season 5), Erin enters the Jefferson County Day beauty contest, despite her parents' disapproval. Of course, she lost. When Erin exits the stage in tears, Grandma's line sums up what I remember about this episode: "I hope it's taught you something." And then in "The Pin-Up" (Season 7), Ben enters a photograph of Erin wearing shorts and wins first place in a newspaper contest. When she became a Camp Lee poster girl, everyone was outraged because it was wrong to be known for your looks. I got it: pretty equals loser.

By the way, remember Grandpa's statue, "Annabel Lee"? She makes a cameo appearance in a scene next to Drucilla's Pond and plays a small part helping Erin convince Grandpa she should be able to enter the beauty contest. Thanks for nothing, "Annabel Lee."

GIVING BACK

As much as I struggled with the body image "stuff," I was also struggling with the messages about what I deserved, and how I needed to give back to feel I deserved my good fortune. I didn't naturally assume responsibility for others, but through my parents' teachings, it became an important part of my life. I became a caregiver, and over the years of striving to "deserve" it all, I felt no matter how much I gave, it was never enough to repay everyone. I believed my value was what I did and gave others. Eventually I gave too much and lost myself. My value became: what can I do for them to make me worthy?

"Give back, Mary B.; you've been given so much," my dad would say.

From a young age, I was involved with charities and nonprofit organizations. Seemed I was often pulling a winning ticket at a fair, or making pancakes at a church fund-raiser. I felt that with so much given to me, it was my duty to pay it back.

When I was still a teenager, I became the National Youth Ambassador for the American Heart Association, promoting healthy eating and physical activity for children.

Years later, when the Heart Association awarded me their Les Etoiles de Coeur (Stars of Heart) Award for my service, they expected me to give a speech at the award ceremony. I was terrified. I couldn't believe they wanted me to speak about getting an award—it seemed gratuitous. A publicist pressured me about my speech, so I tormented myself for weeks to come up with something appropriate to say. I said just that in my speech. It was odd to receive an award for volunteering my time for a worthy cause— something I felt was the right thing to do, anyway.

WHAT DO I SAY NOW?

Part of my responsibilities as a spokesperson was, of course, to do interviews about the association's work. However, this rekindled an old anxiety: what to say in front of the cameras when I didn't have scriptwriters and a director telling me my every move.

I still remember one especially horrifying incident. I was on *A.M. Los Angeles,* and Regis Philbin was extremely tough on me as I stumbled to get all the right points out in the interview.

Later, I went back to *A.M. Los Angeles* again to promote *Midnight Offerings,* and, once again, Regis was there. This time, I said the name of the network where the movie was airing, which was not the network the talk show was on. Regis puffed up about how I was promoting another network on his network, what a faux pas I had made. I felt horrible, like I did something wrong again. In those days, people didn't mention competing networks on air to prevent promoting another network. Heck, back then, commercials hinted at their competitors and never mentioned them by name. Now it's a free-for-all and competing companies use the actual name of the product they are dissin'.

I crumbled there on live TV. Cyndy Garvey was so sweet; she jumped in and protected me from the big, bad Reege. I was afraid of him—and on-air interviews—for years. I just seemed never to get it right, no matter how much I studied the facts. I wish someone had told me I was okay. I wish I had been able to remove myself from the meat hook I hung myself on. Learning to find my "I'm okay" inside myself would take years of self-work and exploration.

In 1998, I was guest starring on an episode of *Diagnosis Murder,* and Regis was also on the set prepping for his own upcoming episode. I still felt a little of the old anxiety, but now I was a grown-up and had found a little of my voice. I went over to him, introduced myself, knowing he would never remember me, and told him how he had frightened me years earlier. He asked me if he was really that horrible.

"To me? Yes!" I realized how stupid it sounded, and we laughed about it. Then he did something I didn't expect. He apologized.

He was so sweet and understanding. I grew up in that moment and realized I could let go of a very old fear. Thanks, Reege.

SPIRITUALITY AND RELIGION

As early as that day in the schoolroom on *The Homecoming,* I started to question my religion and the scary God I was taught to fear and please. In high school one day, I was sitting outside my Christian Morality class, reading Wayne Dyer's *Your Erroneous Zones,* which was much more interesting and helpful to me than the religion class, by the way.

Something clicked in me and I started to explore a more spiritual path toward this God. I have read Dr. Dyer's books ever since.

He has always been a calm bay in the storms of my life. Though I have drifted in and out of the bay, in times of trouble I find my way back, usually through one of his books, or a PBS special. He has always been an inspiration and a reminder of my inner self as connected to Source. It started here and expanded into a metaphysical exploration for the next twenty years. I believe I have come through my challenges because of this connection to Source and returning to my inner knowing self.

Eventually I learned about many different religions. I studied the teaching of the Buddha and other teachers. I embraced my Catholic upbringing while not rejecting others' beliefs if they were not like mine. I expanded to include and add other religious teachings to my foundation. Learning acceptance of other faiths, cultures, people, and backgrounds created the space for me to begin accepting myself.

GOOD NIGHT, RITTER

John Ritter was as sensitive as he was funny. We used to have deep conversations about life, boys, and school. He didn't treat me like I was a little kid. He was a different kind of big brother, less teasing, more listening. He asked me questions about myself, which was different for me. We all adored him. I think I adored him more than anyone else because of how he touched my life. He was so well loved—I know I am one of many.

I was trying so hard to appear perfect to my costars and family, and I thought I fooled everyone. The tears were hidden in the tub after all, right?

One day, we were on location in Frazier Park, filming the Mary Ellen wedding show. "The Wedding" aired November 4, 1976, as a two-hour episode. Someone had said something insensitive to me. As usual, I was injured to my core—I took everything so personally. Not one to address or confront anyone, I walked away. A typical response. I sat down on a rock, alone, raging in silence, hoping to control the storm and not step into the tornado of my emotions.

Ritter came over and sat with me. After a few minutes, he asked if I was okay. I, of course, said, "I'm fine." He realized how upset I was and persisted in trying to reach me. Not very many people asked me how I was in those days, and when they did, most believed the lie of "fine." I was so touched that he didn't give up.

"Do you ever write down your feelings? Keep a diary?" He told me he had kept a journal for years and wrote his thoughts, feelings, and entire stories about whatever was happening. His journal helped him through tough times, and he encouraged me to start one.

That night, I asked my mom to take me to the store, where I purchased the first of many spiral-bound notebooks, and I began journaling. To my surprise, it was easy to write. I realized I had always written in one way or another, from my plays to poems. I had so much to say to this sacred, secret paper.

My first entry was about all the anger I felt from the unkind comment on the set. I wrote about other incidents, all the pressures flowed into my pen and onto the pages. And then, much like that math problem, my anger turned into physical rage. I stabbed the journal. I let it rip. No holding back. I broke my pen.

This started a soul salvation for me. I had somewhere to vent, cry, or even—horror of all horrors—get angry. After the fury wrote itself out, my journaling settled into calm reason. Writing connected me to a place in my soul, back to the peace that I loved. Here is a section of my first entry after Ritter's advice that I should write:

Here I am sitting up on a mountainside watching some beautiful trees and breathing some fresh air. I have been talking to Tom (Bower) and John about numerous amounts of things, having a great time. I am now back in touch with my life and body although I would like to lose a little weight.

The nature here is unbelievable. There is a cool breeze. I have a feeling of peace and happiness, a comforting feeling with nature; little wild flowers, pinecones, trees, dirt, bushes and love. Beautiful creations and an earthy feeling, I am glowing. The clouds are nice too, the sky is blue. Nature is reborn in me. The wind is rushing through the trees.

I am sitting on an old tree stump looking at, feeling and admiring nature. John R and I just had a great talk about nature, us and all. He told me I was special, I am thankful for knowing all I do, and having all the experiences and relationships I have had. My experiences have made me wiser.

Life is such a beautiful thing. Nature is so full of life; I wish everyone could experience life.

My parents didn't have great communication skills. While they never yelled or raised their voices, the tension was so thick in our house at times that you could cut it with a knife, as the saying goes. So learning to deal with anger was a whole new ball game. My tears could turn to rage and still be safe in the benign book of lined pages. When I look back and read them now, I see how conflicted I was, and how badly I needed an outlet.

I have Ritter to thank for being my angel that day. I feel so blessed to have known him. He was one of the kindest, gentlest, naughtiest, funniest men I've ever had the honor to know. He reached out to me with comfort and advice in a time that was crucial to me.

I saw him over the years after he left Walton's Mountain and went on to be a huge star. He always treated me in the same loving way. He made me feel seen and heard—no matter where we were. Years later, he was doing a play on Broadway and I was fortunate enough to be in New York and go backstage to see him. I told him he saved my life that day he started me journaling, and he gave me a big hug. That was the last time I saw him.

I remember the day I heard the news. On September 11, 2003, while rehearsing an episode of his hit sitcom *Eight Simple Rules*, Ritter collapsed and was rushed to the hospital, where he died of a congenital heart defect. I thought of his wife and kids, whose pictures he kept in his dressing room. I remembered the impact he made on me. He helped a very scared little girl off the pool ledge of suicidal thoughts by sitting with me on the side of the mountain that day.

Good night, sweet Ritter.

> *April 21, 1983*
> *. . . here I am starting my second journal. . . . It's been a long time since I was sitting on a hilltop in Frazier Park when John Ritter told me I should start a journal. I thank him for that. He'll never know how much it helped me. Saved my life. . . .*

ELLEN

Will was quite concerned when Ellen didn't show up for work one morning. That was out of character for her. She was never late. When they called her, she tried to answer by knocking the phone off the hook. Knowing something must be wrong, our producers Andy White and Claylene Jones got a driver and headed to her house. There was no answer, so the driver climbed up and saw her lying on the landing. He broke in through a window and let the others in. They called an ambulance. She'd had a stroke.

It was a tough time for us all. Ellen wasn't able to work for the rest of the fifth season, and her absence was felt by all of us, as well as the viewers, until her remarkable return in "Grandma Comes Home" a year later. Rod Peterson and Claire Whitaker wrote a compelling episode that mirrored our own very real excitement to have her back.

Her return to the show as a stroke survivor inspired millions, and the episode is still a fan favorite. She was so brave and an inspiration to others who had suffered a similar loss of speech and use of limbs. Here was a woman who made her living by expressing herself through speaking and movement, now limited to a fraction of her former physical abilities.

She could still use those expressive eyes, and she learned her lines, even though it was a struggle to deliver them. Her personal experience brought a sense of dignity to what also became part of Grandma's story line. She taught us about honesty and portraying your truth. I learned not to be afraid, that she was still Grandma and I could indeed communicate with her.

We all wanted to help her. There would be four or five people guessing what she was trying to communicate. It was really frustrating for her. I would sit back and watch her as she tried to get her point out. Often I could get on her wavelength and figure out what she meant. Her eyes would light up; she would point to me, or whoever figured it out, and say, "Yes, Yes." This was the beginning of me trusting my instincts to assess people and situations. Trusting myself and my own gut feelings felt right to me. This would eventually help get me through life's ups and downs. To this day, I'm able to use this ability as a life coach.

DAD

My dad was never a "doctor" person. His farm life prepared him to take care of things on his own. When he was building a wall in our backyard, a cinder block fell on his hand. Blood was building pressure under his nail. He went to the garage, got a drill bit, and drilled through his fingernail until the pressure released. I asked him later why he had a hole in his nail. He said, "To get the blood out."

He was the same way about pulling teeth. When we were little, he'd ask us if he could just have a look at any loose teeth to "check and see how loose they were." Then he'd yank it out. We caught on to that one fast enough. Subsequent teeth were pulled by our own timing when he tied our tooth to a string and then the door. We got to shut the door when we were ready. I never shut the door, though. I couldn't do it.

My father got sick when I was fifteen. We didn't know there was anything wrong for a long time, as he didn't go to the doctor at first. I came home from school one day and he was sitting alone, in a dark room, which was so scary to me. He was never home during the day, let alone sitting in a darkened room.

I said, "Is something wrong?"

He said, "Yes, something's very wrong." The look on his face and the tone of his voice was unfamiliar. I had never seen him like this before. My legs started to shake.

He told me I had to drive him to the hospital in Pasadena, a good forty-five minutes from our house. I didn't have a driver's license yet. He had taught me to drive when I was nine, but this wasn't sitting on his lap steering down a dirt road, or that deserted highway in Colorado. This was for real, negotiating freeways and interchanges. I was scared, but I knew I had to help my dad. I didn't question or argue. I got my purse, and we left. My journal entry from that day:

> My Dad is in the hospital, he is very ill. He had major surgery yesterday. They cut out his gall bladder because of over 120 stones. He also has over 30 abscesses on his liver which they are draining. He is in intensive care. They say he might die—but I don't want to think negative—my mom is very upset. The doctor said he has a thousand to one chance of living through the night.
>
> Waiting for a phone call is like waiting for death. Every time the phone rings, I jump. Waiting to hear from the hospital. I have a fear in me now. My father is in ICU—a depressing sight. All those machines . . . I hate the hospital, but I must go there because I love him so much. I don't want him to feel alone.

I remember the first time I went to ICU to see him. My godfather, Uncle Hugh, was there and warned me my father didn't look the same. He was unconscious; there were so many hoses, tubes, and the sounds of machines.

I sat down next to his bed and pretended I wasn't scared. I talked about the cards I brought, made by kids in the neighborhood. I chatted on. He just lay there. The only sound was the suction from the machines. I left the room, and as I walked out, my knees buckled. My legs went out from under me, and my godfather caught me before I hit the floor. Then I cried.

My dad had a near-death experience that night. He went through the tube and toward the Light, had a conversation with

Jesus, and came back to tell us about it. He recovered, and when he came home, he was so exuberant and full of life.

He'd wake us up early to go out and pick strawberries for pancakes he was making. He took us even more places than he did before. He went to my brother's basketball games, and with loads of energy, he'd say, "Come on, let's go. Have some fun." As I look back, it was as if he knew he had a short time left. He savored the moments, and without coming out and saying a word about dying, he cherished life.

From then on, a different cloud invaded my life—a cloud of death. I would be out with my friends, having fun and laughing. When I returned, I would pause in my front yard, afraid to go inside. I was scared that when I walked in the door, everyone would be sad because he was gone.

MOUNTAIN LOSS

About a year and a half later, when I was sixteen, my dad took ill again and had another surgery. An adhesion had wrapped around his intestine and surgery revealed colon cancer. He started chemotherapy; he took a turn for the worse and went back into the hospital.

My friends were a saving grace for me at the time. My friend Rozanne DeCampos came to the hospital with me one day and brought her guitar. Rozanne has a great voice and we sang "By My Side" from *Godspell*. My dad loved music and to hear us all sing.

Olivia Newton-John was popular and my dad thought she was cute. He asked us to sing "I Honestly Love You," and then asked me to sing it again, alone. As I sang, he stared out the window. He had a faraway look in his eyes. I watched a single tear roll down his cheek, fall off his chin, and soak into his hospital gown. He stared off as I finished the song; then he reached for his kidney-shaped bed bowl and threw up blood. The nurses came in and asked us to leave. I wondered if we upset him too much, and later joked with Rozanne that it must have been my singing. It was the last time I saw him conscious.

During Holy Week, he took a "turn for the worse," and the doctors said, "There is nothing we can do." *Nothing you can do?* I screamed, but only in my head. Even though I couldn't say the words out loud, I was angry, almost couldn't believe they were giving up. Why couldn't they do something? They were educated, smart, supposed to be able to help and heal. In that moment, I lost my respect for medicine, doctors, and grown-ups. My dad had faith in them—his life depended on them—and now they were saying, "There's nothing we can do." This was a rude awakening for me. I was devastated and so angry that these stupid doctors had given up on my daddy. He should be outside enjoying the nature he loved so much: the roses, the trees, and the grass he planted in our backyard. I hated the hospital: the smell, the walls, the lights. I hated that this was the last place he would see. But I wouldn't leave.

The hospital vigil began. My uncles prayed over him. One brought a loud man who walked around his bed, shouting, "Jesus, drive the cancer out." We prayed for him to cross over soon, so the pain would end.

It was a horribly painful way to die. I did not understand how my God could let a good man suffer such a miserable death. It shook my sensibilities. Hadn't I said enough prayers? Wasn't I good enough to be answered? Why do evil people live long lives and my daddy had to go so young? My dad never hurt anyone, and yet he had to endure this terrible suffering. But like his Jesus, he went through his Stations of the Cross in about the same time frame.

We wanted to help him, but the morphine wasn't enough to cut his pain. His rosary was his constant companion. When we placed the beads in his hands and told him we would take care of Mom and each other, he would relax. My mom left the hospital; she felt he did not want her there, for her to see him that way. The last night was a long one. My brother Michael didn't want him to leave this earth being alone, so we stayed. The hours went on and on, and the gasping for each breath after what felt like hours of silence was like a horror film.

They told us your hearing is the last thing to go, so we told stories around his bedside. We laughed as Michael and my brother, John, imitated him up in the bleachers at basketball games, cupping his hands around his mouth and yelling, "Take it away! Take it away! Take it away!" We talked about his famous pancake breakfasts, his backyard barbecues, the plane trips, and a failed boating expedition.

One of the nurses came in every hour to check his vital signs. "How long do you estimate?" I asked her.

"Just a couple of minutes," she said.

What? I was angry. What if I hadn't asked? She would have just written in his chart and left the room, like every other time.

We all gathered around him and held his hands. The phone rang. It was our mom.

She knew.

He was gone.

We all had tasks, and mine was to take down the cards made by the kids on our block. I thought I was alone in the room, and started to take the pushpins out to pack up all the get-well wishes. Then I heard a rustling behind me. I turned around and saw the nurse pulling tubes out of him. She had pulled back the sheet, fully exposing him. The last sight I had of my dad was the catheter being removed. The image of my daddy lying in the hospital bed in the shadows of the green fluorescent light still haunts me. Later that day, I wrote in my journal:

IN LOVING MEMORY
Lawrence J McDonough
Good Friday, 3:50 AM—1978
My dad died on Good Friday. I was there when it happened. Me, Mike and John were with him from one PM in the afternoon on Holy Thursday until 3:50 AM Friday. We waited there until he left us.

It was an unusual experience. I had never seen John cry before. I cried, too.

Sometimes I feel very lonely and sometimes I feel he is here by my side helping me make the right decisions. I remember a lot of memories, mostly good. I loved my father and told him so. At least I did that. I miss him when I am alone. I remember how he used to hold me when I cried, like I am doing now.

I find it easy to talk of his death. It was dark in the hospital, dark when we got in the car to drive home. Mike and I got in and I turned the key and "Dust in the Wind" was playing on the radio. After we told my Mom how peaceful it was at the end when he died, the birds started to sing and the sun came up. I went to my room, changed and it was light. I lay down, stared at the ceiling and felt the salt water in my ears.

My father died on March 24, 1978. Easter was early that year.

My Walton family came to help and support my McDonough family, and we were together again, this time on a sad occasion. Erin Moran called and cried on the phone with me.

We had an Irish wake for my father, and when Richard Hatch called, he asked what was so loud in the background. I told him, "We're having a party to celebrate my dad's life. It's how we do it here."

People still tell me wonderful stories about how my dad touched their lives. More than thirty years later, I still celebrate and miss him every day.

COMA

I am blessed with the most amazing friends. I am lucky. I had my own high-school friends from Chaminade, and my dear friends from the "Alemany Pack," who went to a nearby school, Alemany High. Carol, Tim, Rozanne, Bobby, Kori, and Tom were there for me when my dad died. I love this story and can laugh still, even though my friends were shocked when it happened.

We had spent days on end in the hospital until my father died. Then there were all the calls and arrangements to make. We had to make a difficult decision whether there would be an autopsy. My mother didn't want him to endure any more hurt, as he had been through so many drugs and surgeries, and she didn't want him experimented on. My brother and I argued that there might have been a therapy that slowed the disease and could be used for future cancer patients. He'd had a rare form, and his death might help someone. What if one of us developed it someday?

It was tough, but Dad went back to the hospital for an autopsy.

My friends knew I needed a break, so they arranged a movie night. I was so relieved to get away from the sadness for a few hours. They picked me up, we all piled into the car; we drove to the movie theater. Knowing I loved a good horror flick, they'd found a drive-in showing *Coma*. The movie started, and my friends realized very soon what the topic was. Tim looked sideways at Bobby; Rozanne looked at Tim; they all watched me.

I kept my gaze focused forward. I didn't want them to think I was ungrateful. As I watched, I realized the plot of the film had elements of the very thing my dad had just gone through.

When the film arrived at the autopsy scene, well, that was it. Tom was obviously uncomfortable. Squirming in his seat, he turned to me and squeaked something like, "Good choice, huh?"

When I started to laugh, they joined me, and the tension melted. They offered to leave, but I insisted we stay and "watch" the whole thing.

I cherish my friends for trying so hard to make it better. They really did, too. Rozanne, Tom, and Tim sang at my father's funeral. Twenty-eight years later, my dear Tim would come full circle and sing at my mother's.

GRANDPA

In April, we were still on hiatus when we got the news Grandpa Will died. It was only a couple of weeks after my dad had died. I couldn't believe he was gone now, too. This was the man who told me he would be on the show forever; he would never leave. Why didn't I know he was sick? Why wasn't I at the hospital with him? I knew hospitals, that I could do.

We all had the opportunity to say good-bye to Will in a two-hour episode, "The Empty Nest." We gathered around the grave in the familiar mountains in Frazier Park and said our scripted "good-byes" to Grandpa. It was a tough show for me to film. We still had Grandma Ellen, whom we thought we had lost, but was back, and now Zeb was missing. It was not only a "good night, Grandpa Walton" moment; it was "good night, Will," our merry leader in the band of players, and "good night" to my own daddy.

As I look back, I can't say I freaked out, but rather I became more stoic as I dealt with each loss. Something in me hardened, and my resolve to be strong and take care of everyone grew deeper. The role of caretaker gave me purpose.

BOZO HAIR

I think I just needed to change something about me as a way to cope, or to feel like I had control of something after my father's and Will's funerals. One thing I did was get my hair permed. It was crazy, but my friends (with thick, beautiful hair) were doing it, and theirs looked so wavy and curly. My hair didn't hold a curl, so I thought it was a great idea. Only thing was, my thin hair permed so tight, I didn't get the soft curls I was expecting, but more of a Bozo look. My hair suffered the loss.

Edie, the show's hairstylist, about had a heart attack when she saw it. "What did you do to yourself?" she cried.

The producers were not happy, either. My long, pretty red hair was now shoulder-length frizz. Edie twisted it away from my face and pinned it back for many episodes, then cut it out as soon as it grew. It was a bad hair time for poor Erin, but it was the first time in my life I ever had a current, popular do. I never got to have the Dorothy Hamill wedge, the Farrah Fawcett layers, or the shag, because they weren't period and our styles had to be appropriate for the show. Maybe there was a little rebellion; gone was the good girl. Bring on the sassy, made-tougher-by-circumstance girl.

. . . I am still scared at times, but I am so strong, independent, mule-headed, loud, opinionated, social, sensitive, outspoken, child-like, giggly and brutally honest.

Later that year, something good happened to me. My first boyfriend. He was in the Alemany group. I did get to go on a date, to his prom, and I felt like a normal girl. I was so happy to have found someone who finally liked me and someone I felt safe with. I felt protective. He was mine, not yours . . . sorry. I didn't want to share him. It was so private, I went to public functions with someone else to throw the press off. After all, hadn't I learned what the press could do to the truth? He was my truth, and I wanted to protect us. He was my first love and put up with an awful lot. I was a scared girl who had lost her daddy and was navigating a rocky path. He was patient and kind, and I learned to love, let go, and trust. I felt alive, loved, and lucky.

7

I FEEL IN-BETWEEN AND FORGOTTEN

I want so much to be normal, to be accepted as whole, as one on some world. Either at work or at school. But I am divided into two pieces. Maybe I don't fit into either world.

My journal tells it like it was. As I got older, it was harder for me to go back and forth from work to school. I first went to Chaminade in my sixth-grade school year. Going to middle school is hard enough, but to begin in March was awkward to say the least. Add in being a kid actor, and you have a recipe for disaster. The rumors started before I arrived, and many of my new schoolmates assumed they knew what I was like because of seeing me on television each week.

I remember standing in the principal's office on the day I checked in, feeling like an alien. I fought to maintain composure as office workers stared at me, and kids walking by in the hallway pointed and whispered. Later, I found out an innocent, nervous mannerism "confirmed" their suspicions. A girl saw me and ran off to tell everyone I was stuck-up. "You should have seen her flipping her hair."

Fortunately, not everyone believed the gossip, and they assigned me a guide for my first day. Caren Cline not only taught me the ropes, she became one of my best friends. We swore on that first day as she showed me to my classrooms that we would be in each other's weddings, and we were.

Some of the kids at school just didn't know what to do with me. That first year, I got hate notes in my locker saying, *Hey, Walton girl, go home.* My locker was ransacked once—not sure why—maybe it was a hazing and it happened to everyone. I knew I was different and how could I expect people to get to know me, since I was hardly ever there.

I craved consistency. I would be at work adjusting to set life, only to have the season end and dread going back to regular school. My journal entries from 1976 reflect my mood. I was a sophomore in high school:

> *I start school on Wed. What a drag. I just want to work. I have 2 weeks left of studio school, then I go back to my own school. What a bummer. I don't like the school scene at all. I hate it.*
>
> *   *   *
>
> *I started school today. What a bunch of bull, lectures on success. School is so cliquey, everyone has a clique. It really bugs me. I have classes with Kate and I am glad. There are so many people I don't know.*

We wrapped our seasons in late February or early March. I would return to Chaminade in the middle of their semester and hope I was at the same place they were at in their studies. Just as I would get attached to my friends and they would get to know me— *poof . . .* it was back to work in late May:

> *I leave here in 2 weeks. Work will be a bummer, I don't want to leave. I want so much to be normal and try to be a part of it all, but I can't. I have not been brought up in a manner such as that. Since I was 9 I was crossed to another world. Was I freaked out as a child? I wasn't, but now I feel as if it's all caught up to me and I am very down and blue. . . .*
>
> *I have always said that the transition from a totally adult world to a kid world never affected me. Also, being switched from studio school to normal school, I lied.*
>
> *I am in studio school for the summer; go to my own school for a month, then to studio school for 5 months, then back to school for 3*

more months. It doesn't really affect me at first but when I have to leave all my friends and all the people I have just started to get to know I get very sad. I never really get to know anyone before I have to leave, then when I come back I have to start all over again.

All I do is cry for awhile and then I feel better, for a short time. Sometimes I get violent, sometimes suicidal. Well, that's life.

I remember at the end of one season—I think I was about fifteen—David and I ran around our second home, which was encased in the padded, soundproof walls of Stage 26. We screamed at it, as if those walls were to blame for our troubles. I kicked and pounded on it with my clenched fists, like somehow I could make it feel my pain of being pulled from one life into the other. When I couldn't scream or punch anymore, I was exhausted, and my hands were red from hitting the imposing stucco exterior walls of the soundstage. No amount of abuse affected the edifice; it stood strong and unyielding in its power. I looked up at the straight, windowless building that held out the real world. I felt dwarfed, helpless.

I started back to work today. I just don't like it there. I don't want to be there. I thought I was the only one who felt that way, but David does too.

I had a love-hate relationship with the show. I was on a rollercoaster ride I couldn't get off, trying to balance the changeup. I went back to work, and accepted my sentence: the seven-year contract my parents had signed years ago.

Lately I have been having fun. I want to work now. I have decided to be an actress. There is a lot of Bull to get through, but I think I can make it if I don't get hung up on it all. If I do I can always look at a leaf, watch a sunset, visit a tree or listen to snow fall.

MY BIG EPISODE

I have been having a great time with the crew and am working harder. Lately, I really want to be an actress but I don't know if I can put up with all the bull involved in it all. I have been acting myself lately, not caring what others think. Maybe that's why I have been having a good time. I just have to overcome my fears and climb over my obstacles. I can do anything if I set my mind to it. I just hope this show is good, really good.

Every season there was at least one special episode that featured one of us. In the fifth season, I was sixteen when mine was "The Elopement." So many episodes were focused on my looks, but I wanted to be known for my talent, not my appearance. It was tough to separate from being just the pretty girl and to be thought of as a serious actress.

I had enrolled in acting classes, and one day while we were filming "The Elopement," I shared that information with Ronnie Claire Edwards. I told her how much I wanted to be a better actress.

She said, "Oh, Mary Beth, you don't need to worry about talent, you have looks!" Getting ahead in the business would be easier for me. She insisted that was the reality.

I felt the rug pulled out from under me. This was a sample of the "bull" I wrote about in my journal. Her comments strengthened my resolve to take even more classes. Acting classes brought me a relief I had not felt before. I had been flying by the seat of my pants for years, and finally I was learning the art.

Ever since that lesson underneath the pepper tree when Robert Butler used the snake story to teach me about the fourth wall and breaking the illusion, I'd hungered to understand my craft. Maybe now I could figure out what was expected of me and *how* to develop a character, dig deep for emotions, and deliver compelling performances. It gave me purpose and focus and something to work toward, and I applied all my class work to every episode.

WHICH BETTY?

Then one day, Ralph Senensky, a wonderful director, brought me to my ultimate choice. Ralph and I had discussed whether children should learn to act, or if it was enough to be a kid. Ralph believed when you got to be a certain age, it wasn't enough just to act like a kid anymore; you actually needed to learn the craft.

He explained it was like walking up to a bridge and deciding to cross over into the grown-up world, where the challenges were tough and the expectations high, or staying on the "safe" side, where you could continue to play around and "get by." Ralph knew I had been working to bridge that gap between the cute child actor and an adult with believability, depth, and scope. I respected his knowledge and sensitivity toward my serious effort.

The set was ready, the lighting done, and they were waiting for "talent," as the performers are called. I was in the makeup room, my hair in rollers, and the AD kept checking in to see when I would be ready.

I looked up at Edie, our hairstylist, as she told him, "Another fifteen minutes, at least." I realized I was the one holding up production.

The hair. Need I say more? There was such a focus on hair, wardrobe, and our overall appearance as we got older. We wore makeup and had 1940s-style hairdos every day. I was no longer the carefree, barefoot little girl in pigtails running around the set.

Ralph himself finally came into the makeup room and asked if I was ready. When the director goes looking for his actors, you know things are getting serious.

"I'm ready, but my hair isn't done," I told him. I felt stupid even as I said the words.

He looked at me sitting in front of the mirrored wall. With measured words, he said, "Well, who do you want to be—Betty Grable or Bette Davis?"

Like a cattle prod, his words stunned me into action. I stood up, ripped the rollers out of my hair, and ran to the set, thinking Bette *Davis.*

In the movie of the week *A Wedding on Walton's Mountain* in 1982, Paul Northridge proposes to Erin. I had a similar decision to make, much to the dismay of our producers. We were filming at the house on the backlot, and Erin is preparing to see Paul and agree to marry him. My hair was nowhere near ready, and we were losing time.

I thought of myself as a no-nonsense actress by then, very practical and production savvy. I decided I would just stuff my hair under a hat. We shot the scene and got on with the day's work.

Later in the week, we were shooting the following scene, and, of course, it had to match the previous one, so again I had to wear the hat. Well, when the footage of me in the hat with no hair showing was discovered, the set was not happy. I must have looked really bad, or maybe I didn't look as pretty as Erin should when getting betrothed, so the order came down: no hat.

How did we fix it without reshooting the entire scene? With creativity. In the final cut, Erin approaches Paul. She removes the hat, and multitudes of perfectly curled hair cascades out. At last, Erin had fabulous, flowing hair—perfect for a marriage proposal.

"WOW, OH WOW"

Because of my acting classes, I started to ask a few questions at work and wanted to understand and participate more in what I was doing in the context of the story lines. I began to act on my impulses, speak about my character, and collaborate about how a scene could be played. Sometimes these baby steps toward expressing my voice were accepted, but not always.

In "The Legacy," Erin encounters Ashley Longworth Jr. for the first time. After flirting with him in the living room of the Baldwin sisters' house, she lets herself out. The script had Erin swooning against the door and saying the line, "Wow, oh wow."

I hated this line and I loathed the "swoon." I felt my character would never speak or act this way. I didn't know how to make it work. Erin was strong and confident; she worked around men in the defense plant and had reached a level of maturity that didn't fit what the director was asking for. I tried to explain, but our director, Gwen Arner, insisted I do it as written. I protested, then felt bad for resisting and belittled for trying to express myself.

If there was an attempt at explanation, I would have accepted the decision. Instead, the AD made it worse, took me behind the set, and gave me a verbal lashing. He told me to stop disrespecting our female director and do what she said. How dare I ask questions or think I knew better? "Don't ask questions, and do as you're told!" he screamed.

So much for having a voice, for working to improve my talent, for growing up in a business that expects you to know everything, then punishes you when you try to be a part of your own journey. I went back to the set so upset I fought to hold back tears at the complete humiliation. Here I was playing a happy scene about being smitten by a gorgeous man, and I had to fake my way through. It went against everything I was trying to accomplish. I felt a failure all over again. Squashed.

Years later, Earl's sister Audrey Hamner, the real Erin, said in an interview she liked my portrayal of her, and how I played Erin. "However," she said, "there is one thing I don't like that Erin did. I would never have swooned over a man and said 'Wow, oh wow.' "

NUMBER ONE

Erin's favorite love interest was Ashley Longworth Jr. That's because Jonathan Frakes, who played Ashley, is one of my favorites as well. In "The Legacy," a script written from a story idea by Michael Learned, Miss Emily mistakes Ashley for his father and believes he has come back for her. Erin, rightfully so, thinks he is her cup of tea, and the games begin.

As hard as this episode was for me to shoot, I couldn't help noticing how completely gorgeous Jonathan was as Ashley in his dress whites. You know, a man in uniform. I could go on and on, but . . . need I? You get the picture.

Jonathan, who later went on to fame as Commander William T. Riker, or Number One, in *Star Trek: The Next Generation,* was my number one favorite love interest on the show. He is a gracious man whom I adored working with. We had chemistry, fun, and shared many laughs.

I was about seventeen when we did our first episode together. There was a kissing scene, never my favorite thing to do. However, Jonathan is such a confident, good person, he was the first actor I felt totally comfortable kissing in a scene, in front of twenty crew members. As it turned out, we even had a good laugh over it.

We were outside one chilly morning, filming the romantic scene leading to our big kiss. Trouble was, when we spoke, you could see our breath, only it wasn't supposed to be winter in the scene. We learned a little movie magic trick that morning; they had us put ice in our mouths to equal the inside temperature to the outside temperature. Voilà, no more fog breath.

As with many romantic scenes, it was very technical, and we both laughed at how unromantic it was to hold ice in our mouths until "action," then spit it out and resume the scene. So there we were, spitting ice and kissing. This was truly an icebreaker. But that's not all.

The scene called for Miss Emily to catch us kissing and watch from afar. The camera setup was like this: us in the foreground, and Miss Emily in the background. Then the camera panned over to Miss Emily, revealing her standing there spying on us. At that point, we were out of the shot. Well, we started to kiss and just kept going, even after the camera focused on Miss Emily and we were out of the shot.

We were "acting" our hearts out. (How could we see that, anyway? Our eyes were closed. Hello?) The crew started clearing their throats; then their coughing got louder and a bit more, well, insistent.

Finally someone said, "Excuse us, but you can stop now."

We broke apart, and I looked up. I smiled innocently (okay, I admit, maybe I blushed a little) and said, "Oh, are we out of frame? Do we need another take?" Jonathan laughed, and for the first time, I felt like a working actress, not a schoolgirl.

The crew gave us a hard time and teased me, but I held my ground, mostly because of Jonathan's solid persona as my scene partner. He helped me step into that role. His grace, class, and humor showed me I could play Erin as she matured.

The second time Jonathan visited the mountain was the following season. I had turned eighteen, and overnight that birthday changed how I was treated on the set. I was able to work longer hours; I no longer needed a guardian; and the "adult" label must have been stamped across my chest, because all bets—at least the rules about how minors could be treated—were off.

While I often had felt uncomfortable whenever there was any sexual tension on the set, it was a surprise to me that simply my being of age brought on a different attitude from those around me. Walter Alzmann was now directing us while we filmed "The Lost Sheep." Walter, who had known me since I was a child, grabbed me and planted his lips on mine to demonstrate how he wanted Jonathan to kiss me. I couldn't scream, push him off me, or even move. Not only because he had me in his grips, but he was the director and to be "respected." Another land mine inside me exploded. He had violated boundaries that made me feel safe and protected. I was embarrassed and terrified.

Someone attempted a joke to lighten things up. We went back to work. The red flag signaling fear waved in my gut. It was amazing how unsafe I felt now that I was an adult. There was no daddy or Cori to protect me. That daunting task fell on me: a girl with no voice to speak up for herself. This was not the first sexual harassment I encountered, and it wouldn't be my last.

A few years later, I would audition for a movie where the director kept asking me to go to his beach house to rehearse. I wasn't stupid enough to go, but he was angry with me for insisting on rehearsing in his office. On the set, he became abusive and screamed at me during the entire shoot. He cursed at me and yelled, "You suck. You suck. If you had come to my beach house, you wouldn't suck." He tried to get me to wear see-through clothes and to do nude scenes. It was horrible.

Later, I heard there were complaints registered against him at SAG, and if he had tried something at his beach house, and I'd reported him, there would be enough to take formal actions against him. Why I didn't feel I could tell anyone is beyond me. But more disturbing was why I felt somehow it was expected or I deserved to be treated that way.

It took some tough blows, some literal, to help me learn to protect and stand up for myself. I'm not sure why it had to get so bad for me to learn, but sometimes it did. A few years later, I was working with an actor who called himself a *reactor*. He "reacted" how he felt, whether it was in the script or not. During a scene that didn't call for violence, I suddenly felt the side of my face burn as a loud crack sounded in my ear. He literally slapped me so hard, it knocked me to the ground. The next thing I knew, I came to on the ground, dizzy, with my head ringing. What did I do? Yell? Scream? No, I went numb, sucked it up, and finished filming the scene.

The director kindly asked the actor *not* to hit me again, and we did another take. I ended up in the hospital a few hours later. I recounted what happened, and the nurse said, "This is serious. I have to ask you something. You have been assaulted. I need to call the police. Do you want to file assault charges?" I started to shake and stammer. How could I do that? She looked me dead in the eye and repeated the question. I was so upset, and my duty to guarding secrets, the show must go on, and my own lack of self-care spoke for me. I avoided her gaze and meekly said, "It was only a movie."

I wasn't the same for months. I was advised to go to meetings and talk about it—I didn't. I did spend months going to a neurologist after the filming was completed. Unfortunately, it took something like this to teach me that no one gets to hit me. Not literally or figuratively anymore. I picked myself up off the mountain with a new resolve *not* to allow myself to be a victim anymore.

The journey for women to grow has been a long climb. All I can think now is that women were still treated differently in the 1970s when I started to work. I carried some tired beliefs that affected me greatly. Now there is a heightened awareness about violence and sexual harassment; back then, women took it and kept their mouths shut, and so did I.

Luckily, with Jonathan Frakes, I felt safe. He was a calming presence. Working with him was a complete delight.

Losing Family

Richard Thomas left the show in 1978, and Michael Learned and Ralph Waite soon followed. Tremendous change propelled us into adulthood. We "kids" relied on the lessons we'd learned from our "parents" to carry the show.

Losing Richard was hard on us. The show just wasn't the same,

In 1961, I joined my brothers and added to the family. My mom was always so pretty. She worked hard to make sure all of us were well-dressed for family photos.
(Author's personal collection)

Mom and Dad on their way to Hawaii in 1967. They look so happy to me. *(Author's personal collection)*

With the *TV Guide*. It was meant to be! *(Author's personal collection)*

With two of my favorite people, my brothers Michael and John, in 1963. *(Author's personal collection)*

Me as a toddler. *(Author's personal collection)*

I loved this red velvet dress. It looks like a future Walton pinafore. *(Author's personal collection)*

First grade photo. Nice bangs! *(Author's personal collection)*

The beginning of ballet recitals. I was a marionette that cut away from her strings for a solo. Hmmm, a sign of things to come? The glue used to paste on those pink sequins burned my skin. Early performance trials, ha ha. *(Author's personal collection)*

Daddy's girl at her First Holy Communion. *(Author's personal collection)*

The Homecoming cast. Patricia Neal and Andrew Dugan played the parents. *(CBS)*

The Waltons cast, season one. This was the first of many. *(*THE WALTONS
© *Lorimar Television. Licensed By: Warner Bros. Entertainment Inc. All Rights Reserved.)*

At the Waltons' dinner table.
(THE WALTONS © Lorimar Television. Licensed By: Warner Bros. Entertainment Inc. All Rights Reserved.)

In Ike Godsey's store with Judy and Kami. I like this one because it shows how comfortable we are as sisters. My elbows are on Kami. *(THE WALTONS © Lorimar Television. Licensed By: Warner Bros. Entertainment Inc. All Rights Reserved.)*

Goofing on the set in 1972.
(Author's personal collection)

With Ellen at a race car event in 1973. She looked different when she wasn't dressed as Grandma.
(Author's personal collection)

Cheerleading practice in junior high. (*Author's personal collection*)

Turning thirteen with a cake my mom made and decorated. (*Author's personal collection*)

On tour with Eric for the show. Love my vest and Eric's groovy shirt, glasses, and necklace. (*CBS*)

Going to the Emmys with my dad. *(Author's personal collection)*

With Erin Moran at my parents' house. Love us here. I'm wearing a silver Taurus the Bull necklace Richard gave to me for Christmas. Still have it. *(Author's personal collection)*

My self portrait of Hog Body. This is how I felt and thought I looked. Very sad to me now.

This is how I actually looked. I was starving in this photo. *(CBS)*

With Patrick Cassidy on *Midnight Offerings*. *(CBS/Paramount)*

With Melissa Sue Anderson. We witches, we couldn't keep a straight face. We kept cracking up during the PR photo shoot. *(CBS/Paramount)*

No fly aways here! *(Charles William Bush Photography)*

The 1980s! The PR years of posters, photos and bathing suits. I can't believe I thought I was fat in this photo. *(Charles William Bush Photography)*

One of my favorite pictures of me, taken by my friend Michelle Laurita. It's the *Top Gun* era. *(Michelle Laurita)*

A different kind of bride. With Bill Paxton in *Mortuary* just before I stuck an ax in his back. *(Author's personal collection)*

With my roomies, Linda Blair and Steve Lundquist. *(The Shevett Studio/Anita & Steve Shevett)*

It was bound to happen. As a nun in *Impure Thoughts*. Thanks to Michael Simpson. I also played a nun on *American Dreams*. *(Michael Simpson)*

With Julia Louis-Dreyfus in *The New Adventures of Old Christine*. *(THE NEW ADVENTURES OF OLD CHRISTINE © Warner Brothers Entertainment Inc. All Rights Reserved.)*

Erin as a bride. (A WALTON
WEDDING © *Warner Brothers
Television, A Division of Time Warner
Entertainment Company, L.P. All Rights
Reserved.)*

Walton Reunion special. I love my period
hair. The beginning of those character roles.
(A WALTON THANKSGIVING © *Warner Brothers
Television Production, A Division of Time Warner
Entertainment Company, L.P. All Rights Reserved.)*

With my darling daughter Sydnee at a Walton fan club reunion. *(Jason Gilmore)*

As director, a proud moment for me. *(Author's personal photo)*

With Senator Roy Blunt and Pam Saraceni. *(Author's personal photo)*

With Senator Kennedy. I treasure this picture. *(Author's personal photo)*

Sybil and me at the FDA. *(Kevin Scott Mathis)*

With dear Patricia Neal at a film festival for *May*. *(Jason Gilmore)*

The beautiful girls (left to right): Sydnee, Kylie and Robyn. *(Author's personal photo)*

With my Don at a Walton reunion in Virginia. *(Author's personal photo)*

and we missed him terribly. They recast John-Boy, but while Robert Wightman was a very nice man, Richard left big shoes to fill. I heard the producers thought people would get used to the idea; after all, it happened in soap operas all the time. But this was John-Boy—the show centered around his character, and Richard had defined the role. Anyone else just wasn't believable.

There were also many hugs and tears shed when Michael left the show in 1979, her tears as well as ours. I have a picture of her with the entire cast and crew on her last day, and she is wiping her eyes. I knew Michael wanted to move on with her career, but I couldn't help but remember what Will had told me so many years ago in that headlock about this being the best gig we'd ever have.

Richard was gone; Will was gone; Ellen was recovering; I was fighting deep feelings of loss. Another rock from this mountain was about to roll away, and her departure would leave a gaping hole.

Ralph stayed with us for a while to lead the way. At least, we had one parent still in place. Then he, too, left the show, in 1981. That left Judy, Jon, Eric, and me as the "adults," and Kami and David to carry on with the teenage story lines.

In some ways, being the "adults" on the show was an honor. We wanted to make the shows as great as they were before, but the format kept changing. A lot of other characters were added, and it seemed diluted. I wished they had let us just continue on with the Walton lives and their mountain, town, and community.

Don't Leave the Mountain

I wanted to broaden my range and work on stage, as my role models had done, so I expanded my training to local theater and joined the Camille Ensemble when I was eighteen. Doing a straight play was one thing, but a musical was a whole different ballpark for me. I loved to sing, but had limited training, and when I compared myself to those around me who were musically talented, I didn't think I was very good.

I had taken piano and voice when I was younger—you'll recall my "interesting" singing teacher who'd told me what it's like to drown—but I never used my pipes other than to sing on the show or an occasional church hymn.

My parents had generously provided us with all kinds of extra-curricular classes and lessons. My brothers even went to my dance studio and took gymnastics and Polynesian classes. They realized I needed to keep up with what might be expected of me profession-ally, but I was so busy, I learned very little about a lot of things. Just enough to get by.

For a girl who wanted to be perfect, this left me timid about doing things in public if I didn't feel ready. I knew I would be judged on the basis of being a "professional," and not just another kid trying her best.

By joining a stage acting troupe and doing *Godspell,* I challenged myself to stretch out of my comfort zone. Theater and television are two different beasts. Working a show every night for a period of time was completely different from memorizing scenes for a day's work, then forgetting them and moving on to the next script.

Singing "Day by Day" was scary for me every time I took the stage. At times, I had paralyzing stage fright. My desire to grow and improve my craft helped me push through my fears.

The Camille Ensemble had a very long and successful run of *Godspell.* When the reviews came out in the papers, I was singled out. It said something like "McDonough should have never left the mountain," or some such crap. The theater directors knew how sensitive I was, and that I would be upset. One even asked me if I was able to go on. Of course, I would! I would never have allowed myself to be driven from the stage—hell, I was usually frozen to it, anyway.

Seriously, I cried and wished my critic ill, like any actor who gets a bad review does. I wondered if he could possibly understand what a huge risk stage acting and singing was for me, or at least ac-knowledge I was doing something to better myself. Why didn't he just shut up? Why couldn't he appreciate my attempt to leave "the mountain"? Idiot.

I was glum on the set the next day and told Michael Learned about my bad review. She said, "You know, I wish these critics were more original and clever in their comments. That is so obvious a thing to say, 'she shouldn't leave the mountain.' A reviewer said the exact same thing about me. So don't worry, he's just not very smart and took the easy jab."

Just like a mother should, Michael made me feel so much better that day. I resolved to keep working hard.

I learned a lot from *Godspell,* and continued to work in theater over the years. I also continued to get some bad reviews. One day, the actress Dana Hill, my dear friend, bought me the book *No Turn Unstoned,* by Diana Rigg. It is a compilation of actors', playwrights', sets', and costumes' worst reviews. It has terrible reviews of award-winning actors ranging from Sarah Bernhardt to Lord Laurence Olivier. I pored over the pages, comforted to know at least I was in good company.

This experience taught me something about myself, though—an even better lesson. I realized I had stored up and placed downstage, front and center, all the negative reviews I'd ever received in my life, while I'd pushed the positives upstage, hidden behind the scenery.

Eventually I would have to find my way out from behind the backdrop.

THE DUMB WITCH

In my teens I wasn't asked out on many dates, so I often spent Friday nights in my Northridge home watching the scary ABC Friday night movie. I loved them and always wanted to be in a horror film. I got my chance when *Midnight Offerings* came my way, even better because I longed to work outside the show.

I met with the movie's director, Rod Holcomb. I was so nervous going in for the interview. This was a whole new arena, because I hadn't auditioned since I was ten. Rod looked me over, and we talked for a while. He was nice and funny, and I hoped everyone in the room liked me.

I had prepared a scene from the movie to audition. I walked the plank again, worried they'd realize I wasn't worthy. Without hearing me read from the sides (part of a script used for auditions), Rod thanked me and said good-bye.

I asked him if he wanted to hear my scene, but he smiled and said, "No, we just wanted to meet you, see what you looked like." Then he made the "camera lens" with his thumb and fingers and "focused" in on me. He winked, and the meeting was over. I breathed a sigh of relief.

I got the part of Robin Prentiss, seventh daughter of a seventh daughter born with the "gift." Yes, I was a witch! How far away from Erin can you get?

Yeah, woo-hoo! I was thrilled to work on an MOW (movie of the week) as we call them in the biz (yes, I'm hip and part of the *in* crowd now), especially since it took place in modern day. I got to wear jeans and cords and sweaters that didn't smell of mildew and mothballs. I felt like I had won the lottery.

They worked around my Walton filming schedule, and I felt even more like a real actress. When I found out I was working with Melissa Sue Anderson, who played Mary Ingalls on *Little House on the Prairie*, I was even more amazed. She had done a lot of MOWs, and I was so excited to be working with her. She was beautiful, really talented, and you know how TV-struck I am.

Melissa was cast as the bad witch and I was the good witch. Or as the review of the MOW said, I was "the dumb witch." Another *turn unstoned*, but I didn't care. I had a blast on the shoot.

We worked for Stephen J. Cannell Productions, and I found out how generous a production company could be. I had heard Lorimar was frugal, as evidenced in our salaries—cheap, cheap! To give you an idea, Willie Aames, as Tommy Bradford on *Eight Is Enough*, made more in his first year than I did in my sixth.

Midnight Offerings was a class act and I learned a lot about being a producer from Stephen J. Cannell. When I produced and directed later in life, I adopted his set policies and felt I treated my crew in the manner I had witnessed from him years earlier. He treated his crew well. For example, there was always food available at craft services; pizzas were brought in on night shoots, even when it wasn't an official break.

Melissa Sue was the star. When we met, her familiar blond hair I knew from *Little House* was different. Her hair was short and dark, but her stunning blue eyes were the same. Melissa smoked, drank Tab, and—to my recollection—ate carrot sticks. She was thin; I was not. She seemed bold and confident. She smoked outright; I hid in my trailer, avoiding disapproval at all costs. She was about my age, nineteen when we filmed *Offerings,* but dated older men. She was dating Frank Sinatra Jr. at the time. I had barely dated. She drove a Mercedes; I drove a Honda Prelude. She was savvy and sophisticated. I was still a geek.

In one scene, Melissa points at me and her powers launch me across the room and into boards piled up against a far wall. I fall to the ground and try to "battle" her with my weak witchy ways. This was the scene they wanted to use for publicity pictures, so there was a photographer on the set when we filmed.

Melissa Sue gave me her evil-witch eye, and pointed her power-wielding finger at me. I glared bravely back. The photographer started clicking . . . and then we started to giggle. Off and on, I'd lose control and break into my cackle, recover, then she'd bust out and we'd lose it all over again. The entire photo shoot had to be taken in between our breakups. I love those pictures: my favorite is the one of Melissa-the-evil-witch completely doubled over in laughter.

I love being on a set, and working with people who come together against the odds to make something creative. We were treated really well, and I was happy to be there. I felt special in this new experience. It wasn't always an easy shoot, but I learned so much.

This movie challenged me in a new way. As the particular scene drew near, Rod asked me how I was going to do "the scream." I went into frozen-I-haven't-got-a-clue mode. I had never had to scream before. There were no evil crows attacking me on Walton's Mountain. No screaming there, and my real-life parents never raised their voices. It was just not done.

Rod encouraged me to go ahead and just yell. I did my best, but it sounded stifled. I felt lame once again and sad that I'd let Rod down with my fear of the unknown.

Patrick Cassidy played David Sterling, the love interest. It was one of his first jobs in the business and I remember rehearsing lines a lot with him. He was nervous and I could relate to that. He was very sweet and we joked a lot. I teased him about being so "Beverly Hills" and called him a snob. He gave me a Gucci key chain for a wrap present. Now that's a sense of humor. The joke was on me, because I was so un–Beverly Hills I didn't know what it was. Valley girl strikes again. I wish I had been as creative in my wrap presents. I gave Melissa a kitchen witch.

I'll never forget when Patrick's mom, Shirley Jones, came to the set. I was really scared and hid most of the time she was there. I mean—hello—Mrs. Partridge was on our set, watching me work—how intimidating. She was nothing but nice. I wish I had spoken to her more.

Patrick and I stayed in touch over the years, and I went to see his local plays, and on Broadway years later. He really grew into a seasoned professional. I felt proud to have been there at the start. It's fascinating to watch people grow in their lives and careers. No one can take away the memories of those early days working together. I cherish them.

Marion Ross was Emily Moore in *Midnight Offerings*. I enjoyed working with "Mrs. C." from *Happy Days,* and had the pleasure of being with Marion over the years at different events, then working together years later on *Where There's a Will* and recently on an episode of *The New Adventures of Old Christine.* She is a delight, a hoot, and very naughty sometimes. She made our set, and everywhere I have ever been with her, a joy. I adore her.

BURNED AT THE STAKE

We were filming at a high school near the beach, and early one morning, driving to the set, I could only see about six feet in front of my car. This Southern California "marine layer" rolls in at night and back out to sea the next morning several months of the year. It was so dense, it was dangerous, and I was relieved I made it to the set.

We filmed all day and into the night. As the sun went down, the thick fog rolled in again, perfect for our supernatural flick.

We were filming the climactic moment when Melissa's character tries to kill me. I was "tied" to the school bonfire pit, with only her powers gluing me to the stake. She had on her witch makeup and a black cloak, and Héctor Figueroa's lighting made the fog even more menacing for an eerie effect that many productions have to use machines to generate. It was totally cool.

I had to scream again, and really went for it this time. It was easier now, though. I was pinned to a burning bonfire, after all. I broke an old mold and screamed my lungs out. Years later, I was cast in more horror films. Have scream, will act.

Melissa and I finished late that night, and we had to be back early the next morning. I lived over an hour away, in good weather, and I knew that by the time I got home through the fog, it would almost be time to turn around and come back. So I decided to stay the night somewhere close.

Melissa decided to join me. Cool, a sleepover! Since we were unprepared, we went around to the different departments looking for overnight items we could borrow. We walked over to the makeup trailer and got a hairbrush, some shampoo, and makeup remover, then some pajamas from the wardrobe department. Someone even gave us some cigarettes.

We made a reservation in a small motel near the beach, nothing fancy. We drove over, and when we checked in, the woman at the desk gave us the oddest look. I followed her gaze and realized Melissa still had her witch makeup on. We must have looked the pair.

We cracked up as we let ourselves into the room. We lit up cigarettes and talked and laughed and smoked and talked. We talked about being on shows and working as a kid. We shared what our sets were like and wearing the wardrobe on a period show. Yuck!

No one knows what it's like to work as a kid better than another kid actor. It's an unspoken bond I have experienced with most child performers I have met. Sitting in that motel room in borrowed pj's, we joked about the "glamour" of show business and what they'd say if "they could see us now."

We didn't want to, but we finally got into our beds because we had an early call time. Gradually we grew quiet, waiting for sleep, and then . . . the foghorn blew. We cracked up again. We knew that foghorn wasn't about to stop with how socked in the coastline was. We tried our best to go to sleep, but I remember laughing every time it blew, every few minutes, all night long.

The next morning, we took our glamorous selves to the supermarket and bought frozen egg rolls and some other food for later that day to share with Patrick. We thought we could heat them up in our dressing room. Now that's a "glamorous" life. I enjoyed every moment of it.

When *Midnight Offerings* aired and I got a negative review, some of my Walton family was not surprised. Sometimes I felt they didn't want me to leave the mountain, either. I was just glad to have gotten off it for a brief moment. Will's words of advice to be grateful for the Walton gig were etched in my head, but I also understood wanting to stretch your wings.

GOING HOME

I went back to Walton's Mountain for many more adventures. In our last seasons, we tackled some tough subject matters I am proud to have been a part of. In "The Obstacle" (Season 7), John-Boy's college roommate, Mike Paxton, played by Dennis Redfield, returns to the mountain a paraplegic.

The family welcomes his return, and in their unique ways help him transition back into normalcy. Jim Bob rigs a car for him to drive, Daddy offers a father's wisdom, and even Grandma inspires him to work through physical challenges by the example of her own stroke. When Erin and Mary Ellen help him get a job at Pickett's, he overcomes his feelings of worthlessness.

Our World War II shows aired shortly after the war in Vietnam came to an end. Disabled veterans from that war wrote me, wishing there were girls like Erin in their own town who would dare touch a disabled man, or look at them without staring in pity. They shared how tough it was to find work, date, and be seen as a whole person, and not just a guy in a wheelchair. They appreciated the hope the story line gave them.

The show addressed many other important issues at a crucial

time for America. In "The First Casualty," Erin's beau G.W. Haines dies in a training maneuver. A few years ago, I met a man who had been in charge of training new recruits for twenty years. He told me that after seeing that episode, he vowed never to have an accident or death on his field, and he never did. His pride and incredible deed left me speechless. It's amazing how many lives the show touched.

PAYBACK TIME

I was twenty, a home owner, and an actress. My mom had helped me pick out a house in Northridge. I lived close to her, but not so far out I couldn't drive to Hollywood and Burbank for auditions. Since my father had passed, I took on more family responsibility. My mother was still grieving, and I felt it was important to stay close to take care of her and my siblings.

I tried to share my good fortune, and a renewed sense of giving back settled into my bones. I had contributed financially to my family before, but my parents never used any of my income to support them. There were only two times my dad asked me if I wanted to help out. Once to buy a diving board and sweeper for our pool; the other was to purchase a motor home. We had always rented a motor home for our yearly trips; now we owned one. I was proud to be able to help out.

I felt I should also give something back to make up for all the time the show kept me away from my family. The trip to New York that John took with Will, me, and the other Walton kids was one opportunity, and so fun for both of us.

My oldest brother, Michael, was away at school, so I couldn't take him anywhere. But my little sister, who had just lost her daddy, was still home. She was the baby of the family and we all felt the need to care for her in our father's absence. Mom was not doing well in her grief, so John, Michael, and I took up the slack. John took our sister out with her friends to try to make up for losing Dad. I tried to teach her all the things I knew Mom wouldn't. I felt like I owed my family and wanted to make it okay for them. I had promised my dad we would all take care of each other. I worked hard to fulfill that promise.

I also felt like I owed them for taking attention away from them. I heard a story that broke my heart. My sister had a play date with a girl who only came to our house to meet me.

I had so much going on in my own schedule and with my own inner struggles, I had no idea that ever happened. This "friend" causing her pain added to the guilt I felt. To make amends, I took my sister everywhere I could. On trips, to parties, the Rose Bowl parade, out with my friends, and later we went to New Zealand and Tahiti to visit our brother, who had moved there for work. I still felt it was not enough. No matter what I did, I couldn't make it up to everyone. This sentiment seeped into my acting career as well.

OFF THE MOUNTAIN

In 1981, we finished our ninth season and wrapped just like every other year, said our good-byes and our promises to "see you next season." Our ratings had actually gone up a bit, so we were satisfied our season was successful.

Then one day my phone rang. "I'm so sorry. Are you okay?"

My heart sank and I thought, *Oh no, now who died?* I said, "What are you talking about?"

"I heard the news and I thought of you immediately. Are you all right? Did you know?"

I didn't know. No one at CBS or the production company had told any of us. After spending over half my life working for them, I learned that the network had announced the show's cancellation in a newspaper article.

All day, I continued to get "condolence" calls. It was like someone had died, made even harder by the callous way we found out. We mourned the end of the show, but how do you end something you have spent most of your life working on? How do you say good-bye to your family of cast and crew when there is no set to go back to, nowhere to assemble and hug and reminisce?

Then the bigger question hit me. How do you move on when

you know nothing else? This road had ended. Whether I wanted to be or not, I was off the mountain, left to wander back to the only road I had left. The Mary life.

But who was Mary, and what road was she on?

Little did I know the road would be filled with boulders, pot-holes, and even a little quicksand.

8

BUT ALL I WANTED TO DO WAS ACT!

To say the least, the cancellation of the show was a surprise and a social shock for me. As much as I wrestled with my identity, so much of my life and my point of reference in life were all from *The Waltons*. My identity *was* the show. I was lost and didn't know what to do with myself.

At first, it seemed like a natural ending. I knew I wanted to act, so my goal was to keep working. I try not to have regrets in life, but I do wish someone had just packed me up and shipped me off to college and dorm life. I had the grades and was a good student. I know my life would have changed course if that had happened, and the hopeless romantic in me wonders what I could have achieved. But I also know there are no accidents in life—everything happens for a reason—so I dreamed of an alternate me in school somewhere back East, while the other me was in this California life.

I did take college courses, but when I landed a job, I left school and my classes unfinished. My professors didn't allow the distance learning, like I'd grown up with. They required I attend every session. In those days, agents didn't want their actors to take vacations, let alone go away for four years. This was before Jodie Foster went away to Yale and then came back to the business, proving it's possible to finish a degree and still be useful to the business. Now it's not only acceptable to take time for college, it's embraced.

Jodie was a star; I wasn't. My agents, publicists, and managers pressured me to focus on getting work. So I stayed in town, not wanting to miss an audition. I didn't have a big enough name to decide how my life should go. I was still bending to the authority figures. I started the uphill climb to keep working in the field I had grown to love.

All I wanted was to be a successful adult in the industry. I came really close. I continued to work, guest starring in many episodics such as *The Love Boat, Picket Fences, Hunter,* and *Diagnosis Murder.* My agent said I was a good actress, and was getting good feedback, but they went "another way."

THE EYE AND ME

I had considered CBS my home, my family network. While on *The Waltons,* I was flown to affiliate dinners in San Francisco, New Orleans, and Washington, D.C. to promote the show. I felt like a princess. I carried my pen, briefcase, and even had cuff links with the eye logo on them. I felt like a team player and was proud to be a part of the CBS "family."

Once a year, CBS always puts on lavish spreads for anyone working for them, and the L.A. dinner was usually in May, on my birthday weekend. I always went until the year when I turned eighteen. I informed the representative from the network I wasn't going, because it was my birthday and I was going out with my friends, instead. Well, I got a meadow of flowers from the president of CBS with a note wishing me a happy birthday and that he couldn't wait to see me at the dinner. I got the message. Dutiful daughter went to the dinner.

Now that my worth to them was over . . . there would be no more flowers. Betrayed by the company I had felt loyalty to, given half my life, I couldn't even get an interview for a pilot. Why couldn't they at least let me try? I doubted myself, but I vowed to work harder.

AGAINST TYPE

When Mark Morrison interviewed me for *US Magazine,* he asked if *The Waltons* was the apex of my career. I was speechless. My greatest fear, spoken out loud.

Now that fear was becoming a reality. I was typecast as the "all-American girl." I hoped the producers and directors from *The Waltons* would remember me and let me read for their new shows, but that never happened. It felt like everyone wanted distance from the show and from me. It was tough, and I took it personally. The community was gone, and the feeling of being personally rejected set in. I doubted myself and tried to get even thinner than I already was, thinking maybe it was my body that didn't fit in.

I went back to getting injections and eating eight hundred calories a day. I lost about fifteen pounds, became weak and felt terrible, but I was proud. Now I would fit in. I went to see my new agent. Maybe he'd like me better thinner and would send me on more auditions.

He looked at me and said, "Now, I think five more pounds and we may be getting close." I was devastated, angry, and hungry. All that starving, no acknowledgment, and I'm still not enough? My rebellion kicked in. Another yo-yo.

KENTUCKY

When I was twenty, I spent a month in Kentucky for a movie I never actually worked in. The director was very cagey and there was a lot of mystery surrounding the film. I auditioned along with a few other actresses, and the director kept a few of us. I called my agent and she said, "Stay. He hasn't cast the film yet." So I did, for over two weeks. He didn't cast me, and the movie was never finished, but I ended up spending another few weeks at the Lexington Marriott Hotel. I even went to the Kentucky Derby while I was there. It was a crazy experience and might have been a waste of time, except I met some people I'll always cherish. José Ferrer was the star of the film. He told so many great stories about working as an actor, I still share them with my students. What a treat.

While we were there, the gracious Nick and Nina Clooney hosted an Easter dinner for all of us who were away from home. Nick and Nina were so kind to me. When Nick was a news anchor in Los Angeles, I got to know them better and they have helped guide me over the years. They even gave me tips for this book. I adore them and call them every Easter to sing "happy anniversary." Their son, George, was hanging around with us to work on the film as well. When we all went back to Los Angeles, we encouraged George to come to California to try this acting thing. "Who knows, it might work out for you," we told him. Who knew?

I was in Kentucky for my twenty-first birthday. George's birthday is two days after mine and we are the same age. As we celebrated at the hotel, he dared me to jump into the fountain in the courtyard. Well, a dare is a dare, and in my book, the one who brought the dare should take the dare on as well. So I got up and ran to the fountain and in I went. So George had to follow me in. For years, I called him on his birthday, remembering a simpler time before he came to Hollywood to be an Academy Award winner. Whenever I see him, he is warm, and it's just like we're twenty years old again.

Once I was doing a *Tiger Beat* fashion layout and asked if George and his cousin could be in the photo shoot with me. I still laugh when I see those pictures; they are so posed and goofy. Aside from that photo shoot, George and I have never actually worked in the same scene, but we have done three shows together. We did a play called *The Biz*. He was in the first act; I was in the second.

When I did a guest appearance on his show *Bodies of Evidence,* he wasn't in my scene, but he did one of the nicest things anyone has ever done for a guest actor on a show. For a day player, it can be a little intimidating going to a foreign set and not knowing anyone.

When I arrived in the morning, the makeup artist said, "Oh, you're Mary. I'm supposed to be really nice to you."

"Why?"

"Well, George saw that you were working today and he won't be here until later, so he told me to be nice to you."

Then when I went to get my hair done, the hairdresser said, "I hear you were one of the people who told George to come out here to L.A.? Thanks."

The same thing happened when I went to wardrobe. She said, "George asked me to take care of you." Without even being there, he welcomed me and made my day easier. He's one of the good guys. When I did *ER*, my scene was with Noah Wiley.

All the Clooneys, including Nick's sister and George's aunt, Rosemary Clooney, would become friends, with their own lessons to teach me.

I once had a friend who betrayed me, and Rosemary sat me down and said, "She's not your friend." She taught me to see who my real friends were and to let go of people and experiences that didn't matter. It would take me years to understand how to do that, but her advice helped me learn to start standing up for myself and cut out the negative.

BACK HOME

To make myself more attractive to my agent, casting directors, and anyone who might give me a chance, I did more theater, and enrolled in Peggy Feury's prestigious acting class. I studied there four days a week. It was like college for acting. I learned so much and pushed myself.

When I was twenty-one, I landed a role in a low-budget horror film called *Mortuary*. I was glad to have the work. I lost nineteen pounds in three weeks for that movie. A young Bill Paxton was cast as the crazy bad guy. Bill was great to work with, and I killed him at the end by putting an ax in his back. Years later, Jay Leno pulled up a kooky clip from the movie to surprise him with when he was a guest. A kind of "what the heck was that?" moment for Jay. Bill identified me in the clip, which was so nice of him. My friends called me. "You were on *Leno*!" It's a claim to fame for me, the only time I've been on *The Tonight Show*.

After I finished *Mortuary*, NBC picked us up for three Walton MOWs. I was so happy to be back with everyone. In one, *A Wedding on Walton's Mountain*, Erin got married. We were looking for a wedding dress for the show, but the wardrobe department didn't have one that was right. My mom suggested I wear her dress. So I walked down the Walton aisle in the dress my mom married my dad in. It was an emotional moment for me as I realized my own dad wouldn't be there if this ever happened to me for real.

I'll never forget Ralph standing with me in the back of the church, looking at me with those familiar baby blues. I felt so much emotion at home again with my family. I looked at him and said, "You know, you're the only dad I have left." I knew it would never be the same again.

In one of the specials, I was helping Ellen say one of her lines. We were at the stove away from the others, and every time we went to shoot, she turned to me and I said her line to her over and over until it stuck in her head. She repeated it until she heard her cue, and then said the line aloud.

When they came in for her close-up, she didn't turn to me. I touched her arm and said, "Grandma." I repeated the line, but she ignored me. I said it again, like I had done before. Ellen was visibly upset. She picked up her cane and hit me with it. The AD and director, who had no idea I had been helping her during every take, jumped in and chastised me for upsetting her.

I was deeply hurt by this. I felt publicly humiliated and shut down. The rapport I thought I had with her, expressed through my desire to try to help, was severed with that cane.

It took me a long time to realize her pride in her work was the root of her actions. She didn't want to appear weak or unsure about a line. She was fiercely proud.

Years later, when I was producing a reunion segment for *Entertainment Tonight,* I was pregnant with my daughter, Sydnee. I brought along an ultrasound picture to "introduce" her great-grandma to her great-granddaughter, and all was mended. Then when Sydnee was born a few days from Ellen's birthday, we bonded even more. Every June we all had lunch with "grandma" to celebrate both their birthdays, until Ellen got too ill to go out.

We had all left Walton's Mountain, but this brief reprise was a gift. A way to reunite and say the good-byes we didn't get to share when we were canceled. I had to grow up and away from the show, but I still wondered how I would manage on my own.

NEW SPIRIT

During the 1980s, I continued to question this God I was taught about in parochial school. I thought back to the rules and rigidity that was contradicting to me. To be Catholic was absolute for me. You either chose to be in all the way, or not at all. I was trying to find the gray, a balance in these two worlds I was living in. To me, there was hypocrisy to it all. I couldn't escape the PR element on either side and I started to see the conflicting messages. Here's an example:

I had done an interview for the Catholic newspaper *The Tidings.* They asked me how my parochial-school experience helped me on the set. It was another *Dinah!* moment. I had no idea how it had helped me, but I knew I had to say something. My dad was staring at me as I thought hard. I told them the only thing I could think of that was true. "I guess memorizing all those *Baltimore Catechism* questions helped me, because I can memorize my lines."

When the article came out, it said something like: "Mary attributes all her success on the show to her nuns and her Catholic school and upbringing."

I was so disappointed—no, I was mad when the article came out. How could they twist my words around like that? Oh, to be young and trusting. This shook my foundation and taught me not to trust the press. Not even the Catholic one.

I wanted less betrayal, trust, and a peaceful spirit—not something else that confused my sensibilities or required me to be perfect, something I could never live up to.

I started to study different religions and spiritual practices. I read every book I could afford from the Bodhi Tree, a New Age bookstore in L.A. I loved Shirley MacLaine's books, they resonated to me. I experienced past-life regressions, consulted with psychics and trance channelers. I studied the kabballah and the Druids of my Irish ancestors. I sat zazen at a temple and chanted with gurus. I received shaktipat and was brushed with peacock feathers. It was a wonderful journey. I meditated and, of course, listened to audiotapes of my dear "friend" Wayne Dyer.

As I studied different religions, I noticed a similar theme. When it came down to it, they were saying similar things, had parallel stories and the same basic "commandments," if you will. A belief in something more expansive in the world and a Higher Source. This Source was less judgmental and punishing than the God I knew. I started to realize there might be forgiveness, acceptance, even a Love I never felt I could receive from the God I was taught about.

While my mother was disappointed at my searching, I did feel she understood in a way. She had always had what she called her "hobby." She loved to hear alien and UFO stories and read books about angels. She, too, had researched many religions before she chose Catholicism. I looked at her Ruth Montgomery books and questioned who I was and how I was connected to it all. Mom and I shared our paths, and the discussions brought us closer together.

I credit my brother Michael with helping me find my love of nature, which connected me to my Source in those early years. He took me outdoors to escape the grind. Today, my brother has been sober for many years. I am so proud of the work he has done in his life to help change me and the world. He is still a grounding reminder of the *God*-ness in all things.

My brother John moved to New Zealand for many years to play basketball, and eventually settled there for several years. I was lucky enough to visit New Zealand, and loved the country. Queenstown is where I bungee jumped off the 250-foot bridge.

While John was away, we sent audiotapes to each other. He would talk to me from atop a glacier or while choosing apples from a roadside farm stand. While I was on Sunset Boulevard, waiting in traffic, I would hold the tape recorder out the window and "interview" the person in the next car. We had so many interesting people on those tapes we sent back and forth. They brought us together while we were ten thousand miles apart.

I treasure my brothers and feel blessed to have them in my life. They have stood by me, and helped take up the slack when my father left us. I am the luckiest little sister in the world.

When I struggled with the business, I looked to nature and found stillness in the peace so far away from the churches I grew up in. I prayed, but it was a different prayer now:

Journal 1984

Here I sit in the beauty of it all. The meadow below me is above the stream. Always I can hear the rushing flow of the water. Flowers spire to the sun. They face the light. They seem to lean the sun's way. The tall grass leans too.

We should all be little meadows reaching toward the light, God's Light. For darkness comes soon enough. A time to contemplate the day and life by God's softer light, the Moon. And when daylight shines again, it leaves yesterday with the moon.

* * *

The stream flows down the hill. I can hear the constant flow of water. It reminds me of the constant flow of life. My life; streaming past boulders, small smooth rocks, trees and flowers, occasionally damming up behind large boulders blocking my way before the gentle release through the boulders, to freedom. Now I stream freely with the rest of my life. The water is in constant motion. May I never be dammed up for long or to where I cannot release to life's flow. May I always remember . . . slow down and remember to learn from how I feel welled up behind boulders in my way.

"IMAGINE NO POSSESSIONS"

In my twenties, I was obsessed with staying in town to try to get work. I worked as much as I could, mostly commercials, and continued to study, but time, and any savings I had after paying off my huge tax debt, was running out. My mother had not done my income taxes correctly after my dad died and didn't save receipts. I was audited and they went back and back. I used the money that had been put aside for me, to comply with the Coogan Act, to pay off the debt. I was twenty-five, had no career, and finally had to sell my house. I gave away, or threw away, anything that didn't fit into a ten-by-ten storage unit. I bought a backpack, got a passport, and headed for Europe. Alone.

When I left, I called it my hegira, an escape from persecution, from the torture I felt from the industry in which I longed to be successful. On this journey, I would learn from many people. One was a wise woman atop a nunnery in Zurich. This stranger and I watched the sunset, and she shared that I was not escaping persecution, that this trip was not a hegira. Since I had stripped myself of worldly goods, and was traveling to find myself—and my path would be revealed—that was a pilgrimage. I decided I was no longer a victim but had chosen this path. It certainly helped me look at the mountain in a new light.

Traveling through Ireland, I spent time with my cousins. I immediately fell in love with the country my father felt so loyal to, yet he'd never seen. My McDonough family welcomed me, took great care of me, and I didn't want to leave. It was the first time in my life I didn't have to correct someone mispronouncing my last name. From Ireland, I flew to England, and then to Continental Europe, where I traveled all over with my backpack. As I sat at an outdoor café in Bruges, a strolling minstrel sang "Imagine" and strummed his guitar. I listened to his broken English, felt a universal connection to him, to the lyrics, and wept.

BELLA ERIN

I slept in youth hostels, on floors, and on friends of friends' couches. I shared my exploration with fellow travelers: *Who am I? Why am I so insecure? But only sometimes. Other times—I feel connected, almost at peace with myself and others.*

I challenged myself to explore a new city every day with only a map, usually in a language I didn't speak. Day by day, country by country, my strength and confidence grew.

I was glad most of my fellow travelers were just out of high school or college, and had never seen *The Waltons.* I wasn't recognized until I got to Italy.

A woman working in the open-air market in Florence was speaking Italian to me about some bric-a-brac I was admiring and suddenly stopped dead in her tracks. "You're Erin Walton!" she screamed in a perfect New Jersey accent. "Have you seen yourself in Italian? You're hilarious. Here's you, 'Mama, Mama, Mama.' Then you run up the stairs, slam a door, and cry. You have to see yourself."

I never did see Erin speak Italian.

SURRENDER

The John Lennon lyrics "Imagine all the people, sharing all the world" became a background track to my journey. I thought I knew what giving was all about until Paris taught me a lesson in receiving.

I believed I owed so much to people to deserve what I had been given. I tended to keep giving to feel worthy.

My catharsis didn't happen until I was leaving Paris. I had a Euro Pass for the train, so I knew I wouldn't need any more francs. I was making my way down through the train station for my departure when I saw a homeless woman asking for money. I thought, *I'm leaving France. I don't need this money.* I reached into my wallet and my pockets and gave her all of the francs I still had. It felt good I could be so free and maybe even help this woman a little.

After I found the train, a conductor told me I would need to buy a supplement ticket. *A supplement ticket, but I just gave away all my francs!*

I trudged back up to the ticket window and found a huge line stretched out from the cashier. It gave me time to panic. The train was due to leave soon. I had no money! Then I remembered I did carry a credit card, so I was okay. The line inched slowly. I watched the clock and tried to think of the correct French so I could ask for the ticket when it was finally my turn. I needed to catch this train; I couldn't afford to stay longer in Paris.

Finally I was next. I opened my mouth, my rehearsed high-school French phrases ready to spill off my tongue. I stepped up and . . . the ticket seller closed her station. Everyone behind me started running to the other open windows. I picked up my backpack and ran, too, but since I had been at the front, I was farthest away and was now last in line.

Unable to speak the language, I was lost as to what had happened. I sweated the time ticking away on the large dial over the lobby, until finally I made it to the ticket seller . . . again. I managed to explain what I needed, and then handed over my credit card.

I didn't understand all the words he used, but I did figure out the supplement was not enough to put on a card. I had to pay in cash. I dug in my pockets and found a small coin I hadn't given the woman, but when I offered it to him, he shook his head. Not enough. I started to cry and tried to explain, flipping back and forth from English to French, how I gave all my money to a homeless woman downstairs, and my train was leaving in a few minutes—and I'm not sure what else I said. He just looked at me and shook his head again. I was helpless, alone, broke, and my train was about to leave the station. *How could it be that I was trying to be so generous, and now this?* I decided giving to others was a bunch of crap.

That's when the miracle happened. An American woman standing in line called up to us, "How much do you need?"

I looked at the cashier; he held up fingers. "Well, I have a little, but not all of it." She passed the coin forward. I was so grateful; I cried with amazement and called out my thanks to her. I gave her coin to the cashier, but he shook his head again. I felt hopeless. I was a stupid American.

Then I heard, "Hey, here's a coin," and several other people in line started to pass coins forward. One man told another about the homeless woman I'd helped, and he dug some change from his pocket and passed it forward. I didn't even know these people had heard me or even understood what I'd been blubbering.

I sobbed as I handed the cashier all the coins these strangers had passed up to me. He finally put up his hand when he had enough and printed my ticket. I cried my thank-you to everyone, and someone said, "Run, you'll miss your train, and that ticket will be no good." I hoisted my pack on my back and sprinted to the platform, and leaped across the gap onto the train as the door closed.

Huffing and puffing after the multilevel dash, I stumbled down the aisle, found an empty seat, threw my backpack up on the rack, sat down, and collapsed. I leaned forward to catch my breath and smacked my head on the tray table's release button. It popped open, and the sharp metal edge sliced my cheek, cutting my face open. So now I was bleeding. I couldn't believe what had just happened, and I started to laugh. I must have looked like a crazy American tourist laughing through my tears, blood running down my cheek.

I wiped my face and realized this had become a true pilgrimage. I had sold my home, given away my possessions, was traveling in foreign lands with nothing but my backpack, searching for some clue as to what my life was about, and what I should do. I had no cash. Then, out of nothing, came everything I needed.

The train pulled away from the station, and I sat in that seat, full of gratitude. I didn't have to try hard, I didn't *do* anything for them and yet people stepped up to help me. I'll never know who those people were, but I still thank my angels. I owe them more than the coins they gave me. *I* was supposed to be the giver, but that day I received. It was humbling and overwhelming. This experience showed me to trust in the Universe beyond all fear and have faith. The Universe provided. It was a turning point for me, not only on the trip, but also in life, such a small moment with a huge lesson.

What would happen if I took all the advice from the many books I read and actually trusted the Universe? Trusting my Source was the new lesson that would challenge me over and over again.

Wikipedia gives this definition: *A pilgrimage is a long journey or search of great moral significance.* The long journey had just begun, and the moral significance in my life would change me in ways I could never have guessed. I realized that day leaving Paris, that giving was something to be shared, not controlled. Not a way to be "good" or "get to heaven." My indulgences were banked, but that would not grant a safe journey. Something more was needed. I started to give back with a new awareness.

YOUNG ARTISTS UNITED

Europe was an incredible learning experience for me. When I returned, I became involved with Young Artists United, a non-profit group dedicated to helping the youth of America make socially responsible choices, founded by *Baywatch* star Alexandra

Paul and manager/producer Daniel Sladek. I soon served on its board and headed the National Speaker's Network.

There were dedicated actors, some celebrities, filmmakers, publicists, producers, and writers in the group. YAU made PSAs (public service announcements) to educate young people. We worked voter registration and getting out the vote. It was an inspiring time for me. I wanted more—giving back had a new meaning and relevance in my life.

We sent speakers all over the country to talk to kids in middle and high schools. We shared our experiences and why we made the choices we did. I booked the tours and helped train the speakers. I learned so much from my time on YAU. It was a place where I felt I actually made a difference. I could tangibly see it at our presentations. It was the first time I was involved hands-on in a nonprofit, not just lending my name, or showing up somewhere to be the celebrity draw. We worked hard and I made lasting friendships with many members.

Alexandra Paul has been an angel in my life. Her commitment and tireless work for others is incredible. When I produced and hosted segments for *Entertainment Tonight* on eating disorders and young women in the entertainment industry, Alexandra told her story with touching passion. She shared her emotional ordeal with bulimia, self-image, and recovery. She was living proof and an inspiration for women everywhere. She still is. I was still struggling with my own body image, my self-worth, and trying to get work as an actress. Her example taught me to move forward in my search for healing with my own food issues. Her depth as a person and actress is why I chose her to play the lead in my directorial debut, *For the Love of May*, years later. Once again, she was inspirational and an angel for me.

Daniel trained me to run the speaker's network and I joined our other board members on an annual retreat. We had gone away for the weekend to plan the year ahead. On this retreat, I had a big wake-up call and a humbling lesson that forced me to face my deepest fears of failure.

We were all gathered at publicist Val Van Galder's parents' beach house. I was presenting my plan, which was nerve-wracking for me. New to this board of directors thing, I was timid and felt deficient. I stood up and plowed through my notes. Someone questioned my plan; I got rattled and became even more unclear in my explanation. Sarah Jessica Parker, who was wonderfully patient, interrupted me and asked me why I was so mad. I was so embarrassed, became more upset, and didn't know what to do. I just wanted to do it right—why were they questioning me? I managed to make it through to the end and sat down. I can't remember much of the rest of the meeting.

Later on that same retreat, Mark Gill, the fabulous producer who worked in PR then, taught me my first lesson on presentation. He walked down the beach with me and explained how I came across as angry. "But I wasn't mad, I was scared," I whined. I felt myself getting angry and defensive, and knew my face had turned bright red. Because of all those years of growing up on the show, I had not been at school or in college to learn how to deal with people or groups, or even to speak in front of a class.

My inexperience felt like quicksand swallowing me, and I didn't know what to hold on to. Mark gave me solid advice on how to present myself. He gently gave me some tips and helped me do a better job. I went back to the group and explained myself.

His lessons were a turning point for me with public speaking. He was a professional; I was untrained. He took time to help me, and to this day, I'm grateful for his kindness, feedback, and friendship.

My second big lesson with YAU came when we were planning a PSA on social responsibility around drinking and driving. There had been recent press coverage of some not-so-responsible behavior of our "Brat Pack" members at the 1988 Democratic National Convention. A videotape was leaked to the press of Rob Lowe having sex in the convention hotel. We had to reshoot a voter registration PSA starring Rob.

Judd Nelson was on our board of directors at the time, and he wanted to use his friends Emilio Estevez and Charlie Sheen for the new PSA. Not wanting to damage the future of that PSA, I threw out an idea for their consideration. "Could we choose actors who are leading responsible lives or don't drink, so we don't have to scrap the PSA if they get arrested or—?"

Judd spoke up, defending his friends, whom I never meant to criticize. He thought they were the perfect people to do the PSA. They were stars, working actors, and kids would listen to them. Then he turned to me. "Do you think you should do it?"

"N-no," I stammered. "I just thought—"

"Well, you can't," he said. "You don't work enough as an actress to matter. People will listen to Emilio and Charlie." Besides, Charlie and Emilio were "in the public eye."

The room went quiet, no one said a word. I couldn't believe my ears. My worst fear had been spoken out loud in front of the people I respected and admired, whom I was working with to make a difference. I was humiliated and devastated. I was the wicked witch melting into the floor. I shut down, and somehow we made it through the rest of the session, but it was all a blur to me.

What happened next was big for me in my growth as a human being. Later that afternoon, the girls were getting ready for dinner. Sarah asked me where I wanted to go, and I said, "I don't know. I don't think I work enough as an actress to pick the restaurant."

The tension in the room broke, and everyone's mouths fell open as I acknowledged the elephant in the room. I was surprised I had the guts to say something, and was nervous that I had opened my trap. Sarah spoke first and made it all okay. "Oh, my God, what *was* that? I can't believe he said that!"

Val jumped in. "I can't believe nobody said anything. I think we were all stunned."

"I was just horrified, I froze," I said. "Why didn't anyone call him on that?"

No one knew, but it didn't matter, the ice had been broken. I was able to be vulnerable with these supportive women and share my fears. As we talked about the "incident," there were gasps and giggles.

I had always taken everything so personally before. This was a first step not to take it in so deeply. Instead of hiding, feeling miserable, and pulling away, I was actually able to laugh a little myself, but it was still a hard-hitting blow to me.

He was the mouthpiece voicing my insecurity, confirming I was nothing. His words were my worst self-esteem nightmare. I wanted to work as an actress so much, it hurt inside. I didn't understand why I wasn't working, or didn't have a powerful enough agent to get me in to auditions, or why the people who knew me didn't let me read for parts on their new shows. I was doing everything I could, but I wasn't enough and this "Brat Packer" had reminded me of that. He was the schoolyard bully, telling me I wasn't enough and could be replaced.

To this day, the YAU girls and I recount this story, Val retells it the best, and we just laugh. It had such an impact on me, I obviously haven't let it go. I so appreciate my girlfriends for sharing my anger at that comment, and for still being aghast to this day. I'm glad I can see the lesson now, but the meaning of his words would echo in me through several more years of self-doubt.

I can look back and see the positive now, but his words forced me to wander the mountain to find out: if not an actress, what did I have that mattered? I wanted to matter. That desire and his words eventually helped me find myself, my inner power, and what exactly I did have to offer the world.

Through YAU, I learned I could give myself to a cause. I had more to offer than a photograph, or that I played Erin a long time ago. I worked behind the scenes, and when I saw a kid touched or affected in a positive way, I was proud to be a part of YAU.

SOAPS

I had a screen test for a soap opera when I was twenty-one. I was excited at the possibility of full-time work again.

Years ago, soap operas were looked down upon in the industry. Everyone wanted to be a movie star. Times have changed. The stigma is gone today and movie stars appear on soaps and pick up Emmys for guest appearances on TV shows. Prime-time television was the next step down, followed by daytime television. Last was the commercial actor. There was a caste system. Many soap actors didn't or couldn't cross over to nighttime or movies. People didn't realize that soap opera actors are the hardest-working actors in the business. They have massive amounts of dialogue to learn every day, and they make it seem easy.

Since most of the soaps were based in New York at the time, I had to make a decision. My agent asked me, "Do you want to be a soap actress?" so I knew that meant the other Coast. I didn't know if I wanted to move, but I did want to work as an actress, so I ended up in New York to see if I liked it there.

I landed a day player role on *One Life to Live*. My scenes were with Phil Carey and Robin Strasser. I told them I'd never done any soap work, and Phil took me under his wing, pointed at Robin, and said, "Be careful of her. She's a shark. She'll eat you alive." Robin laughed, but it didn't do a lot to calm my nerves. I was afraid of blowing my lines. Soaps are known for not cutting, and I had been told, "Whatever you do, don't blow a line. If you do, cover and keep going. They hate to cut!" Talk about nerves. When Phil flubbed a line, I felt much better. I didn't blow any lines that day, but as much as I love New York, I never got to move there permanently. The scene was fun to do because Robin and Phil were so delightfully evil as Asa and Dorian. I played a girl they used in one of the many scams their characters schemed up. They were a great team, and I learned just by watching them. It was also fun to have big hair, fancy clothes, and so much makeup, I was barely recognizable.

Years later, I also did a day on *General Hospital*. I did flub my lines, but not because of the nerves. This was due to a day of preshoot starvation, my blood sugar tanked. It took me a long time to learn that not eating was not conducive to working!

People still remember me from *General Hospital* and ask how it was to work with Bobbie Spencer. Jacklyn Zeman was very nice to me. I played a woman who had adopted a red-haired baby (always the hair). Bobbie came to see me to talk about adoption. The fact that the child had red hair made her character happy, of course. It was a positive statement for adoption in the 1980s.

At one of the soap screen tests, I was excited at the possibility of full-time work again. The casting director told me confidentially, "You're not going to get this part. I know they'll go with looks, but they want to see an 'actress' too. So that's you." I think it was a compliment. At least, I took it that way to confirm what I hoped: I was a good actress. He was right; I didn't get the gig.

It's not too late. Wouldn't it be fun to play a villain!

BLONDE AND ...

The fears continued to plague me, cemented by my agent calling me and saying, "Well, kid, you always get down to the wire on jobs. You're good, but the only thing I can think is, it's not your time. I'm cutting you loose." That was the last conversation I had with the agent I'd been with for years.

I tried to change my image. I was set to do a sexy photo shoot for *Oui* magazine. It seemed like everyone was doing *Playboy* or *Oui* or making a poster. Why not me? When they interviewed me, I was unprepared for the sexual questions. "How old were you when you lost your virginity? Who was it?"

I wouldn't answer. The publicist was angry, and they canceled the whole photo shoot, which turned out to be a gift. Big angels on my side again. Deep down, I knew sexy half-naked pictures was the wrong path to finding work. It wasn't me. I wasn't comfortable; yet the industry seemed to demand it for success. I battled between my professional identity, my personal privacy, and my desire to keep working. I continued to fight against my values as I struggled to establish myself as a working adult actress. I sacrificed a part of me to do what I thought they wanted. I let people abuse me as I bent every which way to mold into an image, a look, a poster girl. I was worn down, and eventually I gave in and took the step I thought would help me and my career.

It was the *Dallas* era, where big hair and big boobs were the order of the day. I didn't go out for as many parts as my friends in acting class, so I knew each audition was important. I remember once, after interviewing for another part, my next agent said, "They went blond and booby with this one."

How many times had I heard *that?* All these comments pushed my "you don't fit in, you're not enough" button. No matter how much I brought to the audition, or how hard I worked, I wasn't thin, blond, or built enough.

I was still studying acting five days a week at the Loft with Peggy Feury. I believed if I truly honed my craft, I would work as an actress. After all, wasn't that what all those comments implied? While I wasn't blond, there was something I could do about . . .

A fellow thespian told me about her breast implants. She had just had hers put in and loved them. I admitted they looked great, and she seemed so confident. She gave me her doctor's name, a reconstructive surgeon who used the latest implants recommended for cancer survivors. I thought this had to be a good thing. After all, don't doctors know best? "First, do no harm," they promise in the Hippocratic oath.

I did not arrive lightly at the decision to have implants. I was worried. I'd never had surgery before. There was so little information, but I met with the surgeon and asked all the questions I thought important. The new implants, made by Bristol-Myers, had a foam coating to prevent hardening and to create a natural feel. The devices sounded nice. They even had my initials, Meme.

One side effect he mentioned was that I might not be able to breast-feed. Breast-feed, are you kidding me? I was twenty-two, and I didn't even want kids. So why would that matter? If I changed my mind, I was bottle-fed. So what's the big deal? Is that all?

"Oh, and you might lose a little sensitivity in your nipple." He told me they'd last a lifetime, and when I was in my coffin, they'd still be "perky."

One wise person told me, "Don't get these, thinking they'll help your career." Hold on, I *was* getting them for my career, and to feel whole and accepted. Everyone wants to feel pretty, attractive, and desirable, right?

I looked forward to feeling better about myself. As uncomfortable as I was with the idea of having something unnatural in my chest, the upside seemed bigger (excuse the pun). I just knew they would help. And I wanted to get my career back on track. So if this would do it, then so be it.

I love acting, being on set, the whole experience. I had grown up loving and bonding with my television family, and wanted to continue working in the world I adored. I cherished working with talented people and facing the challenges of weather, deadlines, even wearing stinky old wardrobe clothes. It's in my blood, in my foundation. I craved returning to what I knew, where I had a true sense of belonging. However, I was so incredibly embarrassed about getting implants, I didn't even tell my mother I was having surgery.

9

BOOBS IN, BOOBS OUT

During the surgery, I woke up and felt a huge pressure on my chest, but other than that, the procedure went smoothly. A friend drove me home. I felt every bump and cried out in pain. Once home, I slept all afternoon and through the night.

The next morning, I woke up with a rash across my back and chest and called the doctor's office. "It's just the bra. You're allergic," the nurse told me.

Allergic to cotton? Despite my fog from the painkillers I was taking, I sensed something didn't seem right about that logic.

THE FUN PART

While my recovery took a bit of time, I did have some fun with my new breasts. Let's be honest. I was twenty-two, and when you have a bad booby image, doing something society says is sexy felt good for a while. It was exciting as I explored this new image of myself.

A new beau called to ask me out to dinner, and I told him I couldn't go out yet because I'd had surgery. After a few tries at guessing the mystery procedure, he said, "Are you like Mariel Hemingway now?"

"Yes, I am," I said proudly. See, I wasn't alone. Other actresses were getting them, so it must be a good thing. Mariel was a beautiful, successful, and talented actress, and I could now consider her a sister in arms. Although I didn't know it then, she would inspire me in many ways in the future.

A dear friend of mine took a series of wet T-shirt photographs of me. Not for a poster or publicity to boost my career, as a publicist suggested. Just for me. I was really trying on my new silhouette, getting used to the attention. It was a *try* at sexy, a *try* at a new body, a new self-image. But trying is not being. Sexy is being connected to your inner beauty. Sexy isn't a costume you put on or a plastic device you put in your chest. Sexy is a feeling from within, a confidence and sense of one's self. I did not know that then.

Unfortunately, with all the inner turmoil, I began to hide my new breasts. I was embarrassed that people would know what I did and judge me. I felt fake inside. The silicone didn't fill the hole in me.

MY SIZE DOESN'T MATTER, ANYWAY

I did get work in my new shape, but not playing sexy women. I didn't get any parts that required me to be revealing, or that had anything to do with the size of my chest. Throughout my career, I have always been cast as the girl next door, playing a young wife or mother. I did *Picket Fences* as an earthy birthing teacher to Marlee Matlin. No big boobs needed for that part. I played a young bride in *The Love Boat,* a bohemian artist in a movie called *Mom,* and mothers on *Hunter, The Secret World of Alex Mack, The Pretender,* and *Walker, Texas Ranger.* I even played a woman delivering multiple babies on an episode of *Diagnosis Murder,* a comedic role I enjoyed. None of these roles had anything to do with bra size.

In commercials, I was not the bombshell or the hot girl in the beer commercial. I was the waitress. I was the Snuggles mother of redheaded kids, with fresh-smelling clothes. I was a Mrs. Butterworth mom who doesn't see the bottle talk. I played a lawyer on *Ally McBeal,* and that did not require a sexy image. I learned all this after my surgery.

Fun Guest Roles

When I do guest spots, I try to be invisible. It's different than being on your own show as a regular. Even though Richard Thomas was the star on *The Waltons*, we never felt upstaged or less important. We were a true ensemble. This philosophy permeated through the story lines and into the development of the characters. We all had worth as actors, as people, and as "family" members. I believe it is one reason the show worked so well, and why we all had such positive experiences working together.

When I guest star, I know I am a supporting player, and I show up, say my lines, and go home. When I did an episode of *Will & Grace*, the cast was coming down the hallway and I pressed myself up against the set to let them pass. The charming and sweet Eric McCormack leaned in toward me and said, "I can see you." I had to smile and learned not to hide too obviously. I saw that same kindness on the second episode of *Will & Grace* I worked on. When I arrived, Eric said, "Hi, Mary, welcome back." I was floored that he remembered me *and* my name. That's class. He made my *Will & Grace* experience welcoming.

When you love a show and get to be on it, you always hope the illusion isn't blown. Like the cast hates each other, or something like that. I was a fan of *Will & Grace,* so it was great to find out they were nice, were true professionals, and were having fun. I felt so lucky to be on the show and a fly on the wall. I even got to share my *In Style* magazine with Debra Messing, which was cool because she was in the issue.

I was a huge fan of *Ally McBeal.* It was fun to meet Calista Flockhart. I tried to be cool and not ramble on about how I watched the show every week. In the makeup room when Jane Krakowski introduced herself to me, I was charmed. She recognized me from *The Waltons* and we talked. It was nice of her to make me feel so welcomed.

It's always surprising to me when casts don't get along or they complain. Some sets are warm and others are so cold. We were taught by our "parents" to embrace all of our costars and even included them in our lunch outings. I remember Will Geer reminding me this is the best gig, to be happy and to make the most of it.

In my mind, my weight was still an issue, and instead of being lean with big boobs, I thought I just started to look heavier. I found a theme song for my life, k.d. lang's "Big Boned Gal." (I love that song and think she has one of the best singing voices on the planet.) Dancing around my living room and singing, *"She was a big boned gal from southern Alberta, you just couldn't call her small"* made me happy. I embraced myself and swayed and laughed out loud, singing my anthem. I felt free, affirmed, and began to accept who I was and what I looked like.

MARY MARRIES

In 1986, I met Rob Wickstrom in an acting class and we fell in love. I had dated guys for years on end who wanted only to be my friend. This was different. For the first time, I had a partner, someone who truly wanted to be with me.

On one of our first dates, he told me he knew why I was here. I was supposed to have his child. I barely knew him and couldn't believe he would say that so early on, but he was right. I learned later a huge part of my life was to be a mother.

We had dated for about six months when he proposed to me. A year later, we celebrated our wedding with close family and friends. My gracious in-laws, Bob and Barbara Wickstrom, came from New York. They are wonderful people and threw us a beautiful rehearsal dinner at the Hotel Bel-Air, one of my favorite places. My mom was there. Rob's sister, Wendy, was a bridesmaid; his brother, Randy, a groomsman. Leslie Winston, my *Waltons* sister-in-law, was a bridesmaid, and, of course, so was Caren Cline, whom I had made a promise to all those years ago.

Since Rob and I were both actors, the wedding took on a theatrical theme. Our friends Dar and Brian made cool-looking clay characters of us for the cake topper. We had a "program" and T-shirts made for everyone. My brothers were listed as "stand-ins" for Mr. Lawrence McDonough. My brothers walked me down the aisle. I saw Richard Thomas in the pew and he winked at me. All my brothers were there. We celebrated with over three hundred guests and then honeymooned in Hawaii.

THE NOT-SO-FUN PART

I continued to ignore my symptoms, and believed if I focused on being a newlywed, everything would work out. But eventually I had to admit to myself something was wrong.

The decline of my health was so slow over the course of ten years that it's hard to pinpoint when it started and what the actual symptoms were. I went to so many doctors for different symptoms, and at that time, no one ever put it together, or wanted to.

Although I broke out in a rash right after surgery, I was right about how illogical it was to think my cotton bra caused such a reaction. Years later, I still had those rashes; so I went to a dermatologist. The rashes were on different parts of my body and across my nose and cheeks. At first, they did seem like an allergy.

Then the headaches began, along with chronic fatigue. I never knew when it would hit me. I could rest, get up, and feel fine; then suddenly I would have to lie down, right then. A few times I had to lie on the floor of wherever I was. I was once traveling with one of those guys who just wanted to be my "friend" and he left me lying on the ground in an airport. He was angry because he thought it was my blood sugar.

Sometimes I would wake up and couldn't lift my head off the pillow. I gained weight and my muscles started to ache; then my joints joined the pain brigade. I couldn't exercise, even if I found the energy. My internist referred me to an endocrinologist, who thought I was depressed, so I went into therapy. My heart developed an irregular beat, so I went to a cardiologist. Scores of doctors, and no one could tell me what was wrong. I started to think I was a hypochondriac. After all, I didn't *look* sick.

Life moved along and I dealt with constant fatigue and muscle aches; then other symptoms followed. My allergy attacks intensified. If I visited a home with a dog or a cat, my nose ran. Next I couldn't breathe, and within twenty-four hours, I'd develop a secondary infection. I'd had allergies before—now they magnified—

and the doctor diagnosed a bad cold and prescribed antibiotics. Some days, I'd wake up so exhausted, I could barely move. My decline was very gradual over the course of ten years. I couldn't figure out what exactly was wrong with me. I went from doctor to doctor, treatment to treatment: internist to dermatologist to chiropractor to cardiologist to herbalist—I even tried a popular multi-level marketed potion—to endocrinologist to hematologist, and finally a rheumatologist. One doctor thought it was all in my head and suggested another psychologist. I actually started to feel I *was* crazy.

THE LIGHTBULB MOMENT

In 1990, I was in a car wreck that ruptured a disk in my back. My teachings said there are no accidents, and that became true about this crash.

My knees smashed into the dashboard; my wrists and arms were wrenched from holding the steering wheel. My neck, back, and joints—all my muscles ached for over a year. I felt crazy for not healing from this accident. I went to more doctors and finally an orthopedist. He asked me to tell him everything. He listened to *all* my complaints, wrote them all down, and when I was finally finished with this laundry list, he took a few minutes to study them. Finally he looked up at me and asked a question that changed the course of my life: "Have you ever had a lupus panel?"

I was stunned. I knew about the disease. In fact, I knew a lot. Years earlier, I had been the celebrity spokesperson for an L.A.-based chapter for lupus awareness. I knew it ran in families, but no one in my family had it. I froze on the table as scary facts about the disease flooded my brain.

"No, I can't have lupus. I have no family history." But all my symptoms . . . Terror struck deep in my heart. He encouraged me to follow up with a rheumatologist.

Something else life-changing happened soon after that appointment. I found out I was pregnant. I was excited and a little nervous. I had always wanted to be ready for motherhood and waited because I felt it wasn't the right time.

I decided to meditate on my fear and procrastination. During my meditation, I saw myself in a raft, going down a river. I had no paddles and had to trust where the water took me. The water got choppy, but I held on. Then the water turned to white water rapids. I was okay; I still held on. After different scenarios with the water, the raft drifted to a calm alcove. I knew I was safe and took a breath. I looked onto the shore and there was a little baby there. I brought the baby into the raft and held it close, knowing we would be okay. The raft took us back to the river and we floated together down the river. I am a very visual person—so this made sense to me. The meditation left me calm with a sense of knowing. (It's those times when I am connected to the quiet and trust, I am my best. In those moments, I listen and see what to do. I feel connected with the Universe and have peace in my heart.) After that, I knew what was next. I finally realized that it was never the "right" time, there could always be an excuse as to why not to have a baby.

I had waited a long time for this. I was thirty years old and the first Walton girl to have a baby. It was an exciting time. My friend Dana Hill had a coed baby shower for us and we had a blast. I was feeling better than I had in a long time. Well, except for when I was around the smell of Chinese food, which made me gag. Also, I love matzo ball soup, but couldn't eat it while pregnant. As soon as I had the baby, I ate it all the time, still do. So funny these things we crave, and that we can't stand what we normally like. I craved Carl's Jr. club sandwiches, and lettuce. At a restaurant one night, I looked at all the unfinished side salads and said, "Are you going to eat that? Don't let it go to waste, I'll eat it." I ate everyone's leftover salads.

Even though I'd been feeling better, I went ahead and made the appointment with a rheumatologist. Everything seemed fine, except my blood work indicated an elevated ANA (antinuclear antibodies), and she told me to check in with her after the baby was born. She never said I might have a disease or complications or any other issues with the birth, so I didn't think much about it. Plus, I was having a pretty "textbook pregnancy." I would find out the reasons why later.

NESTING

Anyway, I was having a baby and we got busy getting her room together, painting it blue, my favorite color. My friend from junior high, Kate Zovich, came over and painted white clouds on the "sky" in her bedroom. I got out the sewing machine and sewed pink-and-blue rabbit curtains for the windows. One day, a little of my dad channeled through me and I started to strip an old chest of drawers. Rob came home and saw me with a mask and gloves on and said, "What are you doing?" I think my nesting instinct had kicked in big-time.

We found out she was a girl and her name was actually "Aubrey" at first. But we usually called her "Baby Wick." So many people were helpful when I was pregnant. My mom was happy; my friend Gwen had a ladies' shower for me. Michael Learned and Leslie Winston came to that one. As with that other intense time in my life, I got crazy with the hair. I cut it all off. What was I thinking? But pregnant women do strange things sometimes. It was a time of joy, generosity, and nesting.

Women with lupus are often symptom-free during pregnancy. The medical theory is that it has something to do with the hormones. What happened after I gave birth is what knocked me for a loop.

BABY GIRL

Sydnee came into the world surrounded by joy, love, and a bit of chaos and celebrity, all of which have followed her since. I still had the heebie-jeebies about hospitals, so I waited until the last minute to go in. Rob and I were put into a very small holding area, where we waited and waited for a delivery room.

Soon I was in the pain of labor. A nurse peeked in and said, "Oh, are you still in here? We need to move you," and left. I was flailing in pain and just wanted relief.

After a while, another nurse popped her head in the door and exclaimed, "Haven't you been moved yet?" Then she left.

The hospital was filled with excitement and activity, and all the nurses and staff were distracted, but not because of me. Magic Johnson's wife, Cookie, was in the room next to ours, delivering their first child. There was a buzz in the atmosphere all around us. Although I've never met her, there's something about being in labor and hearing Cookie's "push" countdown that became part of Sydnee's birth. I'll always remember the press, security men with funny packs, and helicopters flying overhead. Wild.

Finally some kindhearted person found the time to move us to a delivery room.

Sydnee had a low Apgar score. I kept saying, "She's not crying?" The anesthesiologist whisked her away to the incubator, and I panicked. When I finally heard her tiny wail, my heart melted and has never been the same since.

They took her to the nursery while I rested. I lay in the hospital bed, sweating and feeling sick. The enormity of how my life had changed swept through me like a hurricane. The knowledge that I would never be alone again blew through my consciousness. I was now a mother. I knew no matter how old Sydnee got, I would always feel like I left an arm or another part of me behind when she wasn't with me. I sobbed for the loss of my individuality, and for the gift of this beautiful little girl.

I knew in my heart of hearts I was born to be Sydnee's mommy. I adore her. I would die for her. I dried my tears, got up, and wandered the halls (always attractive in those flimsy gowns) to find the nursery. I rolled her bassinet back to our room and kept her with me until we left the hospital.

Many of my Walton family members came with flowers to meet their "niece," the newest member of our "family." When Sydnee was four months old, we went to Schuyler, Virginia, for the opening of the Walton's Mountain Museum, and Michael Learned told Syd to call her "Grammy Mike." I was working as a special correspondent for *Entertainment Tonight* on the museum opening, and we have the cutest video of "Grandpa" Ralph with Sydnee. Immediately she became another member of our Walton family.

POSTPREGNANCY BLUES

When I got home from the hospital, I was extremely sick, and in pain. I had what I now call a terrible lupus flare-up. I wasn't healing. I couldn't breast-feed Sydnee. She had colic and couldn't get any milk from me.

My OB said I wasn't adjusting well to motherhood. I felt like a miserable failure. I cried and cried, and wondered if the implants prevented her from nursing. I remembered the surgeon saying I might not be able to breast-feed, but many women still could. The OB examined me and said I shouldn't have any problems nursing. Rob assured me I was okay and encouraged me not to guilt-trip myself. I wanted so much to do what was right, to be a perfect mother. I called La Leche, and they suggested I use a breast pump. When I hooked up that machine, it couldn't even get any milk from me.

I now believe my inability to breast-feed was God's way of protecting Sydnee from further poisoning. I learned sometime later that certain silicones can cross the placental barrier, and Sydnee may have been exposed during the pregnancy. Some breast milk donation services wouldn't even accept milk donations from mothers with implants. Unfortunately, I didn't know any of this information as I struggled to care for my child through the challenges of my own illnesses.

There were times I was so ill, I couldn't even hold Sydnee. As she grew, I grew weaker. There were days when I couldn't get out of bed. I never knew when I would wake up and not be able to get up. Sydnee learned to get herself up and toddle to my bedroom. She'd climb into bed with me, and for her breakfast, I'd give her the granola bar I'd have waiting on my nightstand. I felt like a terrible mother, unable to make my own daughter her breakfast.

My health continued to deteriorate. I continued to feel the responsibility to support my family. I carried into my marriage the belief I had to do it all. I had to continue supporting and caring for everyone, just as I had been doing for years. I believed my value was in what I did—not who I was—which didn't help.

Having two actors in the same family can be tough, especially if you're not working very much. Acting is not a steady job. Rob had always worked as a waiter, and I was working as an actor as much as I could. Luckily, I was asked to start teaching acting. We had tough times, and eventually I added a telemarketing job and also worked as a waitress and bartender for a catering company. Rob stopped pursuing acting and was trying to find a new career. I worried about making the mortgage, taxes, and insurance; that pressure added to my stress, which weighed heavily on me and on my health.

My illness was crushing me personally and professionally. It hurt my marriage. I felt my life force slipping away, and I didn't know what was happening.

As my physical discomfort worsened, I withdrew into a cocoon. Chronic pain—especially if you are undiagnosed and trying to buck up and hide it—can mentally and physically disable. I was not the person Rob had married, and that contributed to the unraveling of our marriage. Not having the energy to take care of it all made me feel more like a failure. We separated after seven years of marriage, then divorced. It was a terrible time.

It was the beginning of realizing that constant doing wouldn't make it turn out my way. I made a lot of mistakes and learned that trying to control the outcome of a situation doesn't make it work. Trying to hold it all together can help it fall apart, another lesson for me.

We were filming one of the reunions, *A Walton Easter*, at that time. Michael Learned was a great comfort to me. I cried on her shoulder. She and Judy helped me realize I had to be strong for Sydnee.

My health went up and down, and I went to different doctors for the various symptoms and received more prescriptions. No one could tell me what was wrong; they just treated the symptoms with different pills. When I look at the deaths of celebrities recently, I see I could have easily fallen into the trap of taking pain medications, then denial, and eventually dying from the effects on my body. If I had taken all the medications I have been prescribed over the years, I believe I would have been dead a long time ago. A few of the medications I was prescribed were taken off the market when people died from them. Once again, that safety valve caused me to be a "bad" patient and not take the various pills all the time. That safety valve and the fact that I was a mother—and someone depended on me—probably saved me.

My friends had been reading in the press the emerging information about the dangers of implants. I was in complete and total denial that my symptoms might be caused by my implants. I didn't believe I was sick. The doctors couldn't even tell me what was wrong, so I didn't want to hear my friends' concerns. Besides, if it *was* the implants, then my rheumatologist would have told me, right? These were supposed to "last a lifetime," the literature promised. I continued to get worse.

DOWN THE TOILET

During this time, I wasn't booking any jobs. I would go on auditions for commercials and guest spots. I would try to pump myself up for the auditions, but I didn't interview well. I was mad at myself and frustrated at my inability to perform.

I found out I lost jobs because I wasn't the "me" they knew, and I didn't look the same. My hair had been falling out, and I was tired all the time. My agent later told me he was getting feedback that I looked tired, and just wasn't the same. They thought it was because I had had a baby and was sleep deprived, so they didn't say anything to me. I got nervous and tried harder at auditions, which is never good. I also carried my financial fears into the room with me. Desperation never reads well.

I started to run low-grade fevers, like I had the flu all the time. My muscles ached and my joints throbbed. To doctors, it seemed like the flu. I got painful ulcers in my nose, which I couldn't quite explain to a doctor. Every day in the shower, more hair was in my hands and down the drain. I got weaker. I was not the energetic Mary anymore.

I developed lumps in my back and leg. They were hard, rocklike masses under my skin. My dermatologist removed them. She was surprised at how much scar tissue there was in these things, it was so unusual. She thought maybe they were ingrown hairs that created scar tissue. No one thought to test for silicone. Now we know the body walls-off foreign objects with tissue to protect itself. With implants, this scar tissue can harden, causing pain and disfigurement. It's called capsular contracture.

Silicone is like goo. Implants have an oily feel to them. That's the silicone leaking out of the implant. Traces are so minute, they can seep through the wall and travel through your body. One doctor explained it's like the trace of a snail's path. As the silicone migrates through your body, it's impossible to see the slime and remove it all. Later, I met women who had silicone found in their uterus, ovaries, and liver.

While all this was going on inside my body, my career—what little there was—went down the toilet.

VANITY GIRL

Somewhere in my subconscious, I felt if the news reports were correct about the dangers of implants, then my illness was my fault. I blamed myself for years. My situation reminded me of Erin in "The Burnout." Erin begs John-Boy to risk his life and reenter their burning house to save her favorite party dress. We both chose vanity over substance. We both deserved to be punished. *Why didn't I accept myself as I was?*

One day, my thespian friend whose surgeon I'd used called me. She had news she felt the responsibility to share with me. She had been ill and had her implants removed. They'd found a golf ball–sized cyst behind her implant that had never shown up in a mammogram or breast exam because the implant obscured it. She waited a terrifying three days to see if she had cancer. Luckily, she did not. She told me her health had started to improve, and her symptoms had diminished after she had her implants removed. She also told me her son had been ill. This unnerved me; I thought of Sydnee and her physical challenges when she was born, the low Apgar scores, not breathing, inability to suck or swallow properly, and the colic. It's one thing to make a stupid decision that hurts you, but to hurt your baby? Unforgivable.

I hung up the phone, astonished and stunned. What she said had frightened me. I couldn't imagine having another surgery. I'd look at my breasts and wonder, can these really be the problem? It was so hard to make the decision to have them in the first place. Now, to cut myself open again? I couldn't bear the thought. I fought the truth, but soon I was so ill, I couldn't lift my Sydnee. I couldn't walk up a set of stairs without shooting pain in my legs. It was like being stabbed with an X-ACTO knife with each step. As time went on, I felt like my life was slipping away.

I started asking questions, doing more research. One day, I asked my rheumatologist if she thought my implants were a factor in my failing health. She told me it couldn't be the implants, that more than half of her patients had them. Hello? Over half your patients have them and there's a "supposed" link to implants? I still wanted to trust her, like my dad had wanted to trust his doctors.

Then something extraordinary happened. When she left the exam room, her nurse leaned over and whispered to me, "Run! Run and get those things out!" *What does she know? Red flag!*

Now I knew I had to find out the truth. The rheumatologist had referred me to another doctor for a second opinion about whether I should have them removed or not. I was so stiff and weak, I could barely climb onto his exam table. His advice? "You won't feel like a woman if you have them removed. They take breast tissue with the implant removal, so you'll be smaller than you were before. You'll be depressed for two years if you take them out. Don't do it."

I already didn't feel like a woman. I didn't feel like a wife or a mother, either. I felt like a loser, and I was starting to believe it was my own fault. I'd messed with my body. I'd hurt myself and possibly my child.

After the visit to his office, I was in the shower, looking down at my breasts, and I knew I didn't want to be cut open again. I hid, crying tears down the drain, as I had done so often before, trying again to maintain the image of being pulled-together and perfect.

I closed my eyes, asked for help, listened, and then I knew. The highest part of me, you know, the one we don't always listen to, realized the answer. I knew I had to eliminate every possible variable. I felt like one pint of lifeblood after another was being drained from me as I headed slowly toward death. I had to find out if the implants were making me sick.

I read manufacturers' studies that said there was no link. Their bought-and-paid-for research implied I *was* crazy, and my illness was caused by something else. I knew I had to fight to find out what was wrong with me. If nothing else, I had to fight for my baby girl. Sydnee had started to exhibit more odd symptoms.

I had a mammogram and ultrasound. Neither indicated my implants were ruptured. I got a breast MRI. It also showed no proof of rupture, but the doctor told me "off the record" he believed my implants had ruptured.

I was off to more surgeons. One doctor examined my breasts and said, "Those look great. I wouldn't touch them, at least not with a scalpel." (Insert lecherous laugh here.)

The next plastic surgeon just wanted to replace them. "Why do you want them out, anyway?"

"I feel tired all the time. I'm sick, my joints ache, my muscles hurt, and I have no energy."

He said, "You're getting older, that's natural. I feel the same way."

I looked at this balding, older man and said, "Yeah, but I'm *thirty-one*. I'm not supposed to feel this way, yet."

The more women I talked to, the more I found out that I was not alone. The more I read, the more I wanted them out. I didn't care about big boobs anymore. If I had learned anything from working on the show, it was perseverance.

Some of my earliest lessons from the mountain came from witnessing the noble strength of Patricia Neal doing *The Homecoming* after her many strokes, and Ellen Corby's powerful return to the show after her own stroke. Even when Olivia had polio in "An Easter Story," which we filmed in the first season, she kept fighting. And I had watched my own father's display of dignity while he fought cancer.

I'd learned from the best, and I knew how to fight. I began to find my voice, to trust my gut, to rely on my instincts, and to listen to my angels. Unbeknownst to me, I had just begun the battle.

BOOBS OUT

I held to my decision, even though doctors said it wasn't necessary and there was no link. Here's the "crazy" label again. I made the appointment. Unwavering, I told another doctor point-blank, "Look, I don't want to replace them. I'm over it, trust me. I feel like I'm dying. Please take them out." He argued that I would be happier with replacements. I said, "You don't get it. I'm dying here. Just get them out." He finally believed me.

I was so relieved to be taking action to get better possibly. Then my presurgery blood work came back abnormal. I had a coagulation problem, which I later learned is common in lupus patients. The doctor canceled my surgery and sent me to a hematologist. After ten years of falling down this mountain, I was at the bottom, crushed by rocks, sobbing. I just wanted it over.

Finally, on March 17, 1994, yes, Saint Patty's day, I had the implants removed—ten years since my surgery to have them put in.

This time, I had done my homework. I elected to have an en bloc total capsulectomy. That's where they remove the whole implant, with any scar tissue, so nothing leaks out into the chest cavity. I'd heard horror stories of implants being cut open in the chest, spilling the contents. The silicone would have to be scraped from the chest wall, which could take hours. I was also lucky enough to have a mastopexy, a reconstruction to cut away extra skin and rearrange it into a smaller breast.

The surgery took longer than expected. When my doctor cut them open on the tray, he found my implants had completely ruptured inside me. There was no outer shell left, just plastic bits stuck in the silicone like pieces of a ziplock bag suspended in goo. The only thing preventing the gelatinous mess from spreading more was my own scar tissue. However, my body had had access to the silicone seeping out through my healthy tissue for years. *Hmm, wonder where it all went?* Even with the ruptures and reconstruction, the removal was actually easier than the original surgery.

REALITY CHECK

Soon I was fully recovered from the removal procedure; yet I was still sick. The damage had been done. The downward spiral continued, and I wanted to know what was wrong with me. There was a class action suit against the implant manufacturers for the health problems caused by these faulty devices. I needed to submit my medical records, and I wanted my doctor to include in them my diagnosis. I wanted to know one way or another if she was going to give me a diagnosis of lupus. I asked her over and over. Finally she reluctantly diagnosed me, threw a few more prescriptions at me, and told me something that shocked and appalled me.

She told me she really "liked me as a person." She hoped I would continue to be a patient, but she thought I should know that she was being paid by implant manufacturers to testify in lawsuits *against* women like me who became ill with implants. I was livid. How could she? How could she do this to women? And for money? I felt betrayed and deceived. My mind flashed back.

If she had treated me for lupus while I was pregnant, maybe my postpartum days would not have been so horrible. I could have had help. I might have felt less crazy. Women with lupus often have a flare-up after giving birth. I flashed to the image of her telling me I was "stoic," hard to read. Me? The crybaby, the "sensitive" one? It all started to make sense. I had been the trusting sixteen-year-old girl believing her when she said, "There's nothing we can do." Not anymore.

My rage kicked in and I decided there must be something I could do. I wasn't going to take this one sitting down, not again. I could yell, scream, and warn women what had happened to me. I'd been thrown off the cliff and careened on a rockslide headlong to the bottom as my illness hurt my marriage, life, and career. I didn't want the same thing to happen to anyone else.

Sifting through the rubble of my life, I eventually started to find my voice to use the machine I understood. I called *Entertainment Tonight*, and they allowed me to produce a segment on implants. I went on other shows to tell my truth. I immediately started getting letters from women who were sick. I got calls from so many people,

I was surprised and astonished that the harm was so widespread. So much information surfaced about the ways faulty implants had hurt other women, I couldn't process it all.

I reflected on what I'd been through and thought about the surgeon who assured me implants were safe. Why hadn't he warned me? I later found out part of Dow Corning's strategy was to try to influence every rheumatologist and epidemiologist they could. They countered by focusing on epidemiology because it is an abstract discipline, not widely understood by the general population. Part of their defense strategy—fly under the radar screen. It worked. They also got the American College of Rheumatology on their side, and ACR issued a "position statement."

Upon further reflection, I realized if I'd known the deception and the horror I would go through, starting with rashes I would break out in within twenty-four hours of surgery, be plagued with health issues for—let's see, it's been twenty-five years so far—I *never* would have wanted implants.

If I had been told there was a "supposed" link to autoimmune disease, fevers, flu-type symptoms, chronic fatigue, joint pain, hair loss, memory loss, fibromyalgia, muscle aches, and swelling, I *never* would have considered having implants.

If someone had told me that Dow Corning, the maker of implants and the silicone used by other manufacturers, including my Memes, had manipulated their scientific research, or that I might need to have them replaced because they were faulty, I *never* would have wanted implants.

And if I'd known that all implants need to be replaced every nine to ten years—the equivalent of a major surgery every decade until you die—I *never* would have considered them.

If I knew that Bristol would pull the Meme because the outer layer of foam was made from a known carcinogen, TDA, believe me, I *never* would have had implants.

Despite my belief that everything happens for a reason, I wasn't sure what this lesson was about. I knew I didn't want anyone to go through what I endured for the last ten years; I knew I needed to take action on behalf of other women who needed to know the truth.

First I needed time to heal.

10

WHAT'S NEXT?

My experience of healing was a slow road. I would have a good day, and the next I couldn't get out of bed. I never knew when I would have a flare-up and it made life difficult to plan. I hid a lot of symptoms, so I wouldn't alarm my family. Nothing much had changed, right? I was still keeping secrets and wanted nothing to prevent me from getting work.

There's a metaphysical belief that words are powerful, so I started to be very careful about what I said out loud. I knew how serious the disease was. I didn't want to give the disease "power." I was afraid if I said, "I have lupus," it would make it true. Besides, maybe that doctor was right. Maybe I was crazy and didn't have it, after all. I avoided, ignored, and fought lupus for a long time.

Then, after thinking I was tricking the Universe, someone told me she used the words "I am *healing* lupus." The truth is, until I said the words "I have lupus," until I owned it, so to speak, did I start to heal. Once I embraced it, talked about it, only then was I able to start healing and deal with it.

BOYCOTT

About this time, in 1995, I received a call inviting me to participate in a rally in Chicago. They were having a boycott march through the city—complete with a mock coffin to honor the women who had died from their complications of silicone implants. I had no idea women had died. Christy, a group leader, asked me to speak at the rally and a press conference after the march.

Public speaking was not my thing, and radical acts of protest seemed to cross the line for this girl who always wanted to be socially appropriate. I might make someone, even Dow Chemical, the powerful company that brought us Agent Orange, mad at me. Oh no!

However, as much as I worried and argued with myself, I decided to go. I wanted to be with women who had gone through what I had. I wanted more information—to share and to compare experiences. Hey, maybe I wasn't so *crazy*, after all. These brave women had been creating support and research groups, while I was in denial, hoping my illness and symptoms weren't caused by my implants.

I wrote my speech and was reminded that boycotts, marches, and speaking out were rights the founders of our country had given me. I packed my nerve and a bit of mountain strength and headed to Chicago.

The march went well—the coffin was a bit scary—but we weren't arrested, and we attracted a lot of attention. I was fighting my good-girl image all the way. What would people say? Would I be judged or challenged? In downtown Chicago during the rally, someone handed me a bullhorn and asked me to address these brave women. There I was, facing women who were mirrors of me. We all had had implants, were all sick, and we were protesting a company that had lied to us. As I looked in their eyes, I saw myself reflected back and knew my life was changing. I didn't know then how much or for how long, but it was a mountain I had to climb. Get out the ropes, picks, and climbing shoes . . . let the boycott begin.

COINCIDENCE AND FALLOUT

I had no idea what I was up against. I just wanted to help and speak about my own experiences. Several Gulf War veterans showed up in support. They had similar mysterious health issues and weren't having any luck getting their voices heard. Could we all be victims of chemical poisoning? I listened in amazement to one story after another, each so similar. I wondered what had really happened to all of us.

The press conference was a lesson in just how big this game was. I spoke about how Dow Corning had been found liable for their implants. As we handed out a list of Dow products, I encouraged everyone to join our boycott until we learned the whole truth.

The manufacturers just happened to schedule a press conference in the same hotel—at the same time—right down the hall from ours. *Co-in-ki-dink?* No. Susie, one of the organizers, told me this was common. The company had hired a huge PR firm to handle their press. They would find out what the women were up to and plan a counterdistraction. I was a bit taken aback. I would soon learn this tactic was a pebble in the avalanche to come.

THE PRECIOUS GIRL

The experience had taken its toll on my health, career, and marriage. My marriage ended and my health continued to go up and down. I was tired and sick, but I was still a mommy, and Sydnee needed me. She was a great sport, and we became a team and got through it together. Part of our journey in coping with my illness together was writing a story about kids whose moms were sick. She gave it the title, "I Hate Lupus Because It Makes My Mom Boring." It was sad to me she felt this way, but we did our best.

We were quite the pair. Because of a photosensitivity I had developed, whenever I went outside, I wore special sunscreen clothes to cover my body and block the sun's rays. I loved to take her to a local water park once a year and she got used to the hats, long-sleeved shirts, and pants. She helped put on my sunscreen and became accustomed to having the only mommy who went in the water fully clothed with a big hat on. We got used to being different. We both felt silly at first; but we were so glad to be at the park, the staring didn't matter.

When the *Harry Potter* books came out, we'd climb into my bed with our chamomile tea and take turns each reading a page. Fortunately, all of our kooky accommodations to my challenges made us stronger as women and deepened our mother-daughter bond.

The downside was the roller-coaster ride. I was a single mom now and had to get it together. I felt guilty; I wasn't able to be the mom I wanted to be. My muscles and joints ached so much, I wasn't motivated to exercise. Chronic pain takes its toll on your temperament, the meds make you gain weight, and I was miserable. I lost my temper at times and still felt crazy moments.

I remember when I had my first lidocaine shot, deep into my hip. I could walk for the first time in years without shooting pain. I said, "I would be such a nice mommy if I felt like this all the time. I would have so much more patience." The pressure I put on myself to be a model mommy made me more ill. Depression soon set in. I went to a psychiatrist for help with the common depression women with lupus feel, and more meds were prescribed. Then another boulder let loose and rumbled toward me. Sydnee started to exhibit signs of illness.

Sydnee's attention span was off. She was having trouble focusing at school, causing suspicion of attention deficit disorder, ADD. At night, she started to vomit for no apparent reason. She had no fever or flu; yet she would go to bed, lie down, and vomit. She slept with a Tupperware container in bed with her for years.

I found out many of the second-generation implant children were having some of the same symptoms my daughter was having. I was terrified. The mothers could remove their implants, but if a child was born to a woman with implants, it was too late. There was nothing to take out of the children. Their bodies had to deal with the silicone that traveled into their bodies in utero or possibly in the breast milk.

I spoke with and heard of many other silicone moms whose kids had chemical sensitivity, joint pain, lupus-like symptoms, and esophageal issues. Where was the science? One lone doctor doing any research at all on these kids was in New York. Through their PR machine, the chemical company still insisted there was no link to any illness from implants. I found that hard to believe, though. There were too many sick women and kids for this to be a coincidence.

My frustration brought tears that reminded me daily there was a possibility I had hurt Sydnee. I watched her suffer and hated myself, thinking my idiotic vanity could be the cause of my baby's misery. I felt sorry for myself, my lost marriage, my career, my baby girl, and the years I felt lost to illness. I continued to research the history of Dow's own studies. One of the whistle-blowers with a conscience, the dear Tom Talcott, looked into my misty eyes and said, "One day, you're going to stop being sad and start getting mad."

He was right. I decided I'd had enough of the pity party. I vowed to learn more. I thought if I knew what had happened to my body and to Sydnee's, I could fix it. Besides, I wanted to help my daughter and other women and children who might have been harmed.

DOCUMENTING THE TRUTH

I had already been producing films, so I turned my energy toward making a documentary about how these companies were able to sell a harmful product. I enlisted my friend June Dowad, who is a documentary filmmaker, to help me. The more we discovered, the more our heads swam with the information. June and I learned alarming facts in our research.

As it turns out, the silicone implants were grandfathered in for usage when devices came under FDA jurisdiction. We were shocked to find out implants were never FDA approved. How could that be? There was no proof of their safety. The idea was to have studies prove their safety, and approval would follow. These studies were paid for by the manufacturers, and none were long-term. Dow Corning was publicly saying they were safe; internally they knew there were issues with the implants. Internally they would start a study, but the follow-up was not thorough.

The manufacturers began paying for the "science." I learned later that some manufacturers were frequently tipped off before inspectors arrived so they could hide the faulty implants in the ceilings. No implants were adequately researched for their potential to do harm. Many implants had different "recipes" to try to avoid ruptures and leakage.

Were all these different chemical concoctions what gave us so many different types of symptoms, illnesses, and bizarre reactions? How would we ever find out the truth?

THE UP AND DOWN OF ILLNESS

During this time, I worked hard to heal and be the mommy I wanted to be. I relied on my spiritual side, the experience brought me closer to my Source as I was forced to slow down and take stock of my life. I reevaluated who I was and where I was going. I still had the same goals, but my life was forever changed. I wondered why I ever made the decision to get implants, and why women feel they need to change themselves, their bodies. Hadn't I spent most of my life changing myself to try to fit in? From my laugh, to my weight, to my bra size, I had always looked outside myself for approval. Why didn't I ever believe I was enough? I had tried to fill the hole inside me with diets, dress sizes, acting success, and eventually silicone. Through my own boulders of inadequate feelings, I destroyed my health and hurt what mattered to me most.

As I reconnected with my own spirit, I learned about a Source that I didn't need to prove anything to in order to be accepted. A God that was loving, not angry and looking for my "goodness" to be proved at every turn. Could it be possible? It was a difficult concept for me, and it took me far away from the vengeful God I was raised to know.

I started to realize I had more to offer as a person. I began to fill the hole in my self-esteem and worth as a woman and a mother. In my meditations, a mantra came to me one day. It was clear as a bell, like a little voice whispering in my ear: "I strengthen my Faith and trust in Love."

The trust part was the hardest for me, still is. It was hard for me to surrender; I was used to protecting, hiding, and even submitting to the whims of others. I had a lot of work to do to trust. I started to understand that when I did trust, the Universe brought me everything I needed.

Yet, I still felt deceived and abandoned. As the words kept coming to mind, I started to work with them through my resistance;

then I would repeat them more and more. It was a battle, but—somewhere in me—I knew I needed to change. I wanted to find my own strength instead of relying on someone else's opinion of me. Eventually these simple words helped me. I still say them over and over, especially when I can't sleep.

"I strengthen my Faith and trust in Love."

Serendipity would flow when I did trust, and help would appear almost magically in the form of people with advice or suggestions. One day I was stepping off an elevator and ran into Leslie, a lupus activist I'd known when I had been the celebrity spokesperson. We shared the normal chitchat, and she asked how I was. I told her a little bit of what was going on with my health and she encouraged me to call Dr. Daniel Wallace, the respected lupus doctor. He would be able to get to the bottom of what was really going on with me.

Leslie said Dr. Wallace would remember me and I should call. He ran exhaustive tests, studied all my records, and confirmed that I did indeed have lupus. He started me immediately on treatment that reduced my pain and helped me function better. I was so relieved to finally have a doctor treat me and not make me feel crazy. After ten years of not knowing what to do, I was finally getting help. And I was getting more confirmation to our suspicions that something was indeed wrong with the silicone implants. Dr. Wallace told me he had treated other women with implants who had similar health issues.

LUPUS

Lupus is a connective tissue disease that affects the immune system; it's classified as an autoimmune disease. It is the opposite of AIDS. Instead of a deficiency, the body makes too many antibodies and fights to break the body down. Dr. Wallace said it's as if the body is allergic to itself and sends out antibodies against otherwise healthy organs. There are two kinds of lupus: external, or discoid lupus, that affects the skin, and internal, or systemic. Dr. Wallace diagnosed me with systemic lupus erythematosus, or SLE.

Chronic fatigue, sleepless nights, low-grade fevers, mouth and nose ulcers, hair loss, joint stiffness and swelling, photosensitivity, headaches, sleep loss, muscle pain, and dry mouth, skin, and eyes were all symptoms of lupus. I had them all.

Lupus is the prototype of all autoimmune diseases. So when a cure for lupus is found, it will help many other diseases. Fibromyalgia is a symptom of lupus, and I had it. Sjögren's syndrome, a collagen disorder, is a symptom of lupus, and I had it. Chronic fatigue, another symptom, and I had it. It was a bit confusing, since there are entire nonprofits set up for each of these diseases, but I had them all—as many lupus patients do. It's also why lupus is often difficult to diagnose. There are so many symptoms; yet the patient often doesn't even look sick. After all these years, it's amazing to me when lupus is the first thing the fictional Dr. House looks for in a patient. They are always running a lupus panel and ruling out lupus on that show. We've come a long way.

I began to access my spiritual beliefs to get a grip on my intense emotions. I meditated on my body and visualized it being whole and healthy. It was humbling to have my body say, "No more. If you're not going to slow down, we'll make you stop altogether."

Since my body was making too many antibodies, a visual came to me one day. I saw my brain as the office of the factory giving antibody orders to the "machine." It would release them on the conveyer belt. I saw a man running the operation and he was crazy busy making these extra antibodies, so I slowed him down in my visualizations. I even pictured him taking a nap on his desk to slow the process down. Then I saw a regular order come through. He calmly told the machine the perfect amount to send out. This actually calmed me down and helped me toward healing. I felt better, "mind over matter" as they say.

I also sat in quiet meditation, thinking of the peace and calm of nature and places I loved. I cut out pictures to remind me of my favorite things and placed them in my view. I stayed as positive as I could to deal with each flare-up.

While I tried all kinds of potions, vitamins, cleanses, and Eastern medicine philosophies, I never forsook Western medicine when I needed it. Acupuncture was also very effective for me. I created a balance to work with everything to make me better.

My friends and family were an incredible support. My dear

friends gave me acting work to help me keep my health insurance (you know who you are, and I am eternally grateful). I felt blessed to have health care and live in a country with access to great medical care.

Still, it was hard for me to ask people for help. I felt weak and like a failure for having to ask for help. I mean, wasn't I the one who was supposed to be giving back?

I did give back from a very personal place a few years later. Dr. Wallace was forming a group to raise funds for lupus research. He asked me to be the president of what we called Lupus LA. At the time, I was hesitant to add another thing to my plate. I often joked I had to do it, doctor's orders, right? I was glad I did. The other founding members are another amazing group of people I feel lucky to have learned from, and to have worked with for such a worthy cause.

Lupus is a tough disease with no known cause or cure, only treatment for symptoms that can also make you ill. Over a million Americans have some form of lupus. The most affected are women, and the highest incidence is among African Americans or women with Caribbean heritage. Because a cure will help so many other autoimmune diseases, it's an especially important cause that deserves increased funding and research.

THE WOOLLY MAMMOTH

As time went on, it became more obvious there was something going on with my daughter. We had trouble with schools and teachers. Her teachers would trade her out to another teacher after her first few weeks of school. Even for a first and second grader, she got the message she wasn't liked by those teachers. One day before school, she was crying and said, "I just love my teacher so much. I just want her to like me. Why doesn't she like me?" It broke my heart; she sounded so much like me. I didn't know what to do but hug her, love her, and take steps to help her, but she still struggled.

I wish I had a dollar for every teacher who gave us the "look" followed by "She's an only child, isn't she?" What did *that* mean? After dropping her off at school, I spent many mornings seeing her precious face full of confusion and trepidation. I wanted to make it all better for her. I was wracked with guilt for my part in it.

Now it was Sydnee's turn to visit doctor after doctor. I knew what she must be feeling with all the poking and prodding. One of the scariest tests for me was a brain MRI when she was about eight. She told me recently it wasn't scary for her at all, but she thought my approach to the test was cute. I think I was a nervous mommy. Who, me? Overdo it? Try too hard?

I tried to be creative to help her get through it. We had just watched a special on the woolly mammoth. Since you can't move during an MRI, I told her we would play a game. I told her to pretend she was a woolly mammoth frozen in the icy tundra, so she wouldn't move.

"Syd, you're going to hear buzzing and thumping, but those are just the native people digging down to get to you." I thought of the images we'd seen on the television show. "You're also going to hear them singing and pounding their drums, hoping to find you. If you lie absolutely still, they'll bring you out and celebrate you. You'll be your mammoth self."

What I'd really given her was her first lesson in accessing a character for a "role." She followed my every direction and lay perfectly still for the procedure. When they pulled her out of the scary tube, we celebrated "finding" her, and I was so proud of her.

From this test and some others, we found that her brain was slow to fire in some areas. Off to more doctors. I'd been through this round myself and wasn't about to surrender to medications. The typical assessment was ADHD and everyone wanted to put her on drugs. I was against labeling her and medicating her. So many kids were being given pills; I didn't want that for her.

We tried behavior modification, Chinese herbs, acupressure, tough love, and many different doctors and practices. Some worked, some didn't. When it became clear Sydnee was falling behind in school, we worked harder.

Homework lasted hours, and usually ended in tears, hers *and* mine. I tried to help her enjoy the process with creativity, incorporating colorful tactile elements to reach all her senses. We made the solar system in toilet paper one night. Still, she would spin and spin on the floor. One night, I heard her crying and went into her room. Her head was jerking back and forth.

"Make it stop, Mommy!"

My heart died for her. I taught her methods to calm herself by using breathing exercises, visualizations, and meditation.

As a mother, this was frightening to me, made worse because with every symptom, I blamed myself. There wasn't much research being done on the women who had illness after breast implants, and even less for the kids. Sydnee's problems launched me from being sad into being mad. I committed myself to being an advocate for my daughter. I would fight for her the way I wished I had been fought for. When I was young, I'd felt pushed and pulled. I didn't want Sydnee to feel that way. I was a frustrated mommy, and I was tough and overbearing at times. Looking back, I made mistakes and pushed her too hard, but I never gave up. I always held the possibilities out to her, not the disabilities.

Her third-grade teacher called a meeting with Rob and me. She told us Sydnee was very smart, but she needed help. Back to the doctor. We were so desperate this time, we gave in and tried medications. They had horrible effects on her. It was like torturing your own child. She would vomit with one; then another would make her fall asleep. With one, she completely lost her personality. One teacher said, "Where's Sydnee? I don't think these meds are right for her. She's not herself. She's like a zombie."

Even Sydnee realized she was different. We were lucky enough to find a specialist at UCLA Medical Center. He tested her and diagnosed her with Tourette's syndrome. With that came the OCD, ADHD. He was the first doctor who was really able to help her.

She was still having a lot of trouble at school and falling behind. I was against medications, so I tried many things that didn't work, a few that did. Judy Norton told me about one program that helped both of us. The Hollywood Education and Literacy Project helped me work with her using visual aids and other methods to access her particular learning abilities. By achieving mastery of simple concepts before moving forward, she began to develop a better foundation, and her attitude about learning and school in general improved.

About that time, I cohosted a show for the Travel Channel with

Chris Knight (Peter Brady, of course). He told me he'd recently found out he was ADD and wished he had been properly medicated years ago. He explained I should not give up on Sydnee or a medical solution for her. He told me he was convinced his first two marriages would not have ended in divorce if he had known he had ADD and had treated it. He said he could trace the behavior back to his childhood, and he wished he had help then. His words stuck with me.

HAVING A "NO"

People always asked me if I would put Sydnee into acting. Luckily, Sydnee didn't want to act back then. They say we want our kids to have the benefit of our experience. Growing up the way I did, I was no different. Like my parents giving us the dance classes and big Christmas mornings they never had, I wanted Syd to have what I didn't.

I always had a tendency to overexplain everything to Syd, probably a direct result of the way I grew up. Often people who heard me thought I was a wack-a-doodle, but given my experience, I was obsessed she know everything. The pendulum had swung clear to the other side. I can laugh at the overexplaining everything now, but my motivation was to prevent her from having her own *Dinah!* moments. No surprises for my kid. In fact, now I can say I do most of what I do so people never feel as uninformed, frightened, and bad about themselves as I did. I can laugh about it now, and I am sure you are chuckling along with me, but I was a bit crazed.

Sydnee's life was more like this: Picture me down at her eye level. "Okay, Sydnee, now, this is called a birthday party. We will bring this present inside, but it's not for you. When we get there, give it to Katie. There may be balloons, maybe not, maybe decorations. Then you'll play and maybe some games will happen. Then cake will come out with candles on it. We'll all sing to Katie and she'll blow out her candles. Then you will get some cake and ice cream. Katie will open her presents. Then we'll go home, which will be in our car and take about five minutes. Okay? Do you understand?" Blah, blah, blah . . . imagine having me as your mom. I was an admitted nightmare at times.

Another thing I felt I didn't have growing up was a "no." As a result, I gave Sydnee a very strong "no." Sometimes it's hard to have her be so strong in her "no," especially when it comes at me full force, but I wouldn't want her to feel as disempowered as I did.

Over the years, her life has gotten so much easier. I am so amazed at her continued progress and who she has become. She had a tough time, but she is a strong and compassionate person because of all she went through. I am so proud of her, my heart sings. There are so many lessons here about having a kid with a disability, but that's another book. Sydnee is an incredible kid. Her challenges in life have made her a sensitive, caring person. I am so lucky to be her mom and to see the person she has grown into.

11

NUTS AND SLUTS

The more I found out about the dangers of implants from court documents that cited the manufacturer's own data, the more concerned I became. Dow Corning was found civilly liable for failing to disclose to recipients the dangers of their implants. The company's own scientists had raised concerns about suspected problems; yet their PR machine continued to argue against women who questioned the connection between implants and health concerns.

Internal documents indicated that complications reported by women had been suppressed. I found out there had been suspicious links to autoimmune diseases, and an entire community of researchers disagreed on the safety of silicone use for medical purposes for several years *before* I even had implants. Why hadn't my doctor told me any of this information? Terror ripped through my heart. Had I poisoned myself and my baby girl? What had I done by having implants?

The court transcript exhibits included one study I'll never forget. In 1967, Dow Corning commissioned a four-dog twenty-four-month study using miniature silicone implants. They implanted dogs with samples of the devices—like the ones used in women—and examined the subjects at six months, and then at twenty-four months. Well, three of them, anyhow—one of them had died after only eleven months. The necropsy showed it had liver and kidney congestion, and fibrous tissue reactions at the site of the implantation. The other three were killed at the twenty-four-month end to the study. All of them had severe or moderate inflammation at their implantation sites.

This is a small sample in the world of scientific research, and probably wouldn't have received a lot of attention; except that in 1973, Silas Braley, of Dow Corning, published a report of the study. He falsely claimed that there were no differences between the six-month and two-year results on these poor dogs. They supposedly found no adverse reactions upon necropsy, and he also failed to report that one of the dogs had died during the study.

First, I thought about the cruelty to the dogs. Imagining breast implants in a dog still makes me shake and outrages me.

Second, as a consumer, I had been kept in the dark about the company's own studies and research because confidentiality orders in litigation often impede the information from reaching the public. It's protected until a trial. If someone settles out of court, important details may never reach the people who most need to know the information. Unless someone knows to look for the court documents—and knows there is anything to look for—the information doesn't get out.

The other red flag is that if Dow Corning's own scientists had published studies with inaccurate and misleading conclusions, how many other discrepancies and poorly constructed research was being presented as worthy and was putting women at risk?

When women started to get sick, they didn't look for court documents, thinking it was their implants. When I had my symptoms, I didn't think of calling a lawyer. I went to the doctor to get well. So, for years, no one looked for this information. There was no "link" back then, and my plastic surgeon certainly wasn't talking, either.

In 1977, a woman from Cleveland sued Dow Corning because her implants had ruptured and caused her a great deal of pain. Richard Mithoff, a Houston attorney, argued successfully for her case and she accepted a settlement. This case didn't receive much publicity at the time, but the internal documents, lack of scientific research, and compelling argument against a medical device that causes harm was the boulder we women have pushed uphill against the manufacturers, plastic surgeons, and, in some cases, the media ever since.

As silicone implants became more widely accepted and accessible, the detriments to women increased, but apparently corresponding research and long-term studies on their safety didn't keep up. As I read further about the history of the industry, I found out more cases of harm done to women like me.

In 1984, a jury had awarded Maria Stern, who had immunological problems caused by her silicone implants, $211,000 in compensatory damages and $1.5 million in punitive damages to be paid by the maker: Dow Corning.

But I Play One on TV

I started to work a bit more as I got better and was lucky enough to get the role of a lupus patient on *ER*. After filming, the Warner Brothers publicist called me and said he'd heard a rumor I actually had lupus, was it true? I said yes. He asked if he could release it to the press. It was a huge decision I agonized over. I was getting better and I was working again. Did I want to admit to being sick? In public? Would the industry judge me as a risk, unable to work? Who would hire me? Would I lose jobs?

As I learned to do with tough decisions, I meditated. I got quiet and connected with the inner me to find an answer. My thoughts reviewed the letters, the march, faces, and e-mails from the women who had contacted me for help. I thought of my dad and wondered what he would advise. I talked to my mom and she was supportive of anything I decided. She knew how much I wanted to work, but also how important it was to help people. Some of my friends advised against it. "You just started to get your life back—don't do it. You may ruin your career," they reminded me.

When I made my final decision, it was because I believe I was given this experience for a reason. I feel my path is to tell my truth, no matter how difficult. I had donated so much of my life to charities I wasn't personally connected to, now I could actually speak from what I knew. I said yes.

After the *ER* publicity, a *People* magazine article followed. Then I got a call from MSNBC to talk about *ER* on their news show. The broadcast coincided with the release of what we now call the "nuts and sluts" study. The Fred Hutchinson Cancer Research Center reported that women with implants drank more, had more abortions, a greater number of sex partners, and dyed their hair more than other women. So I guess the conclusion was that since we were all trashy women, anyway, it was no wonder we were always getting sick.

Something I had learned in my research of the implant industry was that it's often difficult to get clean "science" when the manufacturers themselves pay for the results. I know this is a standard practice, but I think it sometimes creates a conflict of interest. This happened over and over with implant research; take for instance the "nuts and sluts" study.

Two of the doctors conducting the study had connections to the manufacturers. The *Journal of the American Medical Association,* or *JAMA,* reported that one doctor served as an expert witness defending the epidemiologic methods, which is the research to determine the relevance of silicone implants to women's illnesses, used in proving the safety of breast implants. The other doctor had been retained as a paid consultant to several law firms representing defendants in breast implant litigation. Hello? Do you see a pattern here?

Sensing possible media trouble, I agreed only to talk about my role on *ER;* I would not comment on the study.

I was in an L.A. studio the morning of the show; the anchors were in New Jersey. I sat in the news studio and listened to their disembodied voices speaking in my earpiece. I looked into the camera lens and tried to be personal in this disconnected setting. I was prepared to speak about how honored I was to be on such a great show, *ER*, and to help raise awareness for lupus, a disease I had. That was how I wanted to make a difference.

I wasn't prepared for what did happen. When we went live, the reporters ambushed me. They challenged me about the study and said things like, "Doesn't this make your former comments about implants false?" and "What do you have to say now that science has shown women's lifestyles are a factor in their illness after getting implants?"

They fired one question after another, citing the study, cornering me, challenging me to defend myself and anything I'd ever said about the danger of implants. Luckily, I knew enough about the study to speak to it, but defending myself against these voices in my ear threw me. And besides, I was really interested in speaking about lupus, not the "nuts and sluts" study.

At the end of the interview, I was still connected by microphone to the studios on the East Coast. I addressed by name the guy I had made the agreement with, and sarcastically "thanked" him for setting me up on live television, then threw the microphone on the chair and walked out of the studio.

I shouldn't have been so trusting or surprised they'd broken their promise. I felt the fool; it was humiliating. I still didn't manage the media well.

This would be the beginning of years of public scrutiny and criticism I received for standing up for what I knew to be true. I was a healthy girl. I got implants and got sick. I got them out and got better.

My mind swirled with the decision I faced. I could give up, move on with my life, and hope everyone would forget about any of this so I could go back to the business of auditioning for work. Or, I could get a spine and speak up for myself and other women who were being harmed or who would potentially be harmed in the future. What would happen to my career if I continued speaking out, telling my truth?

My Four-Leaf Clover

When I got home from that interview, my phone rang. It was a man calling from Washington, D.C., and he told me one of the support group women had given him my number. He told me he was working with the sick women and trying to help them have a voice in the U.S. Congress. I was suspicious.

"I'm working with women who've become ill from the implants to give their testimony before Congress and the nation. Here it is,

1996, and we're still fighting for more testing and help for women who have been harmed. Would you be willing to help us? We could really use you in our efforts. Since you are recognizable, people feel they know you. The connection with you would help reach women and their families on this issue."

Talk about lousy timing. After that MSNBC interview, I was in a foul mood and told him I didn't think I ever wanted to speak out on this topic again. I'd never wanted to be a poster girl—I just wanted to work. He said he understood, but his words about the importance in getting the truth out there resonated in me. The reasonable side of me took over and I told him to call me in a few weeks.

His name was Tom Sheridan, and he did call back exactly two weeks later. I didn't know it then, but this Irishman would become my personal four-leaf clover.

Tom told me about an effort to help educate women and Congress, to challenge the implant manufacturers on what they knew about the dangers of the devices, and how long they'd known their potential to harm healthy women.

"Mary, would you be willing to come to Washington to launch the effort in a press conference?"

Wow! Getting the information out to the public was important, but why was it up to me? Wouldn't it be easier to hide under a rock and deal with my own troubles? I'd already experienced one public humiliation in that MSNBC interview. Did I really want more public scrutiny, to be vulnerable with something as private and personal as my breasts, my illness? Did I want to focus on what was wrong, instead of what was good and positive? Where was that rock?

My McDonough upbringing that taught me responsibility to others, and my sense of family I'd learned on Walton's Mountain, kicked in. Too many women had been made to feel insane by their doctors and communities, me being one of them. Women deserved to know the facts I never got to see so they could make educated choices.

"I'll do it," I told Tom. "But only if you can promise me that I won't be ambushed again." He promised, and to this day—fourteen years later—he has kept his word. While I have faced scrutiny, tough press, difficult testimony, and a PR machine designed to eat innocents alive, I was never blindsided again.

No longer the unprepared little girl, I learned the history of the implant developers and their sophisticated marketing machine. I was armed with facts and the truth. This time, I was prepared for the minefields I danced into.

By agreeing to appear at this press conference, I launched myself into a cause I had prepared for after a lifetime of lessons about honesty and giving back, having a voice, and finding one of my life's purposes—poster girl, challenges, public criticism, and all.

THE ENEMY LIST

The press conference was at one of the oldest historical establishments in Washington, D.C.—the Old Ebbitt Grill. I didn't have time to enjoy the ambience and significance of the pub once frequented by Presidents Grant, Cleveland, Harding, and Theodore Roosevelt. I had a speech to deliver and I was nervous. This was bigger than the rally on the street; cameras and microphones were lined up everywhere. People always think because I am an actress, public speaking should be easy. It's a completely different ball game for me. It's not like acting at all. It's you out there, not a character. Besides, I wanted it to be perfect, of course. This was too important to screw up.

There was some commotion at the press conference when the "other side" tried to crash our party. The machine's "people" came to the grill and tried to get in. I was surprised they even cared. Dow had always denied any wrongdoing, so why did they care about this press conference so much? Made me wonder what they were hiding or what they were afraid we might shine light on. I found out they had hired a $10,000-a-day PR firm to defend them. This was fascinating and a bit scary to me. I was just Jane Q.—or now Mary Q.—Public here to tell my story, but the real story only got bigger and more aggressive.

One of the stories could have been generated in a Hollywood script mill, for all its irony. John Swanson had worked for Dow Corning since 1966. In 1976, he had been assigned the task of forming their Business Conduct Committee, designed to prevent unethical activities by Dow employees and its representatives. John was at the conference, and as I learned his backstory, the ironies and bravery of this man astounded me.

In 1963, Dow Corning had begun selling small, gel-filled bags that were believed to be biologically inert for use as breast implants. Within a few years, surgeries to implant the device were one of the most popular kinds of plastic surgery. What patients didn't know for decades—I among them—was that the "safety" testing had been limited to short-term studies on very small groups of animals. Since implants were for many years classified as medical devices and not pharmaceuticals, they had not been subjected to the rigorous testing and follow-up reporting that would have provided consumers and doctors with adequate information for informed decisions. Finally, in 1991, the devices were reclassified, but the damage was done.

In 1974, John's wife, Colleen, had the implants and they ruptured. The gel migrated into her system and she developed burning pain, debilitating weight loss, and chronic fatigue, among other ailments. Colleen's medical bills averaged $50,000 a year. His own wife's illness, stories in the press about other women made sick by the devices, the increasing evidence that Dow Corning had known about possible problems with the silicon gel, made John consider leaving the company. But he was so close to retirement, he and Colleen decided he'd stay. John did advise Dow Corning they should withdraw the devices from the market until proper testing could be done, but they refused, claiming the move would be construed as admission the claims were true. In 1993, Colleen settled with Dow Corning; and three months later, in August 1993, the day he became eligible for retirement, John Swanson left the company.

Now considered a whistle-blower, John was at the press conference encouraging education and research, and lending his expertise to our fight.

We presented some of Dow Chemical's own studies with a timeline showing what facts Dow Chemical knew, and when. For example, there was the "cockroach study." Cockroaches were placed in a petri dish containing silicone, and not one cockroach that crawled out lived long enough to crawl more than a few inches away from the dish. Dow has a pesticide division, so you do the math.

The information was explosive, and the pressroom was packed. I was proud to have the forum to speak, to be part of something purposeful. The last ten years of my life had been sidelined with strife and illness—this was something positive. It was groundbreaking for me, a little scandalous to challenge authority; and it was not just a director or my parent, this was a big company.

After the press conference, we gathered in the offices to await any press requests and see if there was any feedback to the news. Indeed, there was quite a bit of coverage, and a flurry of phone calls disputing our claims started pouring in.

John Swanson looked at me and said, "Well, I guess you just moved up the list."

"What list?" I asked.

"The Dow *enemy* list."

I stared at him, my mind racing. I had heard about a list Dow Corning's PR firm had apparently made of the people, listed in order of grievance, who had publicly challenged them on implants. I thought John was joking. "Oh no, I'm not even on the list. There's nowhere for me to move."

He looked at me. "Oh, you're on the list. The minute you came out in that *People* magazine article, you were on the list. You just moved up a lot today."

I still wasn't even sure it even existed, but I realized I had probably pissed a lot of people off that day. I had a daunting feeling in my gut. I sat back, my heart heavy with the realization I had just taken my first step into the minefield. Well, I was in; somebody start the music.

Now, I know you'll think this is crazy and paranoid of me, but after that day, my phone suddenly developed an eerie clicking sound during conversations. This clicking continued for years. My friends got so used to it, we started to talk to whoever may have been "listening." On the count of three, we would curse Dow. Just in case they were listening!

MY MENTOR

When I was going through my surgery recovery and public stumbling, Sybil Niden Goldrich took me under her wing, and I have been there ever since. She has been my hero and a leader for all women who have had implants. Sybil was the consumer's whistle-blower and led the charge on the dangers of implants.

Sybil had breast cancer, and she had terrible experiences with her own implants after mastectomies. She founded Command Trust Network in 1988, a clearinghouse of information about implants—all of which had been difficult, if not impossible, to find because of the secrecy and lies surrounding the industry. She was instrumental in getting implants taken off the market in 1992, until more research could be done on their safety. She blew the lid off the secrets and raised public awareness that implants had been on the market for years without FDA approval. (Now they have been approved, but I'll get to that fiasco later.) She is a champion for so many women and has led the fight for over twenty years.

I met Sybil when I was thirty-two. She became a touchstone for me in all things, and soon became a close friend as well. I went to her after my first experience in D.C. and told her I was worried about the list and the clicking. She said in her calm, knowing way, "Don't worry. You know whose name is first on that list? Mine."

Sybil's experiences were immortalized in a Lifetime MOW entitled *Two Small Voices,* a powerful story of her early experience with implants and her efforts lobbying for better research and consumer information. She is a survivor and one of the most incredible people I have ever known. She helped me develop a stronger voice, and we have battled through many hearings, giving our testimonies, and attending FDA meetings, rallies, protests, and citizen lobby days together. She is a silver lining to this experience.

CAPITOL STEPS

My next press conference was harder in some ways because it had a larger press response. I was again headed to the nation's capital, this time the Capitol building itself. I remember looking out through the taxicab window at the white dome, huge even in the distance. The closer we got, the more my stomach turned. The dome seemed to be standing guard, hovering like a protective parent hugging its child. The three tiers brought to mind past, present, and future. The columns stood strong, erect, and proud. I could feel the honor, strength, and power represented in these structures. Then the familiar fear returned and my gloved hands tightened on the folder containing the speech I'd written.

People milled about as if it were any other day on the hill. But I knew better. Something big was happening, for me at least. The historic building drew closer and I thought of my dad, who loved this country so much. What would he think if he knew what I was about to do? Would I have the courage the founding fathers had when they risked it all to create this country? Or would I panic? I knew there was no turning back. I was going to tell the world my story in a few minutes, so why be scared?

I braced for the task ahead. Instead of rehearsing my speech, as I normally would, I imagined my father's wide smile, crooked teeth, and searching eyes. I realized I still wanted to please him and hear his words of encouragement. I gripped the pages tighter as if the folder itself could bring me peace and calm my nerves.

My anxiety filled the taxicab; my heart beat faster. I wasn't afraid of the television cameras. Although I still find them intimidating, my hesitation came from taking another step away from the "nice girl" image, the one that kept me quiet, prevented me from asking questions, compelled me to keep secrets and—most of all—ensured that I project the illusion that I was perfect.

Would I be a laughingstock? Would they believe me? Would I be a poster girl and lose my privacy, if not my dignity, forever? What did Mary Beth McDonough have to say that might make a difference? Oh, the doubts.

The familiar warmth of tears filled my eyes and the Capitol, now a blur, beckoned to me. Sybil asked if I was okay.

I said, "I was just wondering what my dad would think if he could see through my eyes right now, if he would be proud of me." Here I was, in my thirties and still wanting his advice and approval. My dad had been gone a long time; but he was still so close to my heart, I wished he were there to hold my hand, to tell me I could do this. Fortunately, I had the next best thing. Sybil squeezed my hand and we stepped out of the cab and headed into the building.

Walking through the historic foyer, I thought of others who had come before me. I passed marble statues lining the hallways that I imagined whispered words of encouragement. I climbed the marble stairs, worn from thousands and thousands of footsteps like mine, all working toward change.

Senator Barbara Boxer was holding the press conference, and Sybil, Jenny Jones, and I were giving our personal stories of our breast implants. The first time I addressed the press, I had presented data on the companies. This time, it was personal; this was me telling my story, my secrets.

With each echoing step, all my emotions mounted. As the chamber doors opened, I saw Senator Boxer smiling at me, and the rows of cameras and lights. The podium was once again stacked with microphones, and all I could think was: *How did I get here? All I wanted to do was act!*

I managed to make it through that day. Senator Boxer's press conference raised awareness and we continued to get the message out, even as women continued to get sick. My next lesson would be an even bigger challenge as we fought against the machine.

MISFILED AT THE FDA

In March 2000, the FDA called an advisory panel to approve the PMA (premarket approval application) for saline implants. Advisory panels were made up of plastic surgeons, oncologists, epidemiologists, and other specialists, as well as representatives from industry and consumer groups. They listened to the data to advise the FDA. The ultimate decision was left to the FDA.

This was my first experience testifying before the FDA. I still felt like a hick who knew nothing about Washington, idealistic enough to believe the doctors on the panel would actually listen to the women testifying, weigh all the evidence, and make an educated decision for their safety and well-being.

Boy, was I wrong. This was politics. This was big business, and the plastic surgeons and manufacturers stood to make a lot of money. They both put a lot into the pot.

The first day of the hearings, before any testimony was even heard, the doctors and the panel took a vote to *approve* saline implants. How can that be? I wondered. No data had even been reviewed. The women's voices had not been heard yet.

I entered the hotel in Gaithersburg, Maryland, and the women were already upset. One woman looked at me and said, "Well, we lost this one. The panel isn't listening. They're done." It felt wrong and unfair, but I would give my testimony, anyway.

It was very intimidating. I was not an expert, just a woman giving her story. I held the pages of notes for my testimony and walked into the crowded room, with rows of chairs, and sat down.

The panel sat behind tables at the front of the room. There was a podium for speakers, and red and green lights to monitor time. I listened as the speakers ahead of me went on and on, most of them going longer than their allotted time, ignoring the red light indicating their time was up. I heard specialists speaking the praises of saline implants and what a necessary product they were, how the scientific research supported their safety, and there was no reason not to uphold their recent approval.

My mouth got drier as each speaker finished, moving me closer to the podium. I studied my pages as my mind raced and hands shook. Finally it was my turn.

As I walked forward, my tongue stuck to the roof of my mouth; and my knees shook so much, I thought I would faint. I gripped the podium to steady myself and faced the bored-looking panel. The green light came on and I thanked them for allowing me to testify. I spoke fast, so I could get my message out. I had a lot to say in a short amount of time.

I challenged the safety of the implants, specifically how they could trust the data presented when they didn't have all of it, because—and here's the unbelievable part—when women called the FDA to report problems or "adverse effects" with their implants, these reports just happened to be filed under a number listed for Waterpiks! This was the first of many unbelievable revelations disclosed during the many FDA hearings I attended.

As I spoke, I watched the faces of the panel members. They showed no concern; something fishy was going on. The green light flashed, warning me my time was almost up, but I had more to say. Since the others had been allowed to go over, I plowed on. The moderator immediately cut me off when the light went red.

"Miss McDonough, your time is up."

I kept talking to get it all into the record.

"Miss McDonough." He started banging the table.

Oh, I got it. If I had an opposing view, then I wasn't allowed to finish. I saw this manipulation over and over again. Sick women were silenced because they ran out of time; while the doctors and paid "scientists" were allowed to speak overtime. I started to feel like I was in the movie *The Insider*, and implants were the new tobacco.

One argument from breast cancer survivors was that since silicone implants were so bad, they "needed" saline implants. However, breast cancer survivors were never denied any kind of implant—even when they were restricted for augmentation in 1992. Oddly enough, six years later at the PMA hearings for silicone, I heard the same argument made in defense of silicone implants because saline implants had been found to be awful.

The panel and experts expressed concern, but to my dismay, recommended approval of saline implants, and the FDA approved them. The panel requested additional research, expressing concern for the high rupture and complication rates, especially for cancer survivors. The data showed 73 percent of mastectomy patients had complications within three years of receiving them. There was concern over the risks because there were no long-term studies. There was testimony regarding the early detection of cancer, because the implants obscured breast tissue in mammograms. Saline implants were found to harbor bacteria, produce mold, and cause infections. However, the panel felt that as long as women knew the risks, they were "reasonably safe and effective."

But who was responsible for getting that information out to women? Officially? No one. So we, the sick women, started to educate the public on the risks by sharing our own experiences.

Since then, we've worked to educate women all over the country. I started In the Know as a support group for women in the entertainment industry who had problems with their implants; soon I realized it was for women everywhere. We received e-mails from all over the world. Women were sick, had complications, and needed help. We organized rallies, press conferences, and marches at the FDA and the Health and Human Services building in D.C. At one important rally at the HHS, we carried our signs requesting the FDA examine the approval process, and the FDA itself. There were obvious conflicts of interest within the departments.

Something I found interesting and conflicting was when Medicare and Medicaid had to cover the expenses of women with illness and damages from implants, they went after the manufacturers to repay the expenses. The government recouped over $20 million from the manufacturers. Now the FDA was poised to approve silicone implants, the very product they had received huge amounts of money for in restitution for payment for women who had become sick with implants.

If a federal agency, in this case the HHS, takes money for damages from a product, doesn't it seem odd that another branch of the same agency, the FDA, is able to approve the very product that just cost them millions of dollars—much less the harm that was obviously done as indicated by the amount spent to care for these women? Even Mary Q. Public, who is not great at math, gets it. This just doesn't add up.

SECRET AGENT MAN

At one rally, as we stood in front of the Health and Human Services offices, a man with a camera came out of the building. He stood yards away from us and, not so covertly, zoomed in on each of us.

Someone said, "Well, we all have our own file now, girls. Watch your step." I couldn't help but feel there was something covert going on and thought of my "clicking" phone. When someone approached the guy with the camera, he would not answer any questions and went back inside. The mystery of activism continued.

SENATORS

Now this is a cool part of the story. As you know, I am in awe of public figures I admire. Here I was in Washington, D.C., in my thirties, learning how to be a citizen activist and meeting with congressional members about our cause. To me, that was incredible in itself. Senator Barbara Boxer was an early champion for women on the implant issue. We appreciated her help and understanding at a time when we were being painted in the press as, yes . . . crazy. I loved meeting her and having our picture taken. It was so cool. This issue has gone on so long, I have a more recent picture of me with her. I'm older and a bit more haggard. But she's wonderful and still working alongside us.

One of my favorite moments happened at a party at Senator Edward and Vicki Kennedy's home. I felt so lucky to be invited, I was beside myself. Vicki Kennedy is a woman of such poise and elegance, you forget you have just met her. She made me feel comfortable in an instant. She's so smart and has the best smile. I could gush on and on.

Oh, and her husband? Only an icon. What he accomplished for this country in education and health care alone was amazing to me. It was an honor to be in their home and meet them. I couldn't help but think of what my dad and mom would say if they knew where I was, if they could change places with me for one second. Now, my dad was a pretty calm guy, but I think he would have had butterflies, too. I looked around the house, petted the dogs, and begged someone to take our picture. I have proudly displayed that picture in my home ever since.

Then the most amazing and unusual thing happened. We were talking about being Irish, my hair, the freckles, etc., and the senator started singing Irish songs . . . to me! Okay, there were other people there, too, but think about it. I'm in the house, the famous-family photos are everywhere, and I was being serenaded by Senator Kennedy. One of the best stories I have, so put the book down now. Just kidding. Senator Kennedy's office has also assisted us for years on this issue. It was so nice to be actually heard.

I also have another photo of Senator Kennedy and me taken a few years later. I always wanted him to sign it, but I felt like the girl with the orange corduroy book. Then the senator was diagnosed with cancer, so I was even more hesitant. Tom Sheridan told me to send it to his office. I did, and just before he died, I received the photo signed *To Erin, Ted Kennedy.* I was amazed he even signed it, let alone to my alter ego. Tom told me that was his Irish humor. I cried for a week when he passed, all the time praying for and admiring how brave and beautiful Vicki was as she mourned his passing.

Having met with his office so many times over the years, now knowing I never would again, I felt an end had come for our country, my activism, and being a voice for the "little guy." How would we climb the mountain without Senator Kennedy championing the way? Something great was gone. Not just an era, but for me, my life had come full circle at the loss of the senator. It felt tied to my father and my roots. I am grateful for all his work, especially because my own daughter was helped by him shaping the Americans with Disabilities Act. I will always remember his smile, singing "When Irish Eyes Are Smiling" with that twinkle in his own.

Senator Dianne Feinstein, another of my senators from California, was also good to meet. We were invited to her constituent breakfast, and we shared our concerns on breast implants. Having two female senators is an accomplishment. Having them both listen is even better.

I have met with many members who didn't care a bit about us, or our issue. There was one senator we were excited to meet because he was a medical doctor. We thought he would understand and be interested, but he didn't hear our story. We were ushered in for a photo with him and ushered out when we tried to tell him why we were there. A month later, I received the photo and his calendar in the mail. Welcome to the world of politics. I wondered again what my dad would have thought—this place he held in such high esteem, a place he taught me made a difference. He believed in Mr. Smith going to Washington, but what about his little Mary?

Meeting Senator Hillary Clinton was another perk. Usually when we had congressional interviews, we met with the staff and they relayed the information to the member, but Senator Clinton was gracious and met with me herself. Someone you see so often in the news can be overwhelming to meet. I shouldn't have been timid, because she was incredibly smart, nice, and knowledgeable about lupus and women's issues. I have to say, of all the senators and congressional members I have worked with in the last thirteen years, there have only been two who knew why I was there before they came into the room. Senator Clinton was one of them. She knew the issue and was willing to help.

After my meeting, I watched her take pictures in the hallway with all the interns (mostly Republican) on their last day on the Hill at the end of their service. They clamored for a chance to get a picture with her. She was gracious and easygoing, and I understood them wanting a picture with her. I did, too. Unfortunately, I didn't have my camera with me that day, but she did sign her book for me and I treasure it.

CONSERVATIVE TALK

In organizing rallies and speeches, I put myself out there for public awareness. One speech attracted the opposing PR firm and the manufacturers' lobbyists. I pointed them out in the crowd and invited them to come up and give their side of the story. After all, this is America, and fair is fair. The PR reps didn't budge, so I picked up the microphone, stepped away from the podium, and went to them. I could tell at least one of them was really nervous I'd pointed them out. They refused to speak and said they were just there to "listen." Or to spy? Mary Q. gets a clue.

One rally found us working with NOW, the National Organization for Women. We were not against implants; we just wanted women to know what they might be up against. We believed women should have all the information that wasn't available when we made the decision to have implants.

When I started this fight, the companies were still saying the implants lasted a lifetime; now, at least, they admit they rupture and need to be replaced every seven to nine years. That's a lot of surgery and expense over a lifetime. Women also need to know the information we obtained from the silicone panel: Implants compromise mammograms, possibly hiding malignancies or other abnormalities. Extra angles need to be shot, or other procedures done, such as MRIs and ultrasounds, taken for more complete coverage. Those tests and extra angles may not be covered by health care plans—further compromising a woman's health even if the implants remain intact. I've known many women who have lost their medical coverage because they had implants.

My daughter, Sydnee, joined me lobbying and at rallies. We had made our own signs, and I think the one Sydnee made stood out with a particularly poignant message: MY MOMMY WAS HURT. I was so proud of her. As I spoke, I said my wish was that she would love the body God gave her and not make the same mistakes I had made due to my insecurities and body image issues. Well, the part about Sydnee loving the body God gave her was quoted in the *New York Times* and across the country.

I started to get voice mail messages about a certain conservative talk-radio host who was slamming me on the air. I was encouraged to call in, but I was in D.C. I had no idea what was going on. Turns out he saw the photo, my quote, and the NOW signs, and he figured I was a representative for NOW, which I was not. He was not a big fan of NOW and decided to air his feelings. His tirade on this "Mary McDonough person" lasted a few days on air.

He hinted "this Mary McDonough" person might be a NOW radical and wondered if "this Mary McDonough" wanted to deny deaf children cochlear implants because that's how God made them. One caller even agreed that "this Mary McDonough" probably wanted to kill babies God made, and wondered if "this Mary McDonough" had had any abortions. I was appalled when I heard the tape. All this flack because I wanted women to know the facts before they made an important decision?

Now, that was a huge lesson for me. Still, to have someone tell lies about me and hear angry listeners call in and say horrible things against me was unsettling. I mean, I appeared on *The O'Reilly Factor,* and even he was more fair and balanced. I loathe how these "shows"—and they are just that—boost their ratings, use misinformation, ignorance, and fear to spur the public into hatred. Mr. Talk Show Host had no idea what the rally was about. He saw a sign, then took a half quote and tried to incite rage in people for his own benefit. What's more sad is that people buy into these shows; they believe what they hear without thinking for themselves and doing their own research.

TOXIC SUBSTANCES

Silicone was still not approved and the manufacturers worked hard to get approval. In 2003, the FDA held hearings in Gaithersburg to examine the data. Two companies had presented PMAs and vied for approval, Inamed and Mentor. There were no long-term studies presented. Many testified on both sides. We asked—no, begged—the FDA to look at the long-term risks in considering the safety.

Then a funny thing happened. Dr. Edward Melmed, a plastic surgeon who had put implants in women until he saw the damage they were doing, came to the hearings to illustrate how harmful a ruptured implant can be. He had seen firsthand the leaking, rupturing, and capsular contracture. With gloved hands, he reached into a container and lifted out an implant he had removed from a woman to show the panel. Right away, two "security" types approached him and there was uproar. He was accused of bringing "toxic" materials into the room.

He said, "It's just an implant, the exact material you're talking about here today." He was physically removed from the room amongst the chaos.

There have been so many wild, incredible, unbelievable experiences with implants, I can't describe them all. A few, like this one, stand out. Some of them rocked my Mary Q. sensibilities, and almost all of them pushed my "justice" button.

Over the years, the goal was to get silicone gel implants approved. The surgeons and manufacturers were lobbying hard. I saw big business at work. The 2005 FDA hearings were a bitter disappointment for the women in many ways. Both sides brought out their experts. A *New York Times* article reported: *The American Society of Plastic Surgeons offered extraordinary support throughout the hearing to the manufacturers. Dr Scott Spear, president of the society, is an Inamed consultant and delivered much of its presentation.* This showed me how much they had to gain.

Women gave speeches on the value of implants, and others told their sad stories of illness and losing everything—including a girl who had lost her mother.

It was explosive in energy. These are a few of the odd goings-on, to me at least.

The hotel was a hostile battleground of those speaking for and against approval. At times, it was like a war. No one spoke in elevators for fear the "enemy" was listening. There were standoffs in the press and in testimony, and plenty of evil glares to go around.

Women were against women. Doctors and scientists were challenged by each other and the media. I felt so much pressure and stress I had a flare-up and could barely walk. The women stuck together, and our goal was simply to testify with our experiences, which we did.

SILICONE SAILS THROUGH

The FDA's own scientists testified there wasn't enough long-term data and research to prove safety. There were still the concerns of what exactly happens when an implant ruptures, where the silicone goes, and what it does when it gets there. There was a ten-year study, but only a few years' worth of data was presented by one of the manufacturers to prove safety rates. Suspicious, isn't it? This from a medical device in existence for over thirty years? So why after three decades can't the manufacturers produce more than three years of data?

A few independent studies, such as one at Tulane University in the late 1990s, showed definite links to autoimmune disease. Dr. Robert Garry, professor of microbiology and immunology, supervised a blind study of 153 women, 110 of them with implants. The results showed the statistically significant presence of an antipolymer, which is an antibody produced to fight off the effects of leaking implants. Dr. Garry said at the time, "What we provided was the first objective evidence that it (a disease resulting from silicone exposure) exists." What we needed was more information like this, as the silicone was used in many medical devices besides breast implants.

Why *did* the panel disregard the FDA's own scientists? Why was a doctor who took money from one of the companies that was seeking approval at this very hearing allowed to stay on the panel? Can you say "conflict of interest"? There were so many questions that the panel never answered.

TOUGH LUCK

As the vote was taken, each panel member spoke. As the *New York Times* reported: *Dr. Barbara Manno, a panel member and professor of psychiatry at Louisiana State University, said the panel wanted to give women a choice of implants.*

"And it isn't to have a choice," Dr. Manno said. "It is to make a choice. And tough luck if it doesn't work out."

This statement brought a loud gasp from the audience. I couldn't believe my ears. Tough luck? After all this time and testimony, approval came with tough luck? Well, I can speak from over twenty years of implant experience: It has been tough luck for me and many women and their families who have been affected by these devices. Yep, Dr. Manno . . . tough luck, indeed.

"REASONABLY SAFE"

During previous approval hearings, the FDA was asked if they had any jurisdiction or power to enforce follow-up studies the panel might suggest or require after the approval of a product, they said no. At the end of the silicone hearings, the panel requested more information and market studies for safety. They recommended more long-term data, the study of silicone and its migration. Then the FDA made an unprecedented move. They placed a set of caveats for the implant makers to follow *after* approval. Since the FDA had no power to enforce or follow up if their own requirements were not completed, these studies still have not been completed.

Since then, both Inamed and Mentor have received approval letters from the FDA and are free to supply silicone and saline implants. The last time I was at the FDA, they were having a difficult time getting the manufacturers to comply with follow-up studies and numbers. They asked us to help them educate women about the studies and encouraged us to "keep up the good work" with the women. This was a depressing and disappointing day for us. We had tried for years to help women get the information, but now Mary Q. felt she had lost the fight. I felt I was a little guy, and big business had won over so many women who were sick, tired, and even made homeless from mounting medical bills.

THE WOMEN

I have met so many powerful women on this journey. Their strength, wisdom, and courage inspired and helped me keep up the fight when it felt like a losing battle. When the world calls you money-grubbing, clucking hens instead of seeing how sick, tired, and beaten-down you really are, it bonds you to each other. That is what happened to us.

One of our proudest moments was to be a part of the legislation to educate about the dangers of implants and improve research for medical devices. Senator Boxer dropped her sponsorship of the Breast Implant and Information Act Bill, so I put my film-making experience to use and made videos to educate Congress. Several women, among them actresses brave enough to speak openly in public about their implant experiences, told their stories. Sally Kirkland, Leigh Taylor-Young, Linda Blair, Judy Norton, and Mariel Hemingway were instrumental in bringing awareness to our struggle.

MARIEL

Mariel Hemingway had been so outspoken on the issue, it was great to meet her finally. She agreed to let me interview her. She shared with me how much she liked *The Waltons* growing up. I was gob-smacked, of course. All I could think of was how I admired her when I was a kid and how great she was in *Lipstick* and her other movies. I told her how I was impressed with her courage to come forward with her story. She made such a difference for me in the implant experience, and it was an honor to interview her for the video.

SALLY

The colorful, dynamic Sally Kirkland made all the troubles worth the while when she told me I had saved her life by going public about my implant disaster. She had seen my *Entertainment Tonight* piece and started to wonder if her own implants were what had made her so ill. She became one of the few women in Hollywood who admitted to her experience with implants. She had suffered constant arthritic pain in her neck, back, chest, arms, and legs; inflammation; inability to sleep because of the pain; capsular contractures so severe she described it as feeling like she had a stiff bar running up her neck. She had her last set of implants out in 1998 and continues to speak to women on this issue today. Like me, she began healing and feeling better physically immediately after her explantation.

PAM

I met Pam Noonan Saraceni on a lobby day, and we have been friends ever since. She is a breast cancer survivor, and I mean *survivor.* She had an implant for reconstruction and developed serious health issues. She had her implant removed and now deals with her life as a survivor, helping and guiding other women. She taught me grace in anger.

She had been working on the issue for a long time when I came on board. One of my first meetings at the FDA was with Pam and other women who had traveled from all over the country to express concern about silicone implants. The head of devices at the FDA took the meeting with us, and it was quite the show. We were nervous, but once we began, it was like a comedy sketch that could have been titled "I Didn't Want to Meet You, I Still Don't, but I Will

Make an Appearance and Then Have My Staff Give Me a Note, Then I'll Excuse Myself, Saying I Will Come Back."

He excused himself and never returned. We were defeated, and felt like this was a big waste of time. This was not the first time we were not heard, but we never gave up. Pam was burning mad and let it be known, in the most classy way, of course. She wasn't emotional, but direct and to the point. Great lesson.

When I started In the Know, I asked Pam to be my coanchor, and she is to this day.

JUDY

Judy Norton, my own Walton sister, also shared her very personal story about implants in the "Breast Implant and Information" video. Judy is such a private person, it was hard for her, but she is my sister and stood by me. I appreciate her wisdom and vulnerability so much. Her support and strength helped me get the information to so many women needing help. She's such a great big sister, I was lucky to have her by my side. When In the Know launched with a press conference in Los Angeles, Michael, Jon, Judy, and Kami came out to support me.

There are many more incredible women I have had the honor to picket with and to walk the line with. You know who you are. I am grateful for all your support and encouragement over the years. It was a privilege doing battle with you.

PROSTHESES OUT!

I'll never forget one of our citizen lobby days on Capitol Hill. Many of us were ill; so it was an especially long day as we walked the halls of Congress.

Many of the women were cancer survivors or had voluntary subcutaneous mastectomies because of family history of cancer. All of us were dealing with the nightmare of faulty implants. We didn't want to stand out or look like the "crazy hens" the press had painted us to be, so the women who had breast prostheses wore them. Also made of silicone, they are uncomfortable and hot, and worn against the skin, they cause rashes and itching for the women wearing them.

At lunchtime, we were escorted to a room in the basement with our box lunches. Someone said, "I am so glad to be sitting down for a minute to get some relief."

Another said, "I would have more relief if I didn't have this stupid prosthesis on."

They all agreed. Then someone said, "Shut the door." In the privacy of our little room, she plopped hers out and bounced it onto the table.

The other women looked a bit shocked, but then someone else popped hers out—then another and another, until the table was piled up with fake boobs. They laughed in relief, and the filmmaker in me wished I had a camera. The visual impact of these women with their prostheses strewn in front of them—the very symbols of the battle they'd come to fight—were literally "off their chests." The image hit me like a train.

I knew I had been allowed a rare glimpse of what these women, who represented countless others, had been through. Laughing and bonding with these women and their common experience was a remarkable moment for me. The impromptu scene that played out in the bowels of our nation's capital reminded me why my involvement, and indeed *all* the efforts of these courageous women, was so important.

A few years ago, I was making a toast after one of our marches in D.C. As I looked around the room, I realized that, besides my Walton and McDonough families, these were some of the most resilient, loyal, and generous women and men I ever had the privilege to meet and learn from. I raised my glass, toasted my implants and the whole experience, trying to put into words how these people had changed and touched my life. Talk about making lemonade.

12

THE MOUNTAIN TODAY

I never wanted to see the complete removal of implants from the market. We wanted a safe implant and to ensure that women have the opportunity to make an informed choice about what they were electing to put into their bodies, especially for cancer survivors. We also wanted to shed light on a system full of conflicts of interest that was seemingly allowed to hide facts from consumers.

I fear that may never happen now. After years working toward these goals, in 2006, the FDA approved lifting the ban on silicone implants. This was quite a blow to all of us who had worked so hard to raise awareness and to ask for long-term research. I reflected on the disregard for what we'd been saying about how ill the devices had made us, how suspicious we were of the procedures, especially given the coincidental circumstances: the very scientists who'd performed testing, and the doctors who defended their safety, were often paid by the manufacturers to tell us there was no connection to our illnesses.

I couldn't wrap my head around the conflicting information. The FDA supported the approval recommendation the panel made without the data the FDA itself had asked for. It felt like years of our work was for nothing. Then the FDA loosened the guidelines, allowing both companies to sell implants. When we met with the FDA to ask about the follow-up studies, they asked Sybil and me to continue to inform women and educate them on their choices.

We still work to educate and inform. I still receive e-mails from women who are ill, wondering if implants could be the cause. My hope is that this book sheds some light on a few events in a controversial and heated debate that taught me to question authority and ask again. I also learned that every individual has a voice, and finding yours and using it wisely can make a difference.

FACING THE MOUNTAIN

Similar to the feelings I'd had when I raised my glass to toast the courageous women and men in the implant movement, I realized what the experience has cemented in me. I was meant to learn how to make the best of a bad situation. The connection to a cause and the people affected was the journey, and "winning" not the destination. It was what it was. That revelation led me to where I am today.

Looking back, I realize I battled my fears and tears all my life, until I met the greatest challenge of all. Facing my fears head-on in a cause I truly believed in—one that affected me down to my very bones. It taught me I could speak up; I didn't have to be alone; I did have a voice, even against those in authority.

Here's something I wrote when I was twenty-one. It's amazing how even that many years ago, mountains were such a metaphor for me:

> *Loneliness is a very sad thing. Everyone finds it on their path of life. But for some it is a rock to climb over. For some, it's not even on the path and for others, it is a mountain. You can't see over the mountain so you start to climb. I climb but it seems I get to the top and I fall down. I tumble with the rocks, sand and gravel which are my feelings, tears and hopes.*
>
> *They swallow me up in the tumble. I am lost and again at the bottom of the mountain. I start to climb all over again. Maybe this time I will make it to the top. If I don't, my soul and spirit will. They will*

fly away into the sky, leaving my body and mind behind to deal with the fears of the mountain.

Looking at this, I see I always had an inner strength to know I could fly, even when I felt I was falling down. My mountains of "stuff" ultimately brought me back to myself, my inner knowing. I listened from every level on the mountain and found my spirit. When I flailed and got swept up in the landslides of my emotions, I felt lost. Now it's a moment-to-moment awareness of where I choose to stand on my mountain and how I look at every rock and boulder.

LETTING GO OF OLD APPROVALS

As much as I believed in what I'd done as an activist, after ten years of undiagnosed illness and fifteen years after explantation, I was even further from my goal of an acting career in Hollywood, which I had yearned for after leaving Walton's Mountain. Now I know my path may not have led me to be a movie star, but it did lead me to find my soul and my spirit:

Some beauty here is still, some in motion. There is the stillness of the mountains, the rocks and trees high above us. The vegetation seems as still as the mountain it is attached to. Yet, we know it is growing. Silently, motionless. Lower we see the deer run, birds fly, ants roam and aspen leaves fluttering in the breeze. Motion and stillness coming together as one. Simply living and abiding each other. We as a race should strive to do the same. To live together in stillness and motion, aware of the other, living together in peace and harmony.

As I watch the water flow approach a boulder I wonder which way it will go and how it decides. In a moment I know. There is no hesitation with the water's flow. It simply divides and meets up on the other side; the water effortlessly slides to one or the other side. Never pausing to make a choice. Simply going its own merry way. I must remember this when I want to stop life's flow to pass boulders I see in my way.

MORE THAN ERIN

I learned to accept I would always be associated with Erin. I also learned to direct my life into other areas I was interested in. I had always wanted to try all aspects of filmmaking, including directing. Teaching acting for years helped me direct actors to performances. When I wrote my movie, *For the Love of May*, I decided to make a short film first as a teaser to the long form. Of course, I pulled all my "family" into the making of *May*. Wonderful June, my dear friend, produced it and asked all her own fabulous friends to help. My brother Michael, a director himself, came to work on the film.

May is about four generations of women who deal with the effects of waiting for Mr. Right. I asked both my "mothers" to be in the film. Patricia Neal was incredible as May, a woman who gets a call from a lost love she has pined over for fifty years. Nick and Nina Clooney let me use the image of their uncle George from a WWII still, and his bomber jacket is a beloved prop Patricia holds. He is Edward, the long-lost love. Rosemary lent me her version of "Sentimental Journey." Michael Learned played Patricia's daughter. When she heard we needed a house to film in, she let us use hers.

I was so scared something would happen to her gorgeous house. I was there the night before, putting away her valuables and breakables, and taping cardboard over her beautiful hardwood floors. I feared a light would fall or a camera dolly tire would scuff them, but Michael wasn't worried at all. Just like a mom to support her kid.

As I mentioned, Alexandra Paul and Alison Arngrim were in the movie, with Annie LaRussa and Karle Warren rounding out the generations. I used Tony Becker, who was Drew in *The Waltons*, for a photo boyfriend. There was only one man in the film, so it was perfect that Jimbo was played by RuPaul. *Out of drag.* I loved the irony of that one. Ru is one of the most beautiful people inside, so he was perfect to play the spiritual counterpart to Alexandra's Emily. He radiates incredible energy. I adore him. I had so much help on the film, it was a love fest all the way around. We shot on 35mm, and won several awards at film festivals. I learned so many wonderful lessons from *May*—gratitude being first on the list—and the project confirmed I adored filmmaking from the director's seat.

MOSAIC OF LIFE

Adding filmmaker to my résumé reminded me that it's never just one thing with me. I remember on a speaker's tour for YAU, my friend Mitchell said, "So much has happened to you, you talk about so many issues, maybe you should pick just one to talk about."

The same thing happened while I wrote this. People wanted it to be just *The Waltons*, or just lupus, or implants, or acting, or activism, but I am not just one element of my life. So, with this book, you get many facets of the mosaic that is my life. I have been a child performer, *former* child performer, nonprofit worker, filmmaker, wife, mother, blogger, activist, actress, writer, acting teacher, and producer.

And now I have a new role. I found my Mr. Right. I'll tell you more about him soon.

MOSAIC IN MOTION

I found healing in communication and shared experiences, and decided I wanted to inspire others through the terrain of their own mountains and molehills, so I became a public speaker and workshop leader. As a certified life coach, I help people realize their true potential.

I never want anyone to be as terrified as I was. I faced so many situations not having a clue. I have combined my coaching and communication skills with acting techniques to teach "Acting for Life." Not just designed for people in entertainment, my acting lessons are for everyone who needs a boost of confidence or just a push toward being the best they can be.

Another tile in my mosaic is my body image workshops: "Body Branding, Getting Comfortable in the Skin You're In."

In all the classes, seminars, and talks I give, my goal is to use my own experiences to prepare people for the most important role they'll ever play: being themselves. All our lives, we audition for new jobs or deal with people and their emotions. I teach communication and confidence, how to look someone in the eye and sell yourself, a product, or a concept.

DON ON THE MOUNTAIN

After being a single mom for eight years, I feel blessed to have found a partner in life. Indeed, I found my own leading man.

Like Erin, I went through some interesting times dating—something I didn't like as a teenager, and enjoyed less as a grown-up. One man dumped me because I had lupus, so you can imagine my hesitance to date. After so many years alone, I met my mate, partner, and love, Don, who is handsome, smart, and very funny. Like Erin, I had had heartbreak and I waited a long time to find love again, until I met Don and his daughters in 2004.

Don and I have mutual friends and experiences from throughout our lives. We were probably crossing each other's paths numerous times, until the right time. Our first date was July 5 and we still celebrate our anniversary on that day. We met at a seafood restaurant and I had steamed clams. I gave him the first one, and that is our tradition now. We have the same meal and I always share the first clam with him. Is that goofy romantic or what? But I am a hopeless romantic.

I had always hated dating and this was no exception. I had a lot of support, though. If it wasn't for my friend Scott talking to me on the phone the whole way, telling me I had to go, I might have turned the car around. I even had my friend Maria Calleia as a backup escape call. When she called during appetizers, Don looked at me knowingly and said, "Is that your exit call? Here, give me the phone." Busted, I handed it over. Now, Maria has one of the quickest wits I know; so when Don answered with a witty barb, she was in stitches and they talked for ten minutes. When he handed the phone back, all I heard before the click was "He's hilarious, have fun."

We found out that we had been in all the same places growing up. My dad developed land in Orange County with automotive centers, restaurants, shops, and strip malls. One of his automatic transmission shops was in Buena Park. We used to go with my dad and walk to Knott's Berry Farm when we were kids.

On our first date, we talked about Los Angeles, my being a Valley girl and Don being from the OC. Turns out Don knew the auto center, he ate at the same Love's Restaurant where I went with my family, and even worked at Knott's. As kids, we ate at the same coffee shops, the Van de Kamp's restaurant, with the famous windmill, and he went to the Pop Shoppe on my dad's property. We had been in the same places all our childhoods.

A few years before our first date, I was shooting a Macaroni Grill commercial. At 5:30 A.M., the trucks and equipment took over the parking lot as film companies often do. Don was an Ironman competitor who would swim, run, or ride a million miles in early-morning training. He was in that parking lot that day, hating that he couldn't find a place to park. We laughed about it later, and I said he should have come over and said hello.

Our ninth date was to one of Miss Carolyn Grinnell's Walton Fan Club reunions in Los Angeles. Picture this: Don has never seen an episode of the show. So here he is with the cast members and fans at a Walton reunion! There was memorabilia piled up on our table for me to sign. One was the cover of a *TV Guide*. He looked at me and said, "You were on the cover of a *TV Guide?*"

I don't think he knew what he was in for. It was even more humorous to see the look on his face when he saw the paper doll book. "Yes, I am also a paper doll," I said. It was refreshing to meet someone who had no idea who Erin was. He wanted to be with Mary.

When my brother John heard I was taking him to the reunion, he asked me, "Aren't you pushing him a little?"

I said, "No way. If he can't handle this, then he can't be with me. Better to find out sooner rather than later." Don was a good sport and listened to all the speeches and stories of how the show touched every person in the room.

I introduced him to Michael Learned at the beginning of the night. After dinner, she pulled me aside and said, "You're going to marry him."

I was shocked. "What? You don't even know him. How can you

say that? I don't even know him yet!" She just smiled, knowing she was right.

I met Don a year before my mother was diagnosed with acute myelocytic leukemia. She loved that he held out his arm for her to hold when they walked together. She was always a lady and loved a gentleman, which Don is. When she was close to the end, he told her in a private moment not to worry because he was going to take care of me and Sydnee. I think she left this life feeling a lot better about my future after hearing Don's reassuring words.

After my mom passed, it was a tough time. Don planned a trip so I could visit my brother and go to Sonoma to get away from it all. While we were at a dinner with my brother John, and my sister-in-law Beth, Don ordered champagne for us, then pulled out a beautiful diamond ring and asked me to marry him.

We merged our families. His daughters, Kylie and Robyn, and Sydnee all got along, and I felt accepted when Kylie and Robyn begged me to marry their dad. All three promised they would get along, clean their rooms, and never fight if we were together. They were young at the time. With three teenage girls, it was pretty wild at times.

Don's also great with Sydnee. He has been supportive and a great sport living with all of us girls. My brother Michael said I should marry him quick before he realized he was living with four women. I always joke that Don and Sydnee get along better than anyone in the house, which was so important to me.

They do gang up on me when they watch the show, which I have now forbidden. Let me explain. Sydnee, who had not seen it, either, and Don started to watch *The Homecoming* a few years ago. Well, that was a big mistake. They got to the "I am not a prissy butt" part, and the howling began. In stereo, they would chant, "Mama, Mama . . . Mama, Mama!" You get the picture. Then they would laugh and go on to other choice Erin quotes. The television went off, and I don't think either one of them has ever seen the whole movie.

The same thing happened with the DVD set of the shows. Robyn was watching with them and they decided to imitate Erin and Mary Ellen in one scene. We laughed, and I forbade them to watch any more episodes, but it didn't stop the teasing.

Life is good and I am happy for us all. Now Sydnee has the sisters she always wanted. Having stepdaughters and merging a family is a whole other book, but we have managed to find fun, enjoy traveling, create new traditions, and have a true sense of family together.

On my first birthday after my mom left us, I was sad when I realized she would not call me at the time of my birth, as she had done every year. Knowing I dreaded the approaching hour, Don sent me flowers and signed the card from my mom. He is a good man who makes me laugh, holds me when I cry, and supports me to be everything I am. I am so glad to be a part of his life and have the gifts he shares with us. I could not have written this book without his love and support.

WHERE I SIT NOW

I feel blessed to have had so many great friends and family over the years. I still act, and having my great friend Kari Lizer, who created *The New Adventures of Old Christine*, create Mrs. Wilhoite for me was a true blessing, and I'll be forever grateful. When Don and I got engaged, she threw the perfect engagement party for us.

I am getting to do more character roles now, and I love it. No more worrying if I have to wear a bathing suit. Mrs. Wilhoite is a mom at the school. She's not tiny or a blonde, like the meanie moms. I joke that she's a bit matronly. Not that I don't worry about my looks and don't have image issues. I think I'll always wonder "Does this butt make my pants look fat?" As an actress and as a woman, I may always worry if I look fat. But today, I work with it differently.

In *Christmas at Cadillac Jack's*, I played Madge, a sassy waitress with an ill-fitting bright uniform. I begged the director to let my eye shadow be bright blue to add an offbeat look.

A VIEW WITH THE MOUNTAIN

Through all my ups and downs, I searched for meaning, the *why* of it all, and my truth. I've stumbled and examined every rock, trying to get off the mountain, or at least *move* it. I worked so hard, I was exhausted. Mama Rosemary Clooney once asked me if I would ever stop searching, exploring, and looking for answers. I didn't understand her question at the time, but I think it had something to do with sitting down and just taking in the view. I get it now.

I finally realized I didn't have to move it at all. I can finally accept my mountain and where I am today, look back and learn from the people I loved and the lessons I learned traveling its many paths. I returned to myself and the valuable lessons of my life. I now embrace every path I took and myself in the process.

I am not perfect and I work daily to accept myself as a whole person who is a result of the combined experiences, good *and* bad.

When I was in my early twenties and first went to therapy, I believed I would be healed when all my emotions were gone and I didn't cry anymore. I thought that would be success. Now I know it's not about the emotions and challenges, but how I deal with them. I've learned about the storms of my emotions and how to avoid stepping into them. And that it is a daily, moment-to-moment process without any expectations of perfection attached. The long journey up the mountain, around and down it, returned me to my roots and what was inside me all along. I found the strength of my own inner Mary/Erin and allowed her to guide me. I listen to her now, instead of trying to change her. I love my inner Hog Body and my outer one. I work on accepting them both. Some days, the old voices rear their heads, but most of the time, I appreciate the journey that led me to my mountain.

Despite the disappointments I have felt personally and professionally, I have learned to trust people—even doctors sometimes—because I have learned to trust myself. I believe in people, the brotherhood of mankind. I still believe in the *God*-ness in people, that they and I will do the right thing if given a chance.

Through my own mountains and molehills, I finally found my inner strength. I learned to "Re-Me," an attitude I've incorporated into the self-esteem and body image workshops for women and girls that I conduct around the country.

I worked long and hard to redefine how I saw myself and how I presented myself to the world around me. It's been incredibly cathartic and healing for me to use my own experiences to teach others the repercussions of "negative branding."

When I was young, there were virtually no resources for girls like me who were uncomfortable in their own skin. I struggled alone and was ashamed. In my workshops, I can share my lessons. Our thoughts and images do affect our lives in every moment. If our choices about ourselves are negative, that's what everyone else sees and experiences. However, I discovered if we each begin with a more positive self-image, we then project that to the rest of the world. Once that new "branding" happens, we're less likely to project or be perceived in a negative way. I see women change their brand and change their lives. They receive more positive feedback, interact more positively with themselves, and have a healthier outlook on life.

THE COLORS OF THE WIND

Indulge me while we go back to Walton's Mountain for a few more memories, and I promise you'll enjoy the trip. In the fall of 1992, The Walton's Mountain Community Center opened in Earl Hamner's hometown of Schuyler, Virginia. All the cast, Earl, his family, and the writers and producers gathered for the amazing event organized by Woody Greenberg. It was huge. This small, two-lane town was bursting at the seams that weekend. Over six thousand fans came out to pay tribute to Earl, the Hamner family, and the show. I heard they had to turn people away from the overcrowded town.

I was especially excited to meet the "real" Erin, Audrey Hamner, and see the other counterparts, the real-life people on whom our characters had been based. It was fun to see Elizabeth and Jason's children. We talked and compared notes, such a rich history of family.

During the opening ceremony, a woman came forward and committed to starting an official Walton fan club. Carolyn Grinnell didn't know what she was getting herself into that day, but she started what is still the Walton's International Fan Club. It continues to grow and holds annual meetings, usually on alternating coasts. With our busy schedules, we cannot all make the trip every year, but whenever we can, we enjoy going back to Walton's Mountain. The cast is still so close that when we are together, we have a blast. So gathering us all up to visit was also fun for our kids, who became like cousins.

My mother donated her wedding dress to the center's memorabilia exhibit. They kept it on display for a few years, with a photo of my mom in the dress the day she married my dad, next to one of me wearing it as Erin.

The community center had brought us back to Schuyler to help raise funds for the center. It would be the first of many trips Sydnee and I looked forward to taking, usually in the autumn, my favorite time of the year, and it is especially spectacular in Virginia. Sydnee loved to collect the beautiful fall leaves and bring a bit of what she called "Jaginya" home with her to California. One year when Disney's *Pocahontas* had come out, she told me, "I have to go get my colors of the wind, Mommy."

Signing autographs all day was a lot of work, but we were honored so many people still loved the show and had an interest in connecting to our "family." Fan club members came from as far away as the U.K. to spend some time on the "real" mountain where it all began. Over the years, we have gotten to know many of them and their own families. We now consider them our dear friends and visit with them off the mountain, too.

As you know, I had a lot of trouble with allergies when I was sick. I've told you about my animal allergies, which did not bode well for Sydnee getting the dog she dreamed of having. We had fish, red-eared sliders (turtles), and a few rats, but no dog for Syd. (Besides, I was never a big animal lover myself; perhaps the bone-crunching cow and the runaway mule had something to do with it.)

Because Sydnee has her own health challenges, she often felt like an outsider, different from everyone else. I felt she needed something to love her unconditionally, something that was hers, with no judgment or pressures on her otherwise tough days. We started researching hypoallergenic dogs. Poodles were high on the list; yet I couldn't really see myself as a poodle person. We put our names on a bichon frise rescue list, but got no calls. Then we tried a rescue shelter. Sydnee fell in love with a little dog, but they decided she would "love the dog too much" and rejected us for adoption. Syd was devastated. I was livid these people let her bond with this little dog, let me put in a doggie door, came to inspect our home, and then said no.

As the Universe always works wonders when we allow it to, Scott Vestal, one of the fan club members who had become like family to us, wrote and asked if Sydnee wanted a dog. If so, he'd like to give her a poodle. *What?* Manna from heaven? Soon, our toy poodle, Runtie Schuyler Vestal, was born, and Sydnee was a happy girl. I am now not only a poodle person, I am a dog person. I love that dog like I never thought I would. He watched over me while I was sick and slept on my lap while I wrote this book. He taught me to open up and try love again.

We not only found new friends and became dog lovers, the fan club gave me another special relationship that filled a particular hole in my life. One night, we were all sitting around after a reunion dinner and I felt a wave of nostalgia. I shared with them how much I missed my dad, who had been gone for several years. I knew he would have loved these Walton reunions.

On the spot, Charlie and Marlene Kruger wrapped their arms and hearts around me, and Charlie and Marlene "adopted" me and Sydnee.

Recently I shared with Dad's brother, my uncle Steve, how much I missed my parents. He encouraged me to talk to them to keep them close. I have found this worked, and I even felt they helped guide the process of this book. I finally realized I didn't need to keep dancing; I had my dad's love and approval all along.

When Sydnee was little, she played my daughter in one of the reunion specials. She didn't know the difference between the show, the reunions, the Hamners, and the fans—everyone blended together as one big family to her. When we were headed to Virginia, she'd say hopefully, "Mommy, we're going to see the Waltons, right?"

She was right. We *are* all the Waltons, really. The "Walton Way," as the fan club calls it. The caring sense of community, family, and support for each other is something we all share, and it comes from the feelings Earl created from that mountain and that live in us still. Even though we stopped shooting over thirty years ago, *The Waltons* continues to touch my life—and the world's hearts—daily.

I believe the closing voiceover from the episode *A Wedding on Walton's Mountain*, narrated by Earl in his beautiful Virginia lilt, reflects the poignancy and mountain strength of the bond between all the families who were brought together by the show, and is a fitting end to this book:

> *"My sister Erin's wedding is as clear in my memory as it is in my mother's, although neither of us was there. And that fact has caused me to marvel many times at the power of the human heart over mere time and space. There was a special bond of love in our family, which brought us to that small church . . . that's as strong today as it was then."*

My wish for you is to appreciate every lesson, and know you have the strength to climb your own mountain. May you enjoy every rock and difficult step, and remember you can always just sit and enjoy the view.

A Special Note from Beverly Nault

MY VISIT TO THE MOUNTAIN

Along with the rest of America, I watched *The Waltons* and wondered what it was like growing up in that familiar clapboard home, its screen door bursting open to reveal three generations living under the same roof. The mountain family, the tree house, lumber mill, old-timey cars, homespun clothes, and gentle story lines that taught values and morals seemed far removed from my own home in 1970s Texas suburbia. I wondered what it was like to be one of those actor-type kids who might as well have been living on a different planet: Hollywood seemed so remote, so glamorous. Except for glimpses of them in teen magazines and celebrity appearances on TV, I couldn't begin to imagine what it was like to be Jon, Judy, Mary, Eric, David, or Kami.

While those kids grew up, so did I. Flash forward: My husband Gary's job brought us to Southern California in 1997. At the time, we homeschooled our two children, Lindsay and Evan. One of the first units we studied was the Great Depression. Because it was so true to the era and cultural experiences, I incorporated reruns of *The Waltons* as part of the curriculum. We were all drawn into the excellent stories, authentic settings, and unparalleled acting by the cast, who truly seemed to love and care about each other.

With the flexibility in homeschooling and their interest in entertainment, Lindsay and Evan began working as paid extras on television, commercial, and movie sets. Evan, with his blond hair and blue eyes, was often "picture picked," which means he was chosen by directors needing a certain look. He'd also landed a modeling job, and was showing promise as an actor on the set. Chosen for many up-close scenes, he logged enough jobs and became a "force," which means his paychecks would go directly to pay AFTRA union dues until he satisfied the fee. He also met the SAG minimum, qualifying him to join. In the summer of 2003, we decided it was time to find a coach to help him take the next step.

We learned Mary McDonough taught acting and we arranged for an audition. We were excited to meet Mary, and even though we'd rubbed elbows with many "names" on sets, we weren't sure what to expect from such a well-known actor.

Immediately Mary put us at ease. She interviewed Evan, agreed to take him on as a private student, and for many months, she taught him how to access a character, interpret lines in a cold read (for auditioning), and imparted as much of her vast knowledge as she could. I imagine it was like drinking from a fire hose for him, she has so much experience in the craft.

Mary shared some of her stories, what her life had been like on *The Waltons,* and what she had been doing since the show ended production. The more I heard, the more fascinated I became with what made this interesting woman tick.

While working with her, Evan signed with a commercial agent and began landing lead roles in community theater. See, I told you she's a good teacher. He enjoyed the biz, but he decided to attend college full-time. When he graduated high school, he no longer auditioned in Hollywood.

With Evan and Lindsay launched, I now had the chance to pursue my own dream: to write for the general market. An assignment in a writing course challenged me to come up with a book-length nonfiction project.

The first and only idea I thought of was Mary's story. I shot off an e-mail and wondered if I would even hear from her. After several weeks passed, I assumed she thought I was a kook for asking. But then I got an e-mail. She apologized that it had taken her so long to reply and explained that she'd been at a speaking engagement. She said the *only* thing they told her was missing from her presentation was the opportunity for attendees to buy her book. (She's also a dynamic speaker. If you ever have the opportunity, go hear her.) So we began to talk about the project.

Mary might say it was the Universe; I felt it was God; and I know you will agree, the decision to write Mary's story was inspired. I assure you, she is as warm, transparent, funny, thoughtful, genuine, and beautiful as her onscreen persona. She tackled the book with the same zeal for excellence she has for every role and project. We are all blessed she agreed to share these stories, thoughts, anecdotes, fond and sometimes painful memories of growing up a child celebrity in a fascinating time in a culture few people have the opportunity to experience.

I'm proud to have had the privilege of writing this book with Mary, to go on the journey with her back to Walton's Mountain and beyond, to be warmly welcomed by the other members of the cast family, as well as the magnificently talented Earl Hamner, Erin's real-life model, the lovely Audrey Hamner, and to join the many fans, old and new, who wouldn't have it any other way but the "Walton Way."

Mountain Blessings,
Beverly Nault

BEVERLY'S
ACKNOWLEDGMENTS

Without many people supporting us, this project may never have made it into print. My mom, Barbara, always told me I could achieve whatever the Lord set on my heart. My sister, Brenda, read the manuscript, edited it, and prayed for us. To my kids: Evan, if it wasn't for you, Mary and I might never have met. Lindsay, your never-give-up approach to life inspired me more than you'll ever know. Mary Jo Nault, you cheered us on. And to my husband, Gary, my sweetheart and best friend, you never doubted that we would make this dream come true.

My mentor through the Christian Writers Guild, Kathy Tyers, your quiet encouragement, gentle instruction, and Christian friendship lifted my skills, faith, and belief in myself. I'll never forget the monthly sessions at the Temecula Critique Group led by Rebecca Farnbach. Also thanks to Ashley Ludwig, Dona Watson, Joanne Bischof, Dan and Denise Harmer, Lynn Donovan, Fred Tingler, Dave Henkel, and Jackie Harts. Elaine Klonicki, Mary and I appreciate your advice and direction as well.

To the other Walton cast members and Earl Hamner, thanks for your insight and support. To all *The Waltons* fans, thanks for keeping us going when we might have given up without your constant reminders you were out there. Kevin Brown, thanks for letting me work on this at my desk when things were slow. Really, they were!

Don, thanks for sharing Mary with me all those long hours. I know you lifted her spirits when things were tough.

And a special word to Mary. I'll forever appreciate your faith that I was the person with whom to take the journey. You accepted my nudges, my ideas, and my probes into the depths of your hidden places. Without your dedication, your incredible instinct and creative talent, these compelling memories wouldn't have the same transparency and honesty. I'll never forget the laughter and tears we shared, our Monday morning phone chats, standing in the rain discussing agents and editors, meetings over breakfast and lunch, the chills I felt when you first read "our baby" to the fans. Here's to all the peaks and valleys we shoved this boulder up, down, and across. My writer-sister and dear friend, thank you for not only allowing me to be a tiny part of the legacy of *The Waltons,* but to labor alongside you during this incredible journey on, around, and up to the peak of "Mary's Mountain."

God Bless,
Beverly Nault

"I tell you the truth, if you have faith as small as a mustard seed, you can say to this mountain, 'Move from here to there' and it will move. Nothing will be impossible for you." —Matthew 17:20

Please turn the page for an extra chapter
of all new, never-before-published
bonus material from Mary!

Many people have asked what it's like to have written a book, my personal story, and for people to read it. Well, it's a lot of things. It's a moment of great pride, a dream come true, and a huge accomplishment mingled with emotion and humility.

Since *Lessons from the Mountain*'s publication, life has not been the same. There's something about putting your life lessons on paper that frees you from them on a personal level, yet at the same time concretes them into existence. Letting your experiences be printed onto a page is like allowing a monument to be built to them. There they are, for all to see . . . forever. No going back now. Exposed. You open yourself up for criticism and scrutiny. There is vulnerability in it. My fears of being judged returned. My thoughts went to: *Will they like it? Is it good enough? Will it help people?*

I looked at Don and knew my simple and private life with him was about to change. I sat on the couch with him one night just before the book came out and we talked about my concerns. There was a part of me that wanted to stay on that couch with him and not change one aspect. I wanted to cuddle with him forever and be small and private. Yet I knew that wasn't going to happen.

My lesson was that it is a book, not a monument. I had the power to turn the page or even shut the book and put it on a shelf. I opened up so many memories and relived them writing *Lessons*. Now I realize all my reasons for doing so were important. I have the amazing honor of knowing people related to my experiences and have been touched and even helped by them. Thanks to all of you who shared your own feelings and fears with me upon reading the book. You gave me strength, and I appreciate how brave you all are.

I opened the book with questions we as cast members are often asked. Now I can add several more about the book itself. One is, why did I write the book, and why now?

I wrote to help others in the hopes no one would ever feel as scared or alone as I had felt while I was growing up. As my dedication said, "For anyone who has ever felt like they were not enough."

Well, sadly there are so many who have felt that way. One comforting aspect of the book has been my own continued discovery that we are NOT alone. I was not alone all those years ago and I am not alone now. So many people felt the same way I did.

But many still push back, and their attacks have been personal.

THE NAYSAYERS

It seems each day I open my e-mail and read another letter from someone who was touched by the book. Those letters have made my days and brought me purpose fulfilled. I can't tell you how nice it is to know the reason I wrote the book has come to fruition. I am forever grateful for you all, and your stories of both trying times, and of triumph.

Yet, with all the great reviews also came the naysayers. It is never easy to read a negative review of your work, but I was prepared for that; I mean, everyone can't like everything, right?

Before the book came out, Alison Arngrim warned me about what might happen. She had been through this with her book. We met for lunch and she told me her experiences and gave me tips. She was pretty spot on predicting what might come my way.

After *Lessons* hit the shelves, the reviews and comments were mostly positive, encouraging, and what I'd hoped to hear from readers and fans.

But then one day, Allison called and said, "Well, you got your first troll and here's how I know."

I was surprised she had found "it," and although I am just now learning about being a tweeter, Facebook "friend," Internet follower, Google alerter or review reader, my trusty friend Alison is a genius. She knows everything. Did I mention she is an encyclopedia and dictionary, as well as just plain smart?

I had no idea where "it" lurked, but my dear detective friend, Nellie, led the way. I say "it" because people and companies can hide behind avatar icons, make up fake names, and post negative comments. Who knows if "it" was really a person at all?

And there, on one of the public review sites, was the first of a few very personal attacks. From the comments, we wondered if this "person" had even read the book. Alison and I had a field day. The most interesting thing for me in the process was, the naysayers ALL mention implants or the manufacturers themselves. Hummhhh?

"Funny," Alison said in that oh-so-Nellie voice. "The ONLY negative posts you got ALL mention implants."

I knew the implant issue might piss people off, but this was so obvious. What we didn't take into consideration while writing was the negative reviews of the book or me personally could come from plastic surgeons or the manufacturers. Since these trolls can hide behind a computer and say whatever they want, it made sense. Alison was sure of it, and we had a great laugh reading these together.

After all these years, breast implants as a topic is still hot, but a personal issue and one I don't take with a grain of salt. If a woman wants them, she should research what she is getting into. I advocate for women having all the facts about them and that proper studies be done on the dangers and affects. These long-term studies are incomplete, and we still need objective scientific research to measure how often women get sick from implants.

IN THE KNOW

As long as we are on the subject, I feel it's important to mention the new findings since the first edition of *Lessons* went to the printer.

The FDA doesn't comment unless they have important information that affects public health. So if they *do* comment, you can bet there's something behind their official statements.

Recently they released *new* findings concerning breast implants. They confirmed implants don't last a lifetime. The devices have been proven to rupture, allowing the saline or silicone to leak into the body. Studies have not been done to see what happens to the body as silicone migrates into glands or organs. Shocking! Wow, I must have had a crystal ball because I'd already mentioned this fact in the first edition. The limited life span of implants is not really news, and we knew this years ago, but the FDA officially commented that all types will need to be replaced every eight to ten years.

Another complication, capsular contracture, is when scar tissue forms around the implant and squeezes the implant. This can be very painful and can also cause breast deformity, often visible to others. Other complications can be rashes, necrosis, toxic shock, swelling, hematoma, delayed healing, breast pain, and chest wall deformity, just to name a few. Women need to monitor their implants vigilantly to ensure they are not causing harm to their bodies.

A dear friend called me after *Lessons* came out and said, "I want to talk to you about the book." She is a cancer survivor and was surprised to read the issues with implants. Since no one told her they would ever have to be replaced, she was concerned. Then she was really upset when the news report confirmed what was in my book. Like many women, she felt uninformed and betrayed by her doctor and the FDA. This makes me sad and outraged all over again.

Another announcement at the time I'm writing this is the possible association with Anaplastic Large Cell Lymphoma. This is a rare type of non-Hodgkin's lymphoma. The FDA believes women with breast implants have a low but increased risk of developing this cancer. This is scary to me. I had never heard of this link before. Like I said, if the FDA reported this, there must be something behind it, and once again, more research needs to be done.

Another frightening revelation on the danger of implants is the recent PIP implant scare in Europe. This implant was removed from the market in 2010 because of high rupture rates. Now it is reported the implants were made with industrial-grade silicone. Women have been advised to remove their PIP implants. This is yet again another case where women are now terrified as to the risks they have taken in getting implants.

I have been talking about the risks and dangers of implants for more than seventeen years. I hope we can all educate ourselves and start to challenge the unrealistic images women are holding themselves to in the name of beauty.

I can't encourage women enough to take their health, bodies, and lives into their own hands. Please, do the research before you make a decision that WILL impact you for a lifetime.

WALTON BOOK SIGNING

My wonderful Walton family supported me so much with the release of this book. It was a bit overwhelming. Their support showed just how lucky I am to have them all in my life. All of the West Coast family members came to my first L.A. signing at Book Soup. Dear June Dowad hosted a wonderful book party. Ralph even drove over two hours to get there. David, Jon, Kami, and Eric all stayed and signed books. What dedication! I am one lucky sister.

So there I stood, reading the book to a crowd of people who love *The Waltons*. As I read, it encouraged me to see Michael smiling and nodding in agreement as I described the dinner table scenes. Then, to have Eric laugh, and Judy cut in with a joke, was hilarious. But the capper was when I read about Ralph singing, "I Shot the Sherriff." He, right on cue, started singing it in the exact way I described. The fans howled with laughter, and I felt so wrapped in gratitude I could have burst. Then Michael told a sweet story about me and it touched my heart. I feel truly Blessed to have them all in my life.

I have a confession to make. In the years before and during the writing of the book, I didn't watch any *Walton* episodes. Why, you might ask? Like all busy moms, I just didn't have the time to watch television while cooking meals, running errands, and helping with homework. It was also good to get away from it for a while. While Erin does define me, she isn't me, so I never felt I had to watch. Yet the show lives inside me, so it has touched my life as much as anyone else's.

While writing, I didn't want to watch the show because I wanted to write completely from my memory. I didn't want an episode to spur an outside influence. For the same reason, I didn't read any other former child stars' memoirs before I wrote mine. I didn't want to be influenced by their memories. I'm now making my way through some of them, and yes, I thought, as I was reading Melissa's, oh-oh, I should have written about that, or during Alison's, Oh-Oh I had that happen, too! I am glad now I didn't read them before *Lessons* was done.

Yet I'm struck so many of us have had such unusual and similar experiences; it is incredible. Paul Petersen says we are all part of The Club. The Club of former child performers, even if there is no official card; only we know what it is like to grow up in the industry. We are all related by that common bond of experience.

WHERE ARE THEY NOW?

Here's a quick rundown of all the family today. Some wrote in their own words, the others were too busy to write before this went to press, but they all send their warmest Walton blessings.

EARL HAMNER, JR.

Since the *The Waltons* ended its long run on CBS, Earl has published more books and short stories. He has also been involved in the creation of many more television and movie projects. From the television series *Falcon Crest* to the film *Where the Lilies Bloom* to the animated film *Charlotte's Web,* his pen still creates magic.

Ever since his classic *Spencer's Mountain,* and *The Homecoming,* the books that launched the legacy of mountain-based family tales, to the scripts, series, and movies he's contributed to, all his books still charm and entertain. His works in print also include *Generous Women, The Avocado Drive Zoo, Goodnight John-Boy, Stories from The Twilight Zone,* and, most recently, a charming tale surely to become a classic, *Odette: A Goose of Toulouse.* The reviews have been fabulous. Order a copy today; I know you'll adore it as much as I do.

I am not alone in my admiration of this legendary talent, especially after becoming an author myself. The Library of Virginia presented him with the 2011 Literary Lifetime Achievement Award on October 15, in Richmond, Virginia. Previous winners have been John Grisham, Tom Wolfe, and William Styron. Congratulations, Earl!

Earl lives in Los Angeles with his lovely wife, Jane, where he continues to write, blog, and communicate with the fans and friends he's amassed from seven decades of legendary accomplishments. Stay in touch with him at www.earlhamner.com.

RICHARD THOMAS

People still ask me, "Where's John-Boy?"

Well, Richard is in New York, where he does a lot of theater, his first love. But he really is like Pa Walton. He has seven kids, just like *The Waltons.* Maybe the show rubbed off on him a little. Ya think?

Recently, I was in New York having dinner with him, his fabulous wife, Georgiana, and amazing son Montana (hey, I can be a proud aunt, can't I?).

Richard said, "Have you watched the show with the girls?"

I told him I hadn't seen it in a long time. "They think it's funny, but we are really too busy to watch."

He said, "You know, I have been watching them with Montana. I hadn't seen the show in years either."

I thought it was so cool they were sharing them.

He went on: "You know, you really should sit down and watch. It's a really good show!"

Richard wrote me the loveliest e-mail after reading the book. He told me he was proud of me, and it made my day. What little sister doesn't want to hear that from her big brother? He said he loved the memories, some of which he'd forgotten, that the book brought back for him. It meant so much to have him enjoy the book. He honored me by joining me at a book signing in New York. It was a great night!

He really has too many acting credits to mention here since he's worked ever since leaving the show when his contract was finished in season five. He's been in plays all over the world, including Broadway and London, in *Twelve Angry Men, Race, As You Like It, Hamlet,* and *Peer Gynt,* to name a few. His screen work runs the gamut from directing to acting to voice-overs. You can hear his voice on many commercials, just about everywhere.

He has also always worked in film. He does movies of the week all the time, and often appears on special episodes of shows. I like when he is a deranged killer. As wonderful as he was as John-Boy, I think he plays the sick, twisted serial killer really well! He is a great actor.

RALPH WAITE

Daddy Walton's life has also been quite busy since the show. His credits run long and varied between movies, theater, and television. The famous baby blooos are a perfect match for Mark Harmon's, in his recurring role as his dad on *NCIS.* His acting range is incredible, because he also played a creepy end-times prophet on the series *Carnivàle,* and has guest-starred on shows ranging from *Grey's Anatomy, Cold Case, The Practice, Bones,* and had a recurring role as Father Matt on *Days of Our Lives.*

On the silver screen, he can be seen in *The Bodyguard, Homeward Bound 2, Sunshine State, Letters to God,* and too many others to mention.

Ralph lives in Palm Springs with his beautiful wife, Linda.

MICHAEL LEARNED

Before *The Waltons* ended, Michael earned an Emmy as Mary Benjamin in *Nurse.* Besides returning to the Walton specials, she continued performing, and appeared in series such as *St. Elsewhere,*

Murder, She Wrote, Living Dolls, Scrubs, and *General Hospital.* She was recently on *General Hospital* playing a cancer patient. Her movie credits, besides *For the Love of May,* include *All My Sons.*

It seems like every time I call Michael to try and have lunch with her, she is off doing a play somewhere. Always busy and giving great performances. I often try to see all my "family" members in their plays, and have over the years.

Michael read parts of this book as I wrote it, and she is always there for me. She is writing a book, and I can't encourage her more. The parts she has shared are incredible, and I can't wait until it is completed.

A NOTE FROM JUDY NORTON

The Waltons meant so much to me. It opened doors for my career that have given me the chance to do things I never dreamed possible when I was young. Personally, it gave me my incredible second family, who mean the world to me.

Since the series ended, I have continued working in entertainment. I've guest-starred on many shows, including *Ed, Stargate SG-1, A Twist of Faith,* and *Millennium.* I had a recurring role in *Beggars and Choosers,* and *The Lost Daughter* miniseries. Another series I'm involved in, *Poker Girls,* has been nominated for several awards, including Best Drama Program at the prestigious Banff World Media Festival.

Besides performing for the camera, I also appear onstage and sing in concert, and have directed in Canada and throughout the United States.

My husband, Bob, my son, Devin, and I live in Los Angeles, where I run, and ride horseback whenever I can.

Mary's book has been an inspiration. Not only do I feel I learned even more about this dear friend and sister, but it allowed me to relive wonderful memories of our many years filming *The Waltons.* Reading Mary's book has sparked my imagination with the possibility of sharing my own experiences of that very special time. So, who knows, perhaps a book of my own is in the future.

I have always appreciated the people who have watched the series over the years, especially those incredibly loyal fans who continue to watch today, and I'm excited that new generations are being introduced to the show. I have a website at http://judynorton. com, and a Facebook page, and enjoy keeping in touch with friends and fans. Thank you all so much for your loyalty and support.

Love,

Judy

A NOTE FROM JON WALMSLEY

I loved reading Mary's book. The first part was a walk down memory lane, revisiting the Walton years. Some of the stories I remember differently, but that's always how it goes. Mainly, I don't think I'm nearly as nice as she makes me out to be! Ultimately, what makes Mary's book a real page-turner are the stories of her struggles with self-image, career, illness, and her fearless crusade to inform women of the dangers of breast implant surgery. Who would have thought that our own "little Mary sunshine" would someday go head-to-head with the FDA and Dow Chemical Corporation? Go, little sister!

My own life since *The Waltons* continues to be an adventure. I have traveled the world as a full-time musician, and continue to make my living playing, recording, and writing music. I'm happy to talk to Waltons fans about the show—just not during a performance, please! I have a beautiful eighteen-year-old daughter from my first marriage, and am currently living on the Southern California coast with the love of my life, my wife, Marion. For updates, fans can reach me at www.facebook.com/jonwalmsleyfan.

Jon Walmsley

A NOTE FROM ERIC SCOTT

When Mary asked me to put a few words down on what we are up to, I smiled. My life is certainly not what I had planned, and yet it is so wonderful and fulfilling.

I am happily married to Cindy for over eleven years now. We got married in 2000. Our relationship is everything I could have hoped for and more. She is not only the best wife, but the best mom for our kids.

Ashley just finished her first year away at college and had the best time. Although it was great for her, we surely missed her on a daily basis, but I am so proud of her. She shows a great promise in her photography, and I look forward to seeing how she discovers her path in life.

Emma is now in fourth grade, learning and teaching me every day. She has an incredible way of looking at everything around her. Now the only question is how to harness it. She loves being a Junior Girl Scout and enjoys spending time with her troop.

Jeremy is in second grade; he just started playing electric guitar, keyboards, and drums. He is a proud Cub Scout (I am his den leader), and we enjoy the activities and outings equally. He loves all sports and reminds me of myself (the good stuff).

Our home is a menagerie. We currently have a dog, two cats, a red-footed tortoise, an aquarium, and a tank of frogs that we raised from local tadpoles. We will keep them until they start making any noises!

On the professional side, I am an owner of a delivery company called Chase Messengers. I have been in the industry since 1984, and although it has changed significantly since those days, I am proud of the way we reinvent ourselves to keep up with the times. I have a wonderful staff that is like a family, and I still enjoy going into the office every day.

My memories of our times "on the mountain" are rich, filled with happiness and pride. Who knows, maybe my side of the story might be in the future?

I thank all of our loyal fans for their continued support of "that lil' thing" we did on the lot in Burbank back in the 1970s.

With Love,
Eric Scott

DAVID HARPER

I enjoyed Mary's book because it really took me on a trip down memory lane. Here's what I have been up to. I still live in Los Angeles. I am a musician and enjoy history, film, reading, and the quiet life. I stay in contact with my Walton family, and my real-life sister, who lives in Arizona. Occasionally, I watch *The Waltons* reruns. I am amazed it is still so popular. Some interesting facts you may not know about me are: I am a big Civil War buff and I study ancient history and military history. I love '60s music. I am also an avid military war gamer. I am glad I have this opportunity to send my love to all the Walton fans, and I plan to attend as many Walton fan club reunions as possible.

A NOTE FROM KAMI COTLER

After *The Waltons* ended, I attended the University of California at Berkeley and earned my teaching credential. I taught in Oakland and in rural Virginia, ironically not far from where Earl Hamner grew up. My husband, Kim, and I lived in Virginia for five years and had a boy, Cotton, and a girl, Callan. We moved back to California to be closer to my family when our son started school, and I became involved in charter schools, helping to open and direct a K–8 school that both the children attended. Most recently, I helped open an Environmental Charter Middle School, an interdisciplinary, project-based, arts-integrated, middle school in an underserved community in Los Angeles.

My husband and I also run a small business selling fizzy bath balls on the Internet. Check out www.bath-balls.com. I have a Facebook fan page and have very much enjoyed communicating with Walton fans on that site.

Love,
Kami

HALF-CENTURY SURPRISES

Just after the book came out, I turned fifty. I've never really thought of age as a big deal. I don't feel fifty, and I don't know what fifty looks like in this day and age. I do know that I have wrinkles and age spots, and I'm holding my menus farther and farther away every day. The truth is, I feel better than I did when I was thirty. So for me, fifty is the new thirty. Besides, I am not a date person. I don't like numbers and don't remember them, so I don't really DO birthdays. If you have a party and remind me, I am great. I'll celebrate all day long. But ask me to remember your birthday . . . sorry. It is a social grace I lack. I convinced myself years ago I have many other graces to make up for this fault.

Don and I talked about my fiftieth birthday and decided to celebrate after the book tour. I was scheduled to be in D.C. on the big day, May 4, 2011. I was so sad when I left to promote the book and make some other appearances on the East Coast. I knew I wouldn't see him for weeks. The longest we would ever be apart.

I spent the day lobbying Congress. I saw Senator Roy Blunt and had a nice visit. Met Congresswoman Tammy Baldwin and spoke to her about women's health and body image in the media. My friend, Tom Sheridan, took me out to lunch in between meetings. I had been out in the rain and humidity, walking all day, and was tired. I just wanted to go back to Tom's for a break before a book signing that night. When I went to hail a taxi, my friend Kevin Mathis took my arm and said, "Oh look, there's the Capitol building." And the taxi passed us by. It was daft, or I am, because I was IN that building earlier. Even I know what the Capitol looks like. Then he proceeded to keep me busy by getting us lost in the city I knew he could find his way through with a blindfold on in a blackout!

One grace I do not lack is timeliness. I am always on time. If not, I am stressed. I hate to be late, and we were running late! When we finally got to the house, I ran from the car, up the back steps, and into the kitchen. I could hear voices in the other room and thought it odd there were so many people already there and I was not even ready! I ran up the back stairs and to the third floor. I got to my room and sensed something was different. I turned around, and there was Don. I screamed and jumped into his arms and started to cry. The best surprise ever.

The party was great. All my D.C. friends were there. Such a great start to the next century! I am so lucky to have incredible friends to celebrate with.

THE SISTERHOOD

From D.C., I went to Dollywood and got to meet Dolly Parton. Such a great moment. She was a doll. It's surreal to meet someone you feel you know. I have seen her so much, just not in real life.

She said, "I feel like I know you. Do you feel like you know me?"

I gushed like an idiot and said, "Yes, I feel like you're my best friend." Something totally lame, but you all know how starstruck I can get. She was so sweet, and we took a picture with the book. You probably saw it on my Facebook page. Great fun.

I have to say I had some wonderful help on the tour. Kyle Michael, Patrick Ing, Stefan Lang, Danny Forbes, Lester Holt, Dennis Wills, Dan Rogers: Your contributions are much appreciated. A shout-out to Wade Tallant for your help with the Gospel Music Hall of Fame. Wade, Jake, Deb, Justin, and Chris for taking pictures of me with everyone at book signings. And to David Pounds for welcoming me back to the mountain in Schuyler. Harlan Boll, we're indebted and grateful for your diligence on the book's PR behalf, and someday I may forgive you for booking me for ten radio interviews in one day.

Tim McAbee was also an angel. He arranged book signings, the Dolly parade, and invited me to appear at a Loretta Lynn concert being held at his venue in Pigeon Forge.

Tim knew I had admired Loretta for more than her music. She is an incredible woman and an inspiration in so many ways. From her tough childhood as the Coal Miner's Daughter to her legendary success as a country western singer, she's taught me the most, personally, by being honest about her own health crises.

She has been one of the few celebrities to talk openly about her breast implants. She is "one of us," a fellow survivor reminded me. Back when I was speaking about my implant nightmare, Loretta publicly shared her own experience. In an interview, she warned, "You women out there that have breast implants, it is dangerous. Have them jerked out." (*Country Weekly* magazine, April 21, 1998) Her blunt honesty about how hers had ruptured and that surgery to remove them saved her life encouraged me to continue the fight.

At the concert, I gave her a copy of *Lessons* and we talked and hugged. I felt like I had known her forever. She is so warm and kind, I adore her. I told her how inspiring she was to me, and to the many sick women with implants. We talked about everything from implants and body image, to *The Waltons,* to barbecue. She invited me to her ranch and I told her I would bring Don and he'd smoke some meat for her. She couldn't have been more embracing.

Her daughters were so nice as well. Patsy's daughter Emmy sang with her grandmother that night. Then she performed a solo she had written. I was surprised it was about body image. Here was this adorable, clear-voiced young girl singing a song that touched my heart, all about looking in the mirror. This endeared me even more to all of them. It also reminded me how far we have to go as women, still worrying about our looks and what's outside instead of inside. Things haven't changed that much. Women and young girls still judge themselves against stereotypes in the media. I hope we can demonstrate to young women they are unrealistic images.

Loretta has inspired many, and I was honored to have those treasured moments with her. Yes, I was starstruck, but mostly struck by how kind and open she was.

Then, Jason Gilmore, another angel and old Walton friend, helped organize my Roanoke book signings. He had promised a quiet, small barbecue at his house one night. But, I walked in to find ANOTHER surprise party! He had invited all my Virginia friends AND many Walton friends from the fan club. I can't believe he organized such a great event. Kathy and David Stamman drove from Ohio; Papa Kruger and his daughter, Leslie, came from Pennsylvania; and Carolyn Grinnell from North Carolina came to help me celebrate. Another great night! Such a lucky girl to have so many good Walton friends.

Another special moment for me was being awarded the Ella Dickey Literacy Award. When I received the call from Reverend Nicholas Inman, I was thrilled with the honor.

I traveled to Marshfield, Missouri, for their Cherry Blossom Festival to receive the award. There I met other recipients who made me feel even more honored. I was in incredible company. Curtis Roosevelt, Annette Dunlap, and George McGovern also received awards.

I loved Curtis's memories of living in the White House, and we talked about going to France. Another person who has invited us to stay with him, or maybe I invited myself—after all, he does live in France. Senator McGovern was so sweet as well. It was my brother's birthday, and I asked the Senator to say hello to him. My brother about dropped his phone when I told him who wanted to wish him a happy birthday. So much fun. The entire Cherry Blossom Festival was a good time. I highly recommend it to all.

The 2011 Fiddle Festival in Branson, Missouri, was another good time. Love the music, food, and people of Branson. Our Walton fans are tried and true, and I never tire of hearing all their stories.

SADIE SADIE

As I write this, I realize the most important decisions and cherished times are while I sit on the couch with Don at the end of a day and we contemplate our girls, home improvements, dreams, work, and even life-changing decisions.

My fiftieth birthday came and went, and the party Don had planned to actually celebrate it was just a few days away. I thought we just wouldn't celebrate it with any big deal. Hey, I was living a dream come true, who needs another form of celebration? But my dear Don planned a dinner party for me in L.A. He knows I miss my L.A. friends, so he chose a great restaurant up there.

I was exhausted from traveling and relieved to have the trip behind me. I was really looking forward to this dinner.

There had already been several surprises, so I asked Don a few nights before the party if there were any more, as I didn't think I could handle another one. He said, "No, maybe a few fun toasts, but no surprises."

Then, for some reason, I said, "Maybe we should surprise *them* and get married. That would be a surprise, wouldn't it?"

To MY surprise, Don said, "We should. I have been thinking about that for a while now."

"WHAT?" I said. "How long?"

"Ever since I started to plan this dinner."

"Why didn't you say something?"

"I didn't want to overshadow your birthday."

Don knows I am not a big birthday party girl, and I assured him I wouldn't mind. He also knows I am highly intuitive, I just know things sometimes, and I said, "Were you just waiting for me to pick up on this?" I guess he was, because he agreed it was something he wanted to do, but only if it was all right with me.

Suddenly it felt like the perfect thing to do. When we had tried to make plans for a wedding before, something always happened. Either someone couldn't travel to be there, or we had too many conflicts, or I would feel nervous, or my mom got sick, or, or, or. But not this time. We realized that even though some dear friends would not be coming and we would miss having them there, they would understand. Besides, everyone really was a little tired of this LONG engagement. My brothers were coming to the party, and all our girls would be there as well.

There were only a few days left, so we put it into the hands of the marriage license department. No appointments were available, but we were told we could try to walk in for a license. We only had Don's lunch hour to get that done. We got there and were in and out in twenty minutes. Humph, somebody is on our side. I think a lot of people in heaven were pulling for us, my parents, to say the least, not to mention my Godfather Uncle Hugh, and even a few Walton grandparents.

Then I said to Don, "*Who* can marry us?" He talked about finding someone to show up from L.A. There had to be people who do this. Then I bolted upright and shouted, "Pam, Pam is a minister!" Who better than my dear Pam, who is such a sprite and filled with love and joy all the time? Pam embodies Don's sensibilities, and my sense of spirituality. She's perfect. But was she even available on such short notice? Another test of the fates. I called Pam, and guess what? Of course she was in town and would just love to marry us.

Well, it was a go.

The next two days were so much fun. Filled with the secret we shared, picking flowers, and assembling something borrowed (Sydnee's hairpin), something blue (flowers) something old (well, I was fifty now!), and something new, my dress (a cute Calvin Klein, not too wedding-like and definitely fiftieth birthday party dress).

Don and I had two days of wonder and bliss, just us celebrating our secret. He is so amazing and handsome, and those days were incredible to share with him. I loved looking in his eyes and seeing them twinkle.

We went to the mall for rings, had champagne, and a special dinner. We wrote our vows and kept them secret from each other, but the hints and humor filled our days with so much joy. I felt so Blessed and happy.

Writing my vows brought me to the important decision I was making and how lucky I felt. I wanted to share the funny things between us, but more important, I wanted to recall the meaningful moment when he assured my mom he would take care of Sydnee and me just before she passed away, which he has done. Don is a good man, and while he can make me angrier than anyone, he then looks at me with that twinkle in his eye and I crack up. Even when I want to stay mad at him, I can't. I know my dad and he would get along really well. Actually, I think my dad probably had something to do with us being together.

After our days of secret fun and planning, the night before the party, we told the girls we were getting married. They were happy and helped us with the big day. I took the girls for manicures and pedicures the next morning. Sydnee wanted to tell the ladies at the salon, but kept quiet. I had ordered a bouquet for myself and nosegays for the girls, and on our way home we stopped to pick them up amid giggles and whispers.

My friends Kate Zovich and Rita Chemente drove up to L.A. with us, and the girls were so nervous about blowing it, they all put their iPods in so they wouldn't let it slip. When we got there, Kate tried to help carry an old brown box I had put the bouquets in, but we jumped on her, afraid she'd see inside, and insisted we'd carry it ourselves.

Later, she said, "I was wondering why you grabbed that box from me and why the girls did not talk at all on the ride up. I thought they were ignoring us," but she laughed. All the girls had jobs to do when we got there, and the ugly cardboard box filled with beautiful flowers was Robyn's job to pre-set, hidden in the corner waiting for the perfect moment.

Don planned a cocktail party for the first hour. My family, my brothers and sisters-in-law, and my Walton family started to arrive. Michael Learned and her husband, John Dougherty, came in and I about burst at the seams. John, Michael's husband, ended up in Don's wedding vows because he never had a conversation with Don in seven years when he didn't ask when Don would make an honest woman out of me.

I had been in the bathroom looking at my vows—yes, I used a cheat sheet—and then the moment arrived. Oh, wow, this is really happening, and both my families are here! Eric and Cindy, Jon and Marion, Leslie Winston, David, Earl and Jane Hamner were all gathered in the dining room along with an assortment of treasured loved ones. After all, one gathers a wide variety of friends over fifty years. I was so excited. So much love filled the room.

I was more excited than nervous. Chelsea Claus, my goddaughter, who shot the cover for *Lessons,* was there to shoot the "party." I looked at her and said, "Just go with the flow, you'll know what to do."

She gave me a quizzical look. I looked around the room and my eyes fell on the happy face of Kari Lizer. I knew she was the trusted one . . . and a professional! I gave her my Flip video, looked her in the eye, and said, "Don is going to do a toast. Will you film the whole thing?" She said yes, and it was a perfect shoot.

Don clinked a glass to announce a toast thanking everyone for coming. He said he didn't know what to get me for my birthday, but thought maybe he would just end a very long engagement. He got down on his knee and asked me to marry him, "right here, right now."

There were screams and gasps, and Kate said, "NO WAY!"

Of course I said, "Yes," and the room turned into a wedding party. People jumped up to help, and we moved to the front of the room. Don asked my brothers to stand up for him. The girls gathered around to stand up for me. Robyn pulled out "the box," Sydnee had our rings, Pam was introduced, Kylie passed out bouquets and boutonnieres. It took two people, George Geary and June Dowad, to get Don's secured to his lapel. Cameras were pulled out. Eric ran a video we had set up in the corner. Pam began, and the door pushed open, and Judy Norton slipped in with a very surprised look on her face when she realized what was happening.

Pam's ceremony was perfect. She engaged the entire room with her spiritual blessings, and we shared many laughs. I have to say, there was so much joy and love in the room, or maybe it was the relief that FINALLY we did it. The surprise wedding factor was huge. It really became our day filled with so much love you could feel it. We have the best family and friends who have supported us through the years of ups and downs; we cherish them anew after sharing this special day with us.

THE FAMILY OF MAN

Extending from that roomful of our close family and friends, I feel a wider connection to the fans, the newer friends, and to all the folks I've met through this book. I've been so privileged to be welcomed and accepted, to cross paths with so many of you who have shared personal and sometimes painful stories. The experience has anchored me in knowing how important it is to share our truths. I feel so Blessed to have received a huge dose of what I call the "family of man."

The spirit of people uniting together has been part of my life for many years. Be it with my family, friends, nonprofit groups, charities, or a rally for women's health issues, I have felt the power of unity. I was surprised to feel that same power about the messages and beliefs *The Waltons* has instilled in so many people. It was overwhelming to me. The love and care people have for this show is incredible.

Michael Learned said to me recently she has had the same experience. She said, "Mary, people love the show." And she's right. There is a reverence for the lessons the show taught, the family values it instilled, and that "Walton Way" I often talk about.

An amazing experience that illustrates the show's enduring ability to draw people together happened when I was headed home after the Grand Ole Opry book signing. I was in the Nashville airport buying barbecue sauce and a shirt for Don, and a woman was also buying her husband a shirt. We started to talk and joke about our husbands and the kooky sayings on the shirts. She shared how she was anxious to get home because her daughter had had a serious accident and was in a coma. She started to cry and asked the sales clerk and me to pray for her.

I said, "How about now?" We held hands and said a prayer right there at the checkout stand.

Then I thought of all the "family" in my social network, and asked her if she wanted over 2,000 more people to pray for her daughter. She said yes, and I told her I would post the request to my Facebook page.

Because my plane was delayed, I was able to go online right away and ask for prayers. Well, you all sent up prayers for Tina Siddle's daughter and entire family. It was amazing. When she got to a computer, Tina logged on to the page and thanked everyone. Then Tina posted that her daughter had awoken from the coma. It leaves me speechless, and in awe about this "family of man."

Many thanks to you all for the uplifting e-mails, Facebook posts, the prayers, interviews, PR, spices, Kahlúa, connections, waiting in long lines at the signings, canned goods, gift books, the hand-carved pen (which I use to sign books), the purse, birthday gifts, candy, cookies, cards, tears, wishes, and hugs. You have made this an incredible experience for me. I will never tire of hearing how much you love *The Waltons*, and Erin.

Thanks for sharing all your "lessons" and the support and encouragement you've shown me, and each other, that's only possible in a true "family of man."